CONVERTS
DROPOUTS
RETURNEES

Converts
Dropouts
Returnees

A STUDY OF RELIGIOUS
CHANGE AMONG CATHOLICS

BY

Dean R. Hoge

WITH

Kenneth McGuire, C.S.P.
Bernard F. Stratman, S.M.

Concluding Chapter by
Alvin A. Illig, C.S.P.

United States Catholic Conference
Washington, DC
•
The Pilgrim Press
New York

Library of Congress Cataloging in Publication Data

Hoge, Dean R., 1937-
  Converts, dropouts, returnees, a study of
religious change among Catholics.

  A study sponsored by the National Conference
of Catholic Bishops' Committee on Evangelization.
  Bibliography: p. 219.
  1. Catholics—United States. 2. Converts,
Catholics—United States. 3. Ex-church members—
Catholic Church. 4. Evangelistic work.
  I. McGuire, Kenneth. II. Stratman, Bernard F.
  III. Catholic Church. National Conference of
Catholic Bishops. Committee on Evangelization.
  IV. Title.

BX1406.2.H59   282'.73   81-15351
ISBN 0-8298-0483-8 (Pilgrim Press) AACR2
ISBN 0-8298-0487-0 (Pilgrim Press) pbk.

United States Catholic Conference
1312 Massachusetts Avenue NW, Washington, DC 20005

The Pilgrim Press, 132 West 31 Street, New York, NY 10001

SPONSORSHIP

THIS STUDY was sponsored and funded by the National Conference of Catholic Bishops' Committee on Evangelization. The members of the committee at the beginning of the study were:

Archbishop Francis Hurley, Anchorage, AK, Chairman
Bishop Victor Balke, Crookston, MN
Bishop Michael Begley, Charlotte, NC
Bishop Joseph Daley, Harrisburg, PA
Bishop Joseph Francis, Newark, NJ
Bishop James Hickey, Cleveland, OH
Bishop Roger Mahony, Fresno, CA
Bishop Edward O'Meara, New York, NY
Bishop Raymond Peña, San Antonio, TX
Bishop James Sullivan, Lansing, MI
Bishop John Sullivan, Kansas City—St. Joseph, MO

During the three years spent in research and preparation of the manuscript, the committee membership changed. The members of the Committee on Evangelization at the time of publication are:

Archbishop Edward O'Meara, Indianapolis, IN, Chairman
Bishop Roger Mahony, Stockton, CA
Bishop Eugene Marino, Washington, DC
Bishop Raymond Peña, El Paso, TX
Bishop James Sullivan, Lansing, MI
Bishop John Sullivan, Kansas City—St. Joseph, MO

While the members of the Committee on Evangelization find the results of this study informative and useful, they do not necessarily agree with every detail and interpretation in the book. Final responsibility remains with the author.

CONTENTS

FOREWORD

With joy and enthusiasm, the Committee on Evangelization of the National Conference of Catholic Bishops presents to the Catholic Church in the United States, to all our fellow Christians, and indeed to all people of good will, a remarkable document of research and reflection.

To relish Dean Hoge's *Converts, Dropouts, Returnees* to the fullest and to appreciate its amazing practical usefulness, it is necessary to be aware of the genesis of the evangelistic spirit, so recognizable in the church today as to be one of the "signs of the times," and a sign too of the presence and power of the very Spirit of God.

Bishops from the entire Catholic world came together in Rome in 1974 to discuss a topic that had been crying for such discussion since the end of Vatican Council II—exactly what it is to evangelize, and what is the role and position of evangelization in the life of the church. The necessity for such discussion was both real and urgent. Perhaps it should have been expected that this question would arise, considering human limitations and the intensity of the mighty currents of Spirit-filled thought that had their origin in conciliar days.

Catholic leaders had become aware of the values to be found in the great non-Christian religions; we came to see that the many communions of Protestants were far more Christ-rooted, Christ-centered and Christ-proclaiming than ever we realized; we awoke to a new awareness of the misery and poverty of so many of our fellow humans. Relief, development, and liberation took on an unaccustomed primacy in our hierarchy of church priorities.

The synod took place, and now the pendulum is swinging back toward the center. With a new appreciation of sound ecumenism, with heightened compassion for human suffering, with greater respect for truth wherever we find it, we grasp with a new clarity the magnificent truth that the mission of Christianity will always and ever have as its first priority the proclamation of the person of the Lord Jesus, the fullness of his message and the salvation that is to be found only in his name.

Pope Paul VI spent over a year weighing the thought that had come to Rome during the 1974 synod. He then issued what Cardinal John Francis Dearden of Detroit has called the document that "could well be the most significant, the most far-reaching in its effects, the most long-remembered of his entire Pontificate." The document is *Evangelii Nuntiandi* (Evangelization in the Modern World).

Since then a new wave of enthusiasm and action for the spread of the gospel has come over the entire church. The people of God are "doing" evangelization. They were not doing it for long before the need became apparent for scientifically accurate information about those who had recently been evangelized or were to be evangelized. Dr. Hoge's study is the answer to that need.

As this instrument is presented publicly, it will help all who are entrusted in the proclamation of the Word to recall the words of Pope Paul VI (*Evangelii Nuntiandi*, #80):

> Let us therefore preserve our fervor of spirit. Let us preserve the delightful and comforting joy of evangelizing, even when it is in tears that we must sow. May it mean for us—as it did for John the Baptist, for Peter and Paul, for the other Apostles and for a multitude of splendid evangelizers all through the Church's history—an interior enthusiasm that nobody and nothing can quench. May it be the great joy of our consecrated lives.
>
> May the world of our time, which is searching, sometimes with anguish, sometimes with hope, be enabled to receive the Good News not from evangelizers who are dejected, discouraged, impatient or anxious, but from ministers of the Gospel whose lives glow with fervor, who have first received the joy of Christ, and who are willing to risk their lives so that the Kingdom may be proclaimed and the Church established in the midst of the world.

Most Rev. Edward T. O'Meara, S.T.D.
Chairman, Committee on Evangelization,
    National Conference of Catholic Bishops
Archbishop of Indianapolis

PREFACE

THIS BOOK reports on unique new research on persons entering and leaving Catholic church life. The study was sponsored by the National Conference of Catholic Bishops, through its Committee on Evangelization. The Rev. Alvin Illig, executive director of the Committee on Evangelization, asked me in 1978 if I would direct a study. We formed a research team composed of myself (an academic sociologist with seminary training), Kenneth McGuire (a Paulist priest with a doctorate in anthropology), and Bernard Stratman (a Marianist brother who is a specialist in communications).

The research plan was simple: Interview a sample of recent Catholic converts, dropouts, and returnees, and listen to their stories. We interviewed about 200 people in each of the three categories, and some we spoke with at length, getting their accounts on tape. This book is the report. We have tried to report our findings accurately and straightforwardly, free of jargon, and with correct interpretations. We write as social scientists more than as theologians; our task was to capture the experiences of these people, not to make recommendations about church policy. Father Illig agreed to write a final chapter in this book, outlining some implications for evangelization in the 1980s.

Our research team worked out a division of labor. All three members—myself, McGuire, and Stratman—designed the study with the help of our advisory committee. All three traveled to the various dioceses to gather the data. Kenneth McGuire and I made the global coding of the interviews. I handled the taped interviews, carried out the data analysis, and wrote the manuscript. A first draft was circulated to the advisory committee and to the Bishops' Committee, and many suggestions were incorporated into the present version.

This book includes thirteen extended accounts of actual experiences of persons as they were told to us. No quotes were changed, except for stylistic clarification. All the people are real, but their names, and the names of their hometowns and parishes have been changed.

Due to space limitations the technical details of the research could not be included in this book. They appear in a 100-page *Technical Supplement,* which has been printed separately. It gives a detailed account of all procedures, marginals on the three sets of data, and all interviews and documents. It is available from the Office for Evangelization, 3031 Fourth Street, NE, Washington, DC 20017, for ten dollars. Copies have also been deposited in the libraries of Catholic University of America, Marquette University, and the Graduate Theological Union (Berkeley).

We thank Fr. Alvin Illig for his support and encouragement throughout the project. Also, we thank Cecilio Morales Jr., who helped immensely in gathering data and interpreting experiences among Hispanic Catholics, and Msgr. James Gaffey, who advised us in interpreting American Catholic history. Diane Martin, Ella Smith, and Beth McLaughlin carried out the coding and keypunching. Kathleen Ferry helped effectively in the writing process. Marion M. Meyer and Angela Ricciardelli were exemplary editors.

We thank the seven dioceses who cosponsored the study—Baltimore, Detroit, Oakland, Omaha, Orlando, Providence, and San Antonio. Especially we thank the liaison persons in each who helped us gather the data—Sr. Sharon Euart, the Rev. Edward Farrell, Sr. Leonard Donovan, Sr. Rosalee Burke, the Rev. Arthur Bendixen, the Rev. John Dreher, and Deacon Rudy Lopez. Over a hundred persons helped with data collection; their names are listed in the *Technical Supplement,* and we thank them. Finally, we thank our advisory committee for the many decisions they helped us make. The members were Sr. Rosalee Burke, the Rev. Don Conroy, the Rev. Eugene Hemrick, Dolores Leckey, Dr. John McCarthy, Dr. William McCready, Dr. Meredith McGuire, the Rev. Philip Murnion, Dr. Hart Nelsen, the Rev. Frank Ponce, Dr. Raymond Potvin, and the Rev. Bernard Quinn.

Dean Hoge

CONVERTS
DROPOUTS
RETURNEES

Chapter

1

RESEARCHING RELIGIOUS CHANGE AMONG AMERICAN CATHOLICS

ANYONE WHO has seriously discussed evangelization knows how many questions and issues can be raised. People ask about the theological definition and goal of evangelization, about its relationship to other church mission, and about proper approaches. They ask what motivates persons to become Catholics and under what circumstances they commonly do so. They ask what kind of individuals are most hungry for gospel truth and for supportive Christian community. They ask if conversions, such as those taking place at Billy Graham crusades, have lasting impact and actually bring people to churches.

Some of these questions are researchable, using social science approaches. Over the years various Christian denominations have sponsored sociological research studies to find out as much as they could.[1] Recently, efforts in evangelization have been expanding in the Roman Catholic Church, so new research to aid evangelization is needed. In 1978, several Catholic groups joined Protestant denominations in cosponsoring a Gallup poll designed to describe unchurched Americans, what they think about the church, and what sorts of outreach they might respond to. Fr. Alvin Illig was part of the planning committee for this study and so was I. The committee met many times to discuss which form of research would best serve the evangelization effort. The results of the 1978 national study have been widely read.[2]

During this process most committee members became convinced of the need for interview studies, in which new converts to various denominations would be invited to tell their own stories. Father Illig saw a need for this sort of study in the Catholic community, and he discussed the idea with the National Conference of Catholic Bishops'

3

Committee on Evangelization. Late in 1978 he asked me if I would direct a study that involved interviewing new Catholic converts. He suggested the study examine dropouts and returnees at the same time. Within a few months initial plans were drawn up.

We began work in January 1979. I was granted a leave of absence from teaching duties at Catholic University of America, and we added Kenneth McGuire and Bernard F. Stratman to the project, to form a three-member team. Since we were interested in persons in the process of change—moving either into or out of church life—we called the project "The Study of Religious Change."

CARRYING OUT THE STUDY OF RELIGIOUS CHANGE

The research plan was simple: Find a representative sample of recent Catholic converts, dropouts from Mass attendance, and former inactives who have returned to Mass attendance, and listen to their stories. Two recent books had reported on interviews with unchurched persons and with individuals who had lately joined churches—J. Russell Hale's *Who Are the Unchurched?* and Edward Rauff's *Why People Join the Church.* At the time we started our work, Rauff was still in the process of writing his book, and we spoke with him to learn what we could from his experience.

Both Hale and Rauff interviewed samples of persons gathered by asking ministers and priests in different towns for names of persons who fit the desired descriptions. This method produced insightful results but no findings that could be generalized to larger populations. The samples were not *representative* of anything. We hoped to overcome this limitation in our study, and also we hoped to gather quantified data, permitting computer analysis. We decided to try to interview 200 persons in each category, the 600 persons selected in such a way that they would be maximally representative of all converts, dropouts, and returnees in the nation.

Other decisions had to be made. We found that the study could not look at specific ethnic groups or regions, since the sample size (200 in each group) was too small and could not easily be enlarged. The most we could do would be to include ethnic groups and regions in proper proportions in the nationwide sample. Also, we gave up the idea of looking at specific evangelization efforts or special situations, such as those on college campuses. The study would have to be limited to a sample of typical parishes, and would look at "normal" processes bringing converts to the Catholic Church or causing people to drop out or return.

4

After reviewing the research literature we presented our initial ideas to a group of priests from the Archdiocese of Washington, DC. We requested that they give us the names of some converts, dropouts, and returnees in their parishes who could be interviewed in a first pretest.[3] We also called together an advisory committee of church leaders and social scientists.

The first round of exploratory pretest interviews was completed by March. We did not know how receptive people would be to interviews about something as personal as their own religious changes, but we found that after initial cautiousness they talked freely. They were happy to tell us their experiences and liked the idea of assisting in a study for the bishops. In the first pretest we found definitional ambiguities, so, for the purpose of our study, we firmed up our definitions as follows:

1. A *Catholic* is a person baptized as a Catholic. Anyone not baptized as a Catholic is not considered one, even though he or she may attend Mass regularly, partake of the Sacraments, participate in parish organizations, or feel like a member of the parish. A person baptized as a Catholic is considered one for his or her entire life, even though he or she may have joined a non-Catholic church in the meantime.

2. An *active Catholic* is a person who has attended Mass at least twice in the past year, apart from weddings, funerals, Christmas, and Easter. Attendance at a charismatic prayer group is not counted, unless Mass was celebrated in the group. Whether the Mass was in the traditional setting or not does not matter.

3. An *inactive Catholic* is a person who has not attended Mass at least twice in the past year, apart from weddings, funerals, Christmas, and Easter. Elderly persons physically unable to get to Mass technically fit the category but are not included in our study. A person who has switched to a non-Catholic church and attends its services (but not Catholic Mass) is considered inactive.[4]

4. A *dropout* is a person who changed from active to inactive status within the past three years.

5. A *returnee* is a person who changed from inactive to active status within the past three years.

These definitions do not include whether a person *considers* himself or herself a Catholic, or whether the person has certain beliefs or personal practices. The definitions are solely a matter of actual involvement in Catholic church life. Other criteria could have been adopted, perhaps including devotional practices or inner states, but they would have been too difficult to measure reliably in this type of study.[5] The level of involvement deemed adequate for being active is minimal. It was adopted because it was the same one used in the Gallup survey of unchurched Americans, and because a minimal definition was seen as being preferable for evangelization theorists. In fact, the definition of active sounded too minimal to a number of people we interviewed. Some persons told us they were inactive, but when they became aware of the definition we were using in the study, they said, "Well, by that definition I guess I'm an active Catholic!" and they chuckled.

We discussed with the advisory committee how we could assemble representative samples. Getting a sample of converts would be easy since each parish has a list, and we could interview all converts for the past two or three years in a sample of parishes. But how could we find the dropouts and returnees? One idea was to ask priests and parish councils in selected parishes to assemble lists of persons fitting our categories. But this had a major weakness in that no one could claim that they know a representative group of such persons. Another idea was to make calls randomly to households on parish census lists, asking each if anyone there had stopped Mass attendance in the past three years or had returned to Mass attendance. We decided to try this approach.

Canvassing by Telephone

We carried out a trial run of the canvassing procedure in two parishes in the Archdiocese of Washington.[6] The random calling was well received by the parishioners if we explained how we had gotten their names and why the parish was helping in a study. We located quite a few dropouts and returnees, but many refused to be interviewed, often because of the inconvenience it entailed.

We discussed the refusal problem with the advisory committee, and they suggested we consider telephone interviewing rather than personal interviewing at the people's homes. This would cut the refusal rate and also the costs of interviewing. We carried out another pretest and found that indeed the refusal rate was lower when we asked for a telephone interview, not a personal interview. Therefore, we decided to use telephone interviewing. (For more details on the pretests and interviews, see Appendix A.)

Selecting Parishes

Another problem was how to assemble a sample of parishes in which to work. We thought we would need about thirty. We decided to work in seven dioceses, asking each to select four or five parishes for the study. Selection of dioceses should ideally be done randomly, but this was impossible, since we needed at least one research-oriented person in the diocese who would help us in setting up the data-gathering process. We assembled lists of researchers and acquaintances in a large number of dioceses, then picked seven dioceses that were geographically representative of the nation—Providence, Baltimore, Detroit, Orlando, Omaha, Oakland, and San Antonio.

We asked each diocese to pick four or five parishes that would be representative of the diocese and that also had good parish census data. Thirty-two were selected. They were indeed diverse, including parishes in inner-city ethnic neighborhoods, new suburbs, and small towns. Whether by picking parishes with relatively good census data we biased the sample is unknown. The reason they had the census data was sometimes merely that the pastors happened to believe in house-to-house calling or that the parishes had efficient secretaries. So the bias is probably slight. During the data gathering we interviewed one priest in each parish to learn as much as we could about the parish.

Gathering the Telephone Interviews

One or two members of our research team traveled to each of the seven dioceses between October 1979 and February 1980, staying seven to ten days. Our goal was thirty interviews in each category in each diocese, which totaled 210. But we fell behind in several dioceses and ended up with 210 interviews with converts, 182 with dropouts, and 198 with returnees. Since random search methods were used throughout, the reduced sample sizes introduce minimal distortion.

In the Archdiocese of San Antonio many of the interviews were conducted in Spanish. Also, we discussed definitional questions with Hispanic experts and adopted solutions maximizing uniformity with those used in the other six dioceses (for details see Appendix A).[7]

Biases

Several biases crept in. First, no one not belonging to a family with a telephone was included in the study. This is a small bias today. Second, some categories of persons refused more than others. Among the new converts, refusals were only 5% to 10%. Among the returnees they were about 10% to 20%. Among the inactives aged 18 to 22 years they were about 45% to 55%; among the inactives aged 23 or older they were about 20% to 30%. The high refusal rate among young persons resulted from family tensions regarding the church. Some of the young

7

people felt guilty about being dropouts; others seemed uneasy about being interviewed at all regarding religion and the church.

Taped Interviews

We taped extended interviews with twelve persons in each category. This was done in three areas—middle Atlantic, Midwest, and New England. I interviewed seven people, then hired interviewers to do the rest. An interviewer was the same sex as an interviewee. We tried to choose people, usually from the lists of those already interviewed by phone, who seemed to fit the main types in our typologies. The taped personal interviews were sixty to ninety minutes long, plus a second short interview with follow-up questions, often done by telephone. (The second interview was not done with all thirty-six persons.)[8]

PAST RESEARCH AND THEORY

Past Research

Past research on Catholic converts and dropouts is sketchy, since few studies have been done. Joseph Fichter's large study of parishes of Louisiana, done in the early 1950s, is one of the best. In twenty-three urban parishes he analyzed the adult converts and found that about 75% came to the church in connection with interfaith marriages.[9] He summarized his research experience with church dropouts and identified five kinds of adult dropouts:

1. Some dropped out due to family disorganization. This was especially true of those with lower income, where separation, or demoralization of the marriage led to a breakdown of religious practices.

2. Many left the church after a mixed marriage. Approximately 30% of the marriages in these parishes were religiously mixed, and in a small fraction of the marriages the Catholic partner joined the other church.

3. In more than 40% of Fichter's interviews with dormant Catholics there was mention of the priests, such as "The priest terrified me; we were afraid of him when we were kids." Some persons remarked on the priests' aloofness, lack of cordiality, boorishness, autocratic methods, and so on.

4. Some individuals told of "traumatic experiences" with the church, such as disappointment with priests, teaching brothers and sisters, and other laypersons. It was said that these church people "set a

8

bad example." Some of the criticism was tied to rejection of church teachings about birth control.

5. Drifters are those who left the church but could not present clear reasons why. Often they said they "just lost interest" or "gradually stopped going to church." Two distinct types of drifters are the elderly who seem to have become wearied of all aspects of life, and the social strainers who have immersed themselves in the scramble for status in the larger society.[10]

Ruth Wallace analyzed more than 3,000 persons who enrolled in an inquiry course in a Catholic information center in Toronto. Those who joined the church after completing the course tended to be those with Catholic spouses, fiancés or fiancées, or friends; interpersonal influences were crucial.[11]

An important study done in Protestant churches in Canada bears on our concerns. Reginald W. Bibby and Merlin B. Brinkerhoff worked with ministers of twenty evangelical churches; they reviewed all the converts to those churches over a five-year period. Most of the converts came from other evangelical churches or were children of members. Less than 10% came from outside the evangelical community, and they came mainly through intermarriage or from other churches. Conversions from the secular sector were almost nonexistent, hence Bibby and Brinkerhoff called their report "The Circulation of the Saints."[12]

The most recent study is that done by Edward Rauff.[13] Rauff interviewed 180 persons who joined churches within the past ten years after being unchurched for at least five years. He discerned twelve main influences bringing people back to the church, of which the numerically largest (in the 180 interviews) were (1) a desire to strengthen the family or create family unity, (2) the inspiration or influence of other persons who were religious and witnessed, either silently or verbally, to their faith, (3) the loving fellowship of church groups that the interviewees visited and liked, (4) the effect of personal crises that unsettled their lives, and (5) the experience of visiting churches on special occasions, such as weddings, visits to friends, or musical programs. Rauff talked to people joining all kinds of Christian churches, and he lumped together what we are calling converts and returnees. Yet the categories he derived and the experiences he related are important.

If we turn to research on dropouts and disidentified Catholics, we find a few more studies. The Fichter study, described above, is one of the most thorough. Several studies have been done on Catholic church dropouts among youth, the best of which is by John Kotre.[14] Kotre interviewed 100 graduate students in and around Chicago (mean age was 24), all of whom had attended Catholic colleges. Fifty considered

9

themselves in the church and the other fifty saw themselves as outside; Kotre called the two groups "in" and "out." He discovered that the main determinant of whether a person was in the church or not was family life and parent-child relationships. Persons who had left the church usually did so during college, and tended (1) to have one or both parents who were not practicing Catholics; (2) to have more instances of family disruption, such as divorce, separation, or alcoholism; (3) to see their mothers as less warm and loving; and (4) to feel less identification with parental standards. Interestingly, college experiences, including courses on religion and the church, were less important predictors of in or out status than these family relationships.[15]

The 1978 Gallup survey on unchurched Americans asked unchurched people if they ever had been active in churches, and if so, why they became inactive. Table 1.1 shows the results. Among unchurched Catholics, 41% reported that they dropped out when they grew up and started making their own decisions, 39% said it was when they found other interests and activities, and 35% stated that they had specific problems with the church or its teachings. These are the three main reasons given.

The data from this Gallup survey were analyzed thoroughly by David Roozen, in an attempt to understand church dropouts better.[16] He concluded that about 42% of Catholics drop out of church attendance for two years or longer sometime in their lives. Over half the dropping out occurs in the teen years and early 20s, and the more highly educated young people tend to drop out relatively more often. Of the dropouts, the majority return sometime in their lives.

Hale interviewed 165 unchurched persons in six geographically diverse counties.[17] He presented his conclusions in an anecdotal style, and his findings are difficult to summarize. He discerned eleven different types of unchurched persons, of whom the majority were dropouts from church participation. He concluded that, as a general rule, "unchurchedness is linked to societal alienation, or lack of bondedness of persons to one another in their neighborhoods or settlements." Many of the persons he talked with either felt like outsiders in their communities or were transient persons just passing through the area. Hale found that the main decision point concerning church involvement or dropping out is early or middle adolescence.

Two research studies of United Methodist dropouts furnish more information on dynamics of Protestant congregations, which are, on the average, less than one tenth as large as Catholic parishes. John Savage led an interview study of United Methodists who had retreated from active church involvement after being highly involved for a number of years. He discovered definite sequences in the processes of

10

TABLE 1.1

1978 GALLUP POLL: REASONS FOR DROPPING OUT

	Catholic Preference Persons	Protestant Preference Persons
Thinking back to the time when you began to reduce your involvement with the church, can you tell me which of the statements below best describes the reason? Pick as many as apply.		
When I grew up and started making decisions on my own, I stopped going to church.	41%	19%
I found other interests and activities that led me to spend less and less time on church-related activities.	39	35
I had specific problems with or objections to the church, its teachings, or its members.	35	24
I moved to a different community and never got involved in a new church.	25	30
The church was no longer a help to me in finding the meaning and purpose of my life.	25	15
I felt my life-style was no longer compatible with participation in a church.	25	12
Work schedule	17	21
Divorced or separated	7	4
Poor health	4	11
Another reason	5	10
Don't know or no answer	4	6
Total*	227%	187%

*Totals add up to more than 100% due to multiple responses.

Source: Gallup (1978a:51).

becoming apathetic or bored, leading to dropping out of the church. Usually, in the beginning, some incident produced a sense of uneasiness, most commonly conflict with the pastor, with a family member, or with another church member. If the conflict went unresolved for a time, the sense of anxiety spread to other areas of life, so that worship attendance, interest in the church, and even thinking in religious terms receded. After several weeks, if no one from the church reached out to the person, he or she got a feeling that no one cared or that nothing could be done about the situation. Typically, the person would then reinvest his or her energies elsewhere.

Each of the 23 persons interviewed in the non-active group indicated that no one from the church had ever come to find out why they were losing interest or had dropped out. It reinforced their belief that no one cared, and that they were not missed. One third of this group cried during the interview, indicating the intensity of unresolved feelings.

When the individual begins to move away from the church, there is expressed a considerable amount of grief mixed with the anger. The church, for most of these non-actives, was a very important object in their lives. They still talk about it as being "their" church and "that minister (or other persons or situation) is still there and they cannot return until he/it goes away."[18]

In another United Methodist study Warren Hartman interviewed United Methodist ex-members and asked their reasons for dropping out. He found the most-mentioned reason was their failure to feel they were accepted, loved, or wanted. They felt they did not belong, and that others did not demonstrate any real concern for them. The second most-mentioned reason was some kind of personal situation, including illness in the family, changes in work schedules, transportation problems, or lack of support from other family members. The third most frequently mentioned reason was a feeling that the church was not relevant—sermons were poor, worship was boring, and church people were apathetic. Hartman summarizes:

A deep yearning to be accepted and loved by others in the church and church school is a dominant and recurrent theme among all persons. Church growth may be more closely related to a sense of acceptance by a warm, supportive Christian community than by any other factor.[19]

United Methodist research may not fit the Catholic Church exactly. We believe relationships with other parishioners were more important for the United Methodists in these studies than they are for typical Catholics. Nevertheless, the dynamics found among United Methodists undoubtedly occur to some extent among Catholics, and one would expect these dynamics to describe one portion of the Catholic dropouts.

Theories of Religious Change

A good research study not only describes the phenomena observed, but also sharpens concepts and theories for understanding them. The most helpful conceptualizing and theorizing for our task come from sociological analyses of recruitment to religious groups and to social movements in general. Theory in this field is well developed, and several key parts are outlined below.

The most influential theorizing has been done by John Lofland and his associates, in connection with a years-long study of recruitment of an American religious movement that they call Divine Precepts (a fictitious name). From observing this group for many months Lofland and Rodney Stark set forth seven factors that, in their accumulation, accounted for conversion of a person to the movement. The seven are conceived roughly in the imagery of a funnel—that is, a structure that systematically reduces the number of persons available for recruitment.

The seven factors are divided into two sets: predispositions and situational contingencies. For conversion to occur, a person must:

1. Experience enduring, acutely felt tensions
2. Within a religious problem-solving perspective,
3. Which leads him to define himself as a religious seeker;
4. Encountering the Divine Precepts at a turning point in his life,
5. Wherein an affective bond is formed (or pre-exists) with one or more converts;
6. Where extra-cult attachments are absent or neutralized;
7. And, where, if he is to become a deployable agent, he is exposed to intensive interaction.[20]

The first three of these are predispositions and the others are situational contingencies. Lofland and Stark believed that the seven steps have general applicability for many religious groups. If the predispositions are present in a person, this person is a candidate for recruitment to any of a range of religious groups. The direction this person goes depends on the situational contingencies, which are affective bonds between the person and others already in the group—relationships of trust, support, and affirmation. The theory explicitly sees personal bonds of this type as necessary for recruitment to occur. No one was brought to the Divine Precepts solely through theological teaching or Bible study.

In 1977 Lofland updated the theory and made some changes in the seven-step model. He argued that the concept "turning point" was not theoretically useful, since "everyone can be seen as in one or more important ways at a turning point at every moment of their lives."[21] Also, the concept "tension" was only moderately useful, since a researcher cannot prove or disprove that one person was feeling more

13

or less tension than anyone else at a particular time. Tension is "virtually universal in the human population." So Lofland simplified the model by de-emphasizing the first and fourth conditions. He did maintain the second condition as being important—that the person has a religious problem-solving perspective. This means that he or she already sees the world in the world view of the religious group. For the Divine Precepts, this meant a biblical view of reality; for other Christian groups, it means the general acceptance of the Judeo-Christian view of God and humanity. None of the converts to the Divine Precepts came from the secular community, with its own world view (mainly Marxist or Freudian today). This finding coincides with Bibby and Brinkerhoff's discovery that new members to Protestant churches usually have a Christian identity beforehand; none come from the secular subculture.

It is important to Lofland's theoretical viewpoint that both predispositions and situational factors are necessary for gaining converts. The predispositions are feelings within an individual of a need for personal meaning, personal affirmation, or justification. Persons with such sentiments often speak of meaninglessness, a feeling of personal void, or sense of sin. The feelings may be weak or strong at any time in the person's life, depending on events or conditions. A person without such feelings has traditionally been called hardhearted or not ready to receive the gospel.

If the predispositions are present, situational contingencies are crucial. These are personal relationships that facilitate the person coming into one or another religious group. Lofland calls a person feeling predispositions but lacking a facilitating person a seeker. A seeker often investigates one religious group after another until a facilitating person succeeds in bringing him or her into a group as a full-fledged member.

During the introductory, or courtship, period other personal relationships the person has may pull him or her away from the religious group. Lofland included this in the sixth condition of the model—that "extra-cult attachments are absent or neutralized." If the person feels an attachment to another religious group, there is much less likelihood that he or she will convert, due to the competing relationships. This is why a person committed to one religious group rarely converts to another unless the relationship to the first is somehow weakened or broken off.

A second major model for recruitment to religious movements is that of Luther P. Gerlach and Virginia H. Hine, based on their studies of Pentecostal sects.[22] These researchers stress that the deprivation theory—that socially deprived people are the ones joining religious movements—failed to explain the recruitment patterns they observed.

14

Rather, the persons who joined Pentecostal groups were persons with preexisting ties to sect members. Most prominent were kinship ties, such as with spouses and siblings. Also important were ties with neighbors, friends, workmates, bosses, employees, and distant relatives. Gerlach and Hine did not stress the predispositions for joining a sect; they argued that the necessary predispositions (or motivations) are found in many people, and besides, such predispositions are hard to measure. Rather, they stressed the mechanisms by which certain people out of these large numbers in fact joined the groups. The crucial mechanism was positive personal relationships. Recruiting in the general public or in public places was, by contrast, ineffective. Mass meetings and leaflet campaigns were effective only as adjuncts to the personal communications of members with people they knew.[23]

The main difference between Lofland and Gerlach-Hine is on the question of predispositions. Gerlach and Hine did not deny the possible role of predispositions, but merely said they found no explanatory power in any analysis of converts' predispositions. This is because predispositions were similar to feelings held broadly in the population and also because the feelings were intensified and focused in the very process of becoming a Pentecostal member, with its new affirmative personal relationships and new experiences. Our judgment, as we argue below, is that predispositions must be part of the theoretical model.

But first, let us ask if these theoretical models apply to the Catholic Church, since they were developed mostly from observation of new religious groups and sectlike bodies. Two researchers have studied the question and have concluded that the models apply to conventional faiths (that is, faiths having little tension between themselves and the surrounding society) as well as to sects. With this we agree. Rodney Stark and William Sims Bainbridge pointed out that the Gerlach-Hine model fit the Catholic Pentecostal movement converts in two separate studies, and they argued that the importance of interpersonal bonds is even greater for conventional, mainline denominations than for exclusivistic sects, since the latter attract numbers only from restricted populations having certain predispositions, mainly strong feelings of personal deprivation.[24] David A. Snow and his associates came to the same conclusion.[25]

The Mormon Church, which has experimented with many means of evangelizing new members, explicitly recognizes the importance of social networks and personal relationships. A practical manual on recruiting new members written in 1974 outlines thirteen steps in reaching out to new people and bringing them into the Mormon faith. Early steps are directed toward building close personal ties; at this point in the relationship the Mormon faith should not be discussed. Only after personal bonds are built, through doing things together with the potential recruit, helping him or her, and discussing common life problems, should the Mormon invite the person to a Mormon church service. And only when the person asks questions about the Mormon faith should the evangelizer suggest that he or she do some Bible study with a Mormon missionary. The most promising persons to be recruited are married couples concerned about family life, and a Mormon couple in similar circumstances is the most effective evangelizer for them.[26]

Theories of recruitment to social movements are comparable in logic to the theories of religious recruitment. The older theory gave most emphasis to the predispositions of broad categories of people that "explained" the rise or growth of certain social movements within these groups. Sociological theories of "structural strain," and psychological analyses of alienation and relative deprivation were developed in this tradition.[27]

The newer theory resembles Gerlach and Hine's exclusive attention to networks of people who facilitate recruitment. A recent statement of this point of view by Snow and his associates indicated the importance attached to interpersonal relationships rather than psychological states or ideology:

> It is important to emphasize that people seldom initially join movements per se. Rather, they typically are asked to participate in movement activities. It is during the course of initial participation that they are provided with the "reasons" or "justifications" for what they have already done and for continuing participation. . . . We would thus argue that the "motives" for joining or continued participation are generally emergent and interactional rather than prestructured.[28]

For an understanding of religious change among Catholics, a simplified process model based on Lofland appears most accurate and most useful. Figure 1.1 depicts such a model, which fits both past research and the data gathered in the present study. It is a flow chart showing three conditions, or decision points, in the process of becoming a Catholic convert. The first condition is that the potential convert have a Christian world view. Past research indicates that few persons who do not have this world view become members of Christian groups. The second is that the person have a felt need, at least minimally, inducing him or her to take Catholic teaching seriously or to participate in a Mass or a group activity. We include this in the model even though Gerlach and Hine found the idea too vague for theoretical

16

FIGURE 1.1
THREE SUCCESSIVE CONDITIONS
FOR BECOMING A CATHOLIC CONVERT

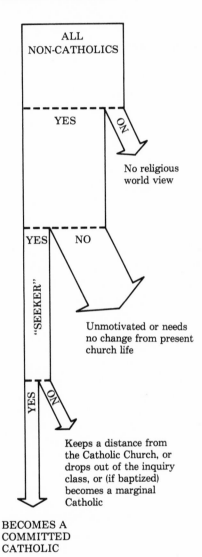

PREDISPOSITIONS

CONDITION #1: Has a religious world view. (In America the majority of people have this.)

CONDITION #2: Has a felt need for spiritual life or church involvement, or a change in them. (The proportions here are unknown, and they vary from year to year. Persons with needs satisfied in another religious group are in the "no" category here.)

FACILITATING RELATIONSHIPS

CONDITION #3: Develops affective bonds with a priest, religious, or church leader and with members of the parish. (The proportions here are unknown. The splitting-off process may occur prior to the inquiry class, during it, or after baptism. In the last case, the person becomes a marginal Catholic. In general, bonds with both priests and laity are needed.)

ALL NON-CATHOLICS

YES — ON

No religious world view

YES — NO

"SEEKER"

Unmotivated or needs no change from present church life

YES — ON

Keeps a distance from the Catholic Church, or drops out of the inquiry class, or (if baptized) becomes a marginal Catholic

BECOMES A COMMITTED CATHOLIC

use; we have found many cases in which felt needs increased dramatically from one month to the next because of events in the person's life. Often the death of a loved one, a family crisis, or an unpleasant experience in another church gives the person new felt needs, leading him or her toward looking into the Catholic Church.

The third condition is a summary of the facilitating relationships and lack of competing relationships discussed by all theorists. We have seen instances where a person became a baptized or confirmed Catholic but never achieved any affective bonds with a priest or with other persons in the parish. Usually such a person becomes marginal and, after a time, inactive.

Many converts to the Catholic Church come after intermarriage. The model is correct for them, but it is not too helpful for increasing understanding. In many cases of intermarriage, condition two is really a felt need for marital happiness and family unity more than a personal spiritual need, hence conditions two and three blur into each other.

Theories of Life Cycle Development

We looked at adults aged 18 and older who underwent religious change. Perhaps the change is one element in a broader change in life, so that it can be understood only within the structure of the larger event. This possibility prompted us to review adult life cycle development research. We hoped that deeper understanding of religious transitions might be achieved by interpreting them within the life cycle. The work of Daniel J. Levinson is the most prominent in this field, as an extension of Erik Erikson's theories of the stages of life.[29] Levinson and his associates studied forty men between the ages of 35 and 45, in four occupations. The survey identified the main developmental tasks these men faced in their 20s, 30s, and 40s. The choices made in each decade and the consequences of the choices for later development are illustrated in Levinson's book. We find the general idea convincing and the task of understanding religious change in such terms promising. To anticipate a bit, we did not find clear matches between our data and Levinson's theoretical stages. We did find evidence of midlife crises, prompting a rethinking of one's commitments and relationships. But no closer correlation between our data and Levinson's was visible.

Perhaps we should not have expected any relationship to appear on its own, without our explicitly probing for it. Or perhaps because Levinson's work was with men and the majority of our subjects were women, the age patterns are different. We believe the idea of adult life cycle stages is still fruitful, but somehow our study was not successful in relating to it.

A theoretically important concept of Levinson's is life structure. It means the total structure of involvements and areas of participation in any period of life—especially marriage, job, community, family, and kinship. The structure must be coherent if the person is not to be burdened by unending conflicts in himself or herself, or within the family. When one important element in the structure changes, others must also change in time.

One or two components have a central place in the life structure; others are secondary or marginal. Central components have the greatest significance for the self, and they strongly influence the choices made in other aspects of life.

> The components most likely to be central in a man's life are occupation, marriage-family, friendship and peer relationships, ethnicity and religion. Leisure may also have a central place, when it serves important functions for the self and is more than a casual activity. Playing sports after work or watching sports on TV is a serious matter for many men. We found that occupation and marriage-family are usually the most central components, though there are significant variations in their relative weight and in the importance of other components. Work and family are universal features of human life.[30]

In short, analysts of religious change must be careful to look for relationships between the religious change and change in central components of the life structure, especially work and family.

Parish Factors

From past theorizing it was clear that evangelization should be conceived of as matchmaking—a process of matching people and religious groups. Good research should therefore start from both parties in the match. Our study is limited in this respect, since we are looking at individuals much more than at Catholic parishes or groups. We can learn a few things about successfully evangelizing parishes by asking the converts or returnees to describe the parishes they now are active in, but this is not sufficient.[31] Another type of research should be done that begins with parishes and religious groups attempting to reach out, and that studies the processes that actually produce new members. We were not able to do this, but someone else should.[32]

The present study has another limitation, in that it starts almost entirely from the accounts given us by the interviewees and is largely limited to the perceptions made by the interviewees. What they failed to see—perhaps some very important things—we will also fail to see. For example, we noticed that the convert-making rates in the Catholic Church varied widely from region to region, since our experiences were so different from one region to another. This led us to look into the topic more systematically (see chapter 2). But no individual convert was aware of this pattern. In short, all individuals perceive the world

19

from where they are, and subtle social forces are invisible to them. Only through systematic historical study or systematic data gathering can subtle economic or social factors be discerned. In our study we have missed many of them.

AMERICAN CATHOLICISM IN THE EARLY 1980s

A study such as ours must be understood in its historical context. Otherwise its findings may be seen as more universal than they are and its implications for coming decades too precisely drawn. Our data were gathered in 1979-80, not 1959-60 or 1999-2000. This point in the history of American Catholicism is unique, and it can be understood only by looking back in time, especially to the 1960s.

The 1960s will pass into history as a major transitional point in the history of American Catholicism. John Cogley has called this watershed "the most dramatic, critical ten years in American Catholic history."[33] A series of sociological studies has led Andrew Greeley to see the decade as one of "extraordinarily profound and pervasive change."[34] Two key events propelled American Catholics from one historical stage to another—Vatican Council II (1962-65), which renewed the church in the spirit of aggiornamento, and *Humanae Vitae* (1968), the encyclical on human love that, among other things, repeated the church's traditional teaching on birth control. Both events made a permanent impression on American Catholics.

A brief look at the period preceding the 1960s may help contextualize the decade's events. The central point is that the preconciliar church in America was shaped during its immigrant era, which spanned the years from 1830 to 1960. For more than a century the church absorbed millions of newcomers—first from western Europe, and later from southern and eastern Europe—men, women, and children speaking a variety of languages and representing a spectrum of cultures but all united in one faith and in the desire to find in the New World new homes and better lives. The rise of the immigrant church is a complex story, but one may select three broad themes in it.

First, the immigrant church was an overwhelming physical presence. Despite their poverty, these strangers and their children built—and staffed—new parishes and institutions of every sort. The growth of parochial schools was the most obvious evidence of this institutional expansion. These schools started out modestly in the early nineteenth century, partly to protect the faith of the immigrant children from the mainly Protestant influences of the public schools

20

and partly to preserve the language and culture of the homeland. The enrollment grew steadily until a peak in the mid-1960s, when Catholic elementary and secondary schools accommodated more than 5.5 million children, a figure that constituted the largest private educational system in the world.

Parishes, schools, and colleges grew up on all sides. Most church leaders in the later nineteenth century believed that the survival of the Catholic church depended on developing institutions parallel to those in the host society and on involving Catholics in them. For instance, Cardinal Dennis Dougherty, in his first ten years as Archbishop of Philadelphia (1918-28), opened ninety-two parishes, eighty-nine parish schools, three high schools, fourteen academies, a women's college, a preparatory seminary, a retreat house, an orphanage, a school for the hearing-impaired, and other institutions and hospitals.[35]

This institutional presence consisted of more than raising imposing buildings; it also meant the blossoming of religious vocations for males and females in the Catholic community, producing leadership for these manifold institutions and programs. By the mid-1960s the American Jesuits alone constituted a quarter of the society's world membership, and in Minnesota, St. John's Abbey gathered the largest Benedictine community in the world.[36]

The second theme concerning the immigrant church is that its physical presence intimidated many native Americans and fueled suspicions that, as members of a monarchical religious body, Catholics would subvert the foundations of the Republic. These suspicions found expression in several—occasionally violent—outbreaks of anti-Catholicism. The anti-Catholicism hurt and confused Catholics who had sought America as a Land of Freedom and Opportunity. It was the source of a strong sense of alienation and unwelcome—what some historians have called the siege mentality.

For many Americans, the fear of Catholicism lingered well into the twentieth century. A key testing point of the assimilation of American Catholics into the national fabric occurred during the election of 1928. A variety of factors have been attributed to the defeat of Alfred E. Smith, the first Catholic to be nominated for the Presidency, but undoubtedly the religious factor was very important. Al Smith lost in his bid for the Presidency because he had been an altar boy and still professed the faith of his immigrant parents.

The third theme related to immigrant Catholicism in America is its striking centralization of authority. Although the early hierarchy experimented with collegiality, after the 1890s the influence of Rome gathered strength. The church was strongly centralized throughout the first half of the twentieth century.

The decades prior to World War II were a time of growth in

21

numbers and in affluence, as the immigrant groups pulled themselves up in standard of living and education. After World War II new underlying social forces began to affect the church. The affluence of the laity rose to hitherto-unknown levels, and suburbanization began. Thousands of young Catholics began leaving the city neighborhoods they grew up in for the promise of homes in the suburbs, with trees and flowers and middle-class comforts. The Catholics of the fifties were well-educated, young, ambitious, child-oriented, and at home in American culture.[37]

The dramatic events of the 1960s could not have happened if social pressures had not been building up. Symptoms of change appeared in the 1950s. First, serious questions were posed concerning Catholic schools and colleges. A national debate focused on a question raised by the leading historian of American Catholicism, John Tracy Ellis: Why have American Catholics, despite their commitment to supporting a network of schools at all levels, failed to contribute substantially to the intellectual life of the country? Perhaps, he suggested, the value and purpose of these schools should be reexamined. Perhaps they have not provided an education of excellence; perhaps their contribution has been only to foster a ghetto mentality, that state of mind which has detoured many Catholics out of the mainstream of national life.[38] Second, there was a new movement for liturgical renewal that gathered much strength. It proposed liturgical changes having more communal aspects, more lay involvement, and more adaptation to the culture. Third, sociological studies appeared showing that, in terms of income, Catholics had become equal to Protestants. Some Catholic ethnic groups were shown to be successful in American economic life.

In 1960 John F. Kennedy was elected President of the United States. He had an immeasurable impact on American Catholics, for he made them feel proud of their religion and secure about their status as fully American. His example neutralized most of the earlier attitudes by non-Catholics that the Catholic Church was somehow dangerous. Both Catholics and non-Catholics felt new openness to each other.

The Vatican Council and After

The closing of the Vatican Council II, in December 1965, marked the inauguration of a new era. The new directions were path-breaking. The council affirmed the ecumenical movement, endorsed religious freedom of conscience in all nations, and expressed openness and some optimism regarding modern secular systems of thought. The council also mandated liturgical innovation, encouraged the religious orders to update themselves and their missions in the context of modern society,

22

and asked for establishment of decision-making procedures involving broader participation—including senates of priests in each diocese and parish councils in each parish.[39]

Three years after the council closed, another important event in Rome affected American Catholics: Pope Paul issued *Humanae Vitae*. While this encyclical affirmed the dignity of human life, it also reasserted the traditional ban against mechanical and chemical contraception. There was opposition in many nations, including the United States. Observers have debated which had the greater effect, for good or harm, on American Catholicism—the council or the encyclical. Andrew Greeley concluded, based on sociological surveys, that the council's effect was positive for the church, but that this effect was undone by the negative effect of the encyclical against birth control. Greeley argued that the encyclical had led to a loss of respect for church authority.[40]

In the decade following the council, events occurred in rapid succession. The Mass was changed from Latin to English, priests celebrated the Mass facing the laity, and the laity became more involved in the liturgy through hymn-singing and as extraordinary ministers at the altar. New music and art styles were tried. Abstinence from meat on Fridays was abandoned, and some older forms of devotion were deemphasized. New forms of confession were allowed, including communal absolution and face-to-face dialogue between penitent and priest. Publication of the Index of Forbidden Books was discontinued. American Catholics had reached maturity and were ready for changes. In Greeley's words, "the Vatican Council occurred just at the time when the youngest generation of Catholics marked the definite end of the immigrant era."[41]

Some parts of the institutional church were strongly affected. The priesthood felt a sort of identity crisis, and thousands left. Women's orders questioned their cumbersome dress code, and the majority either modernized their dress or abandoned the habits entirely in favor of secular fashions. They democratized many of their structures and ventured into new forms of ministry, abandoning the older assumption that their role was confined to staffing Catholic schools and hospitals.

Mass attendance began dropping in the late 1960s. Most of the decline was due to indifference among youth. Figure 1.2 depicts trends in weekly church attendance for both Catholics and Protestants within three age strata. Whereas Protestants developed a moderate generation gap in the late 1950s that has persisted with little change until the most recent polls, Catholics experienced a widening generation gap throughout the 1960s and 1970s. As the figure graphically describes, the result is a recent convergence of Catholic and Protestant practices.

But not all the trends were downward. New forms of church life

FIGURE 1.2
PERCENT ATTENDING WEEKLY BY AGE STRATA, CATHOLICS AND PROTESTANTS

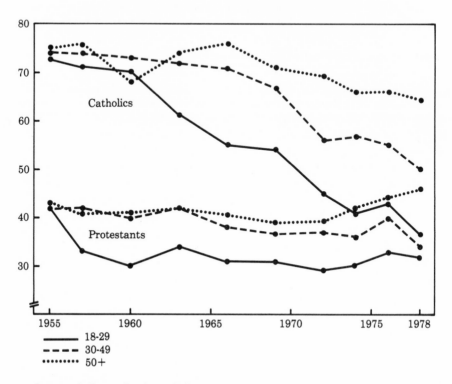

Catholics

Protestants

18-29
30-49
50+

Source: Gallup polls, from Gallup (1978) and Roper Center. Two or more polls combined in each year plotted.

emerged. Democratic structures mandated by the council slowly appeared; first priests' senates in the dioceses, then parish councils of elected lay leaders. The office of permanent deacon was reintroduced after centuries of disuse; the office gained momentum in the mid-1970s, and the number of permanent deacons increased dramatically in a few years. A charismatic prayer movement arose—unexpectedly—in the late 1960s, and new forms of retreats were attracting a massive following, especially the *cursillos* and Marriage Encounter.

The dizzying pace of change decelerated during the 1970s, so that by the end of the decade, there was evidence of a steady return to normalcy. But it was not the normalcy of the pre-Vatican era; it was the stabilization of a different era, one that was new in the history of American Catholicism.

A sociological law states that any group undergoing rapid change splits into factions or parties based on differing attitudes toward the direction or rate of the change. This phenomenon occurred in American Catholicism, producing a polarization that is commonly labeled young versus old, but which is probably better described as pre-Vatican versus post-Vatican. By the mid-1970s the progressive post-Vatican party won acceptance in most segments of the church and enjoyed the backing of the majority of laity.

To sum up, the 1960s saw a great reversal, in which the ghetto Catholicism of the immigrant era was replaced by a middle-class Catholicism that embraced American culture. Many of the changes after the council consisted of trimming off the excesses of Old World styles, authoritarian structures, and clericalism. Others represented a gravitation of Catholics away from religious docility to a new urge to be selective regarding beliefs and exercises.[42] This new stance, Greeley proposed, is typical of the communal Catholic, that is, one who regards himself or herself as genuinely part of the Catholic community and tradition but who declines to allow the institutional church, notably the magisterium, to influence his or her life.

The Early 1980s: Ethnicity

In the 1920s U.S. Congress drastically restricted immigration. The massive flow of immigrants into the American Catholic Church stopped. Currently, the majority of Catholics in America are two or more generations removed from the immigrant experience and have been fully exposed to the dominant culture. Yet the ties of the past have retained such a hold on certain groups within the church that, even after years of residence in this country, they continue to have a distinctive ethnic identity.

The exact sizes of the recognizable ethnic groups in American Catholicism are difficult to determine—especially since U.S. government figures on Hispanics are vague. Our best estimate of the breakdown of American Catholicism by ethnicity (not counting persons who say they are mixed or American) is based on research by Harold Abramson and Andrew Greeley, and on published reports of Hispanics in the church today.[43] The largest group is probably the Hispanics, comprising about 20% to 25% (although this is only a guess), followed by the Italians, making up about 18%. The Irish are about 15% and the Germans are about 14%. The Polish are about 10% and the French (including French Canadians) about 9%. Finally, the English are about 3%, the blacks about 2%, and all others about 6%. The Hispanics are both the oldest ethnic group in American Catholicism—dating from the Spanish missions in the American

25

Southwest—and in a sense the newest, since the dramatic increases in their numbers came only in recent decades.[44]

Hispanics are the only large, new immigrant group in American Catholicism. They are arriving in great numbers each year and are destined to influence the church in far-reaching ways in the future. They comprise several distinct ethnic groups that have Spanish language and culture in common but unique national traditions. About 60% of Hispanic Catholics are Mexican-Americans; the next largest group, the Puerto Ricans, with about 14%. The other 26% are composed of various nationalities, including Central and South Americans, Filipinos, and Spanish.

In the past the Hispanics have suffered exploitation from other Americans. Today they are concerned about maintaining their language and heritage in a culturally pluralistic America. Although in the past they have had disproportionately meager representation within the American hierarchy, greater numbers of Hispanics are now enrolling in seminaries, where they are forming pools of future ministers to assume leadership of these communities.

The Early 1980s: Church Life

Many of the pell-mell changes in the church have now slowed down, so that Catholic church life in the early 1980s has generally returned to a near-equilibrium. Mass attendance continues to decline slowly, but this trend does not come near the 25% to 30% drop in the first decade after the council. Seminaries and religious orders have nearly stabilized their numbers.

Nevertheless, adjustments are going on. In 1979 Andrew Greeley and his associates repeated surveys done in 1963 and 1974, and the results indicated that significant changes are continuing. In the area of sexuality, Catholics (like other Americans) were opting for more and more personal freedom. Opposition to contraception, divorce, and premarital sex declined considerably between 1963 and 1979.[45] Attitudes about church authority also changed, with fewer Catholics believing that Jesus directly handed over the leadership of the church to Peter and the popes, and fewer believing in papal authority.[46]

Approval for the changes since Vatican Council II is high. A 1977 Gallup poll found that 67% of American Catholics approved of the changes.[47] Ecumenism is also high; three recent studies found that Catholics are more ecumenical in their attitudes than Protestants.[48]

New forms of spirituality have appeared in the years since the council. The charismatic renewal movement dates from 1967, and by 1980 about 2,800 prayer groups were active.[49] Marriage Encounter came to the United States from Spain in 1967 and mushroomed

26

throughout the American church. Thousands of couples have taken part in the weekends and have felt new commitment to serve the church. The Cursillo movement (emphasizing weekend spiritual retreats), also from Spain, began in California in 1962 and spread to all sectors of the church during the 1970s.[50] All three of these movements are highly personal, involving participants in small supportive fellowships, with de-emphasis of clergy-lay distinctions. Each manifests the vitality of the church and may indicate future forms of devotional life.

Chapter

2

WHO ARE THE CONVERTS?

To UNDERSTAND the patterns of convert-making, we carried out two
levels of analysis: first, the analysis of broad statistical trends; and
second, the analysis of the 210 individuals we interviewed. We
examined the statistics on adult converts in the *Official Catholic Directory*
and found definite regional variations. To compare the regional rates
we computed the ratio of converts per 1,000 active Catholics for the
total United States as well as for the nine regions defined by the U.S.
census. Figure 2.1 shows the ratios in the nation, in the two regions with
the highest rates, and in the two with the lowest rates.

Convert-making is most active in the central states and least active
in the New England and the Middle Atlantic states. The most
important explanation for these regional differences is in the rates of
intermarriage. Intermarriage rates are highest where Catholics are a
small percentage of the population and where no social barriers
impede social mixing of religious groups. The east south central
region, which has the highest convert per 1,000 active ratio, includes
Kentucky, Tennessee, Alabama, and Mississippi. The west north
central region, which ranks second, includes the Dakotas, Nebraska,
Minnesota, Iowa, Kansas, and Missouri. The individual states with the
highest ratios in 1979 were Oklahoma, Arkansas, and Tennessee.
These are states with small Catholic populations and virtually no ethnic
neighborhoods or enclaves. The states with the lowest ratio in 1979
were Rhode Island, Massachusetts, and Connecticut, where Catholic
neighborhoods are distinct and intermarriage rates are low.

Figure 2.1 shows that convert-making has become more difficult
since the 1950s. The greatest slowdown was in the 1958-to-1975 period.

FIGURE 2.1

CONVERTS PER 1,000 ACTIVE CATHOLICS
IN THE TOTAL U.S. AND IN THE CENSUS
REGIONS WITH HIGHEST AND LOWEST RATES,
1950 TO 1979

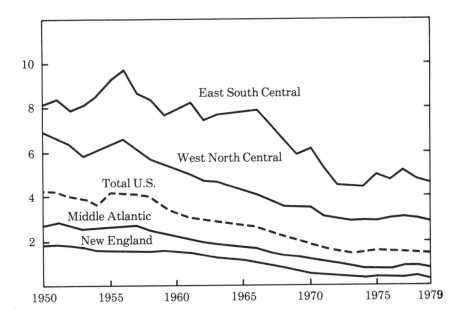

Source: Kenedy Directories 1950-1979. The four regions shown have
the highest and lowest rates in the 1970s.

The rate in the total United States was 4.3 per 1,000 Catholics in 1950,
3.9 in 1958, 2.1 in 1969, and 1.6 in 1979. This decrease has been
gradual and steady, indicating it is a product of underlying social
factors more than specific church policies. The most crucial social
factors are rates of intermarriage and decisions about converting or not
converting after intermarriage. (The topic is discussed in detail in
chapter 4.) Here we may note that although intermarriage has
increased during the 1960s and 1970s, the number of Catholic adult
converts per 100 intermarriages has decreased during these years. The
latter trend is important in understanding the downward slopes in
Figure 2.1.

Our major analysis was based on the 210 interviews. We asked the
pastor in each of the thirty-two parishes where we worked for the list of
converts in the past three years. In four dioceses the converts in the
four to six parishes totaled thirty or more, but in three dioceses they did

not, necessitating our interviewing converts in neighboring parishes as well.

The number of adult converts varies from parish to parish as well as from region to region. We have no statistical study of this, but in our experience the parishes receiving the most converts are those located in neighborhoods where relatively well-educated young adults reside, provided the churches relate well to such people. Relating well entails the churches carrying on programs and styles of worship that the people like and having staffs that relate well to the people. One special type of parish receives many converts—a parish in a black neighborhood that relates authentically to the black culture and the black worship idiom. We experienced several such parishes, and they receive many black converts.

Description of Converts

Since few of the converts refused interviews, we have a reliable picture of who the adult converts are. The lists given to us had 60% females and 40% males. Our completed interviews listed 62% females and 38% males. This sex ratio is similar to the sex ratio of persons attending Mass in a typical parish.[1]

The interviews had 85% whites, 10% blacks, 2% Hispanics, 2% Asians, and 1% others. To check on the racial composition of all Catholic converts, we conferred with the National Office of Black Catholics and the Commission for the Catholic Missions Among the Colored People and Indians—the two national offices with the most reliable information. The latter estimated that 8% of recent adult converts are black. Experts in both offices agreed that the number of black converts to Catholicism has declined since the 1960s. One reason is that Catholic schools have been closing, and Catholic schools have been agents of evangelization, since they were often attractive to blacks as alternatives to public schools. Some of the black parents later converted. Another reason is that the ideal of integration is weaker now in the black community than it was in the 1960s, and fewer blacks come to the Catholic Church desiring a racially integrated religious community. Sr. Mary Ellen Quilty, of the Commission for the Catholic Missions Among the Colored People and Indians, estimated that the number of black converts in 1979 was half what it was in about 1965.

Most of the converts are young adults. The top part of Figure 2.2 depicts the ages of the converts when they joined the church. Forty-six percent are between ages 20 and 30, and 26% are between ages 30 and 40. They are relatively well educated; 23% have college or graduate degrees compared with 12% among active Catholics in 1978.

30

FIGURE 2.2
AGE OF CONVERTS AND RETURNEES

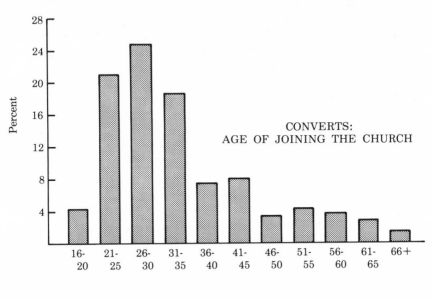

CONVERTS:
AGE OF JOINING THE CHURCH

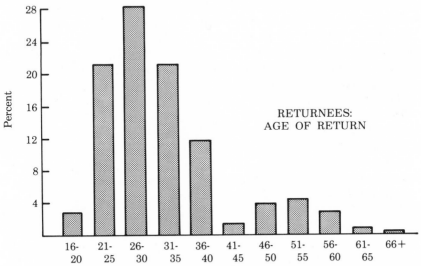

RETURNEES:
AGE OF RETURN

The converts belong to all ethnic groups, but the number of Italians, French, Polish, and Hispanics is much lower than among active American Catholics. In our sample, 1% are Italians, 1% are French, none are Polish, and 2% are Hispanics. Disproportionate

31

numbers come from ethnic groups largely outside of American Catholicism: 15% are English or Scottish, 8% are African, and 8% are Scandinavian. Twenty-one percent give their main nationality as mixed.

REASONS FOR BECOMING A CONVERT

At this point we need to insert a short explanation of how we handled the interview information. A main purpose of our study was to discern the main motivations causing people to become converts, dropouts, or returnees. Such a question requires some human judgment in addition to the answers given to our specific questions. Hence, the two persons on our research team with the most pastoral and research experience made global judgments about each person interviewed. We made judgments about the principal predispositions (or motivations) for the change, the principal facilitating persons or relationships, and the principal facilitating events. The coding scheme allowed more than one predisposition, facilitating person, and facilitating event per person.

We trust these global judgments—which we call global codes—as the most reliable way of discerning this important information. Throughout this book we refer to global codes. They are similar to the raw information given us, but in some cases they differ a bit, for theoretical reasons yet to be discussed.

Both the interview responses and our global codes agreed that the major reason for becoming an adult convert to the Catholic Church is intermarriage. The current marital status of our sample is 84% now married, 3% separated or divorced, 10% never married, and 3% widowed. Of the persons now married, 71% are in their first marriages and 29% are in their second or third marriages.

In the global coding we looked at each case of a person becoming a convert after intermarriage, and our best estimate is that 83% of the converts came largely due to intermarriage. But marrying a Catholic is not in itself a motivation for conversion to the Catholic Church; many non-Catholics marry Catholics and never change. So the actual decisions are made by other factors than just intermarriage as such. Most priests today, when counseling mixed-religion couples about marriage, do not recommend conversion if family pressures appear to be the main reason for doing it.

In the global coding we were able to identify one or more predispositions in 95% of the cases (one in 60%, two in 31%, and three in 4%). We were able to code facilitating persons or relationships in 91% of the cases (one in 50%, two in 41%). We were able to code facilitating events in 73% of the cases (one in 60%, two in 13%). (See Table 2.1, page 34.)

We discerned four predispositions. The most frequent is concern for education or religious training of children being reared Catholic; this is present in 45% of the cases. Second is concern for a marriage to a Catholic person (38% of the cases). Because these two were so similar we never coded both for any one case. The two add up to 83%. The other principal predisposition is a feeling of void, spiritual need, lack of meaning, or emotional depression; this was present in 40% of the cases, usually in combination with concern for one's marriage or concern for one's children. The most common combinations of predispositions were the second and fourth (15% of all the cases) and the first and fourth (9%). That is, conversion most often occurred when a person was married to a Catholic, had children being reared Catholics, felt concern for them or for family religious unity, and also had feelings of void, spiritual need, lack of meaning, or emotional depression. A combination often precipitated a decision to look into converting.

Most conversions are facilitated by personal relationships—in our sample clearly in 91% of the cases. The most common facilitators by far were Catholic spouses, or fiancés or fiancées. The second most common were priests, relatives, and in-laws. Frequently, both spouses and relatives were influential.

Finally, Table 2.1 shows facilitating events that were factors in the decisions to convert. The most common event was marriage. In 8% of the cases the death of a loved one was a factor, because it influenced the converts' religious viewpoints or introduced them to new relationships in the family or parish. Personal and marital crises, and illnesses were present in 15% of the cases. Child-related events, such as a new birth, baptism, or beginning school or Confraternity of Christian Doctrine (CCD) were present in about 14% of the cases. Seven percent converted after moving to new communities or changing to new parishes. Eight percent did so after having important religious experiences. (We coded religious experiences separately only when the person emphasized them and when they occurred apart from other recent highly stressful events in the person's life.)

These facilitating events were occasions for undertaking some new pattern of behavior. The majority of the events caused changes in predispositions, but some caused changes in facilitating relationships. Often they produced changes in the total life structure of the person. The presence of facilitating events in most of these cases demonstrates that any person's readiness to become a Catholic convert is greatest after some shift or movement in his or her life—a point often noted by specialists in evangelism or church growth.[2] Another implication is that persons who have moved into new communities are the most receptive

TABLE 2.1

PREDISPOSITIONS AND FACILITATORS FOR CONVERTS

	Percent
Predispositions	
Married to a Catholic or about to marry a Catholic; feels concern for the marriage (concern for children is secondary or absent)	38
Has children being reared Catholic and feels concern for their education or religious training, or for family religious unity	45
Dissatisfied with another church; recently withdrew from it, and the dissatisfaction is still significant; desires a new church	9
Feels a void or spiritual need in life; feels emptiness or lack of meaning or emotional depression	40
Other	1
Total	133
Facilitating Persons or Relationships	
Catholic spouse, fiancé, or fiancée	63
Relative or in-law	14
Children (if children took a conscious role in facilitating)	6
Friend or neighbor	9
Priest	17
Other parish staff	5
Charismatic group	5
Marriage Encounter	7
Television programs or reading (not including books in inquiry class)	3
Other	3
Total	132
Facilitating Events	
Marriage, remarriage, or upcoming marriage	21
Annulment of former marriage or death of former spouse	3
Death of loved one	8
Marital or family crisis	7
Serious illness or personal crisis (including serious illness in the family)	8
Birth or baptism of child	7
Child entering Catholic school	4
Child entering CCD or making First Communion	4
Moved to new parish or community, or changed parishes in same community	7
Had religious experience	8
Other	7
Total	84

34

to affiliation with churches during the first few months. After six months or so, behavior and commitments tend to harden into forms less easily changed.[3] The importance of facilitating events furthermore indicates that receptivity to evangelization by any person changes from time to time, depending on life events. The mission field is forever being renewed.

What Influenced Them to Become Converts?

We asked the converts a series of questions about possible influences on their decisions to become Catholics; then we asked them to estimate the importance of each influence. The percentage estimating each influence as very important is shown in Appendix A, Table A.2. The numbers in Table A.2 are somewhat lower than those in Table 2.1 above, since we included some items in the global code even if the persons did not rate them very important, but if the total interview demonstrated their effect.

The most influential persons clearly were spouses, in-laws, and priests. Thirty-four percent reported that a personal problem or problems in the family had been influential in their decisions to become Catholics (10% said that the problems were very important), and we asked which kinds of problems they were. The most common were death of a loved one, family or marital crisis, and personal illness.

Of all the converts, 37% had children between ages 0 and 6, 48% had children between ages 6 and 18, and 19% had children over age 18. We asked all those whose children were school age if the children were in public, private, or Catholic schools. Sixty-two percent replied public; 2%, private; 31%, Catholic; and 6% reported that some were in public and some in Catholic schools. We asked those whose children were younger than school age which schools they would prefer their children attend: public, private, or Catholic school. Seventy-one percent said Catholic schools.

We asked all who had children of school age if their concern for their children's education influenced their decisions to become baptized Catholics, and 12% of the sample responded that this concern was very important. Then we asked if the children were factors in any other ways, and 18% said yes, very important. "How?" The overwhelming answer was a desire for family religious life and family unity.

In the lower part of Table A.2 we see that other influences were present for a few converts: participation in charismatic prayer groups, Marriage Encounter, radio or television programs, and religious reading. They are of secondary importance in the overall.

Most of the converts had been active in other churches. Eighty-five percent said they received religious training as children, and 83% said they attended Sunday school or church two or three times a month or more when they were in elementary school. This finding agrees with all earlier research showing that most new members of Christian churches already possess a Christian world view.

We asked in which denominations they had had training. The responses were Baptist, 24%; Methodist, 17%; Lutheran, 15%; Presbyterian, 11%; Episcopalian, 7%; Catholic, 3%; Jewish, 2%; Pentecostal, 1%; and all others (mixed, multiple religions, or unspecified Protestant), 18%. The 3% reporting Catholic religious training had attended Catholic schools or catechism classes sometime during their youth, but due to some family influence, residential move, or the like, had never been baptized or confirmed Catholic. In general, the converts came from all branches of Protestantism and Judaism, more or less in proportion to the sizes of these groups in the nation.

We asked if the converts had ever been active in any churches prior to becoming baptized Catholics. Sixty-three percent answered yes. When we asked which denominations, they reported the same distribution as for their training (noted above). Next, we asked if they were active in these other churches until the time they became Catholics. Sixty-seven percent replied no. We asked them at what ages they had dropped out of active church life, and they said it was in their teens and 20s—20% said between ages 10 and 15, 42% said between ages 16 and 20, and 27% said between ages 21 and 25. Why had they dropped out? The most common reasons given were "married a person of a different denomination" (26%), "moved" (20%), "unhappy with beliefs or practices" (16%), and "rebellion; out on my own; drifted away" (10%). In short, two thirds of the converts who had been active in other churches had dropped out of church life some years ago, and the reasons for dropping out had mostly to do with their experiences in adolescence and young adulthood.

John Lofland and Rodney Stark spoke of seekers, whom they defined as persons having personal predispositions to church involvement but lacking facilitating persons or relationships that would bring them into active church life. We tried to estimate how many of the converts in our sample could be so defined in the years prior to becoming Catholics. We asked, "In the years before you became a Catholic, did you seek religious truth in various places and look into various kinds of teachings?" Thirty percent said yes. We asked these persons, "For how long a period?" Thirty-four percent said two years or less, 25% said three to five years, 18% said six to ten years, and 23% said more than ten years. We were surprised by the large number who replied yes to this question; apparently, many persons in our society are seeking religious truth in various places but not finding personal satisfaction.

Some people have histories of religious switching, and we wondered if this were true of the converts in our sample. We asked, "Did you switch from one denomination to another at any time?" (This was apart from their recent conversion to Catholicism.) Fifteen percent said yes. The ages of switching were mostly between 10 and 25. Why? The main reasons were "moved" (19%), "marriage or relatives" (19%), "unhappy experience with the church or minister" (15%), and "friends" (12%).

Finally, we asked every convert who had been active in another church, "Did you feel a dissatisfaction with the other church or religious group?" Fifty-three percent said yes. What was the main dissatisfaction? The main ones given (as we categorized them) were "dissatisfaction with doctrine or practices" (39%), "did not meet my needs or offered me no help" (30%), "unhappy experience with the church or minister" (9%), and "not part of the group or did not fit in" (9%).

As noted earlier, one predisposition for converting to the Catholic Church is dissatisfaction with another church earlier, leading the person to withdraw from the first church but to desire membership in a different church. We estimated that this was an important predisposition for 9% of the converts in our sample. As an additional check we asked all the converts who said they had felt dissatisfaction with other churches or religions whether the dissatisfaction was a factor in their decisions to become Catholics. Fourteen percent said that such dissatisfaction was very important in influencing them. This is higher than our global judgment of 9%. This occurs because some interviewees stressed this factor even though they had withdrawn from the other churches as long as ten years earlier. We believe that our estimate of 9% is more accurate.

A predisposition toward changing churches because of dissatisfaction with an earlier church does not lead directly to one's becoming a baptized Catholic. Other outcomes are equally likely. For example, if a United Methodist becomes disillusioned with his or her church and breaks away from it, he or she could become a Baptist, a Presbyterian, a Catholic, or no church member at all, depending largely on facilitating persons or relationships. To some extent it also depends on doctrinal factors and worship style.

We asked the converts several questions about the parishes where they were baptized. First, we asked if they had participated in these parishes for a time before becoming baptized, and 84% said yes. For how many years? Forty-seven percent said one year or less; 20% said two years; and 33% said three years or longer.

We asked, "How did you choose *this* parish rather than another parish?" For 59%, the answer was simple—these were their home parishes, the closest parishes, or the only available parishes. Eighteen percent said family members belonged to the parishes, and 3% said their boyfriends or girlfriends belonged to the parishes. Adding up these figures, it seems that 80% had their choice of parish determined by geographic or familial factors. A few had selected parishes on other grounds—5% said their friends belong there, 4% said they liked the priests, 2% had participated in special groups or programs in these parishes, and 1% had selected these parishes due to good parish schools. The rest gave various responses difficult to code.

Next, we asked the converts how they first had contact with the leadership of these parishes. We were interested in personal or parish factors that facilitated relationships with the clergy. The majority (52%) said they first met the priests after Mass or after classes, or they went to the rectories to see the priests. Fourteen percent said they met the priests through their spouses; 8% said they met the priests through their friends; 5% said through relatives; and 3% said through boyfriends or girlfriends. Eleven percent said they met the priests through child-related programs, such as baptism, CCD, or school. Finally, 3% said the priests had contacted them. Most of the initiative in creating relationships with the clergy came from the converts and their families.

All the converts had completed inquiry classes that lasted between three and ten months. Some of the classes were held in groups, and some were done personally, between the convert and a priest or deacon. We asked if they liked or disliked their instruction classes. Ninety-two percent said they liked them, 1% said they disliked them, and 8% said they liked some parts and disliked others.

We asked those who liked the classes what were the best parts. Three kinds of answers were given. Thirty-two percent said they liked the instructors. Another 32% said they liked the openness, the friendliness, or the good communication. Also, 28% said they found the classes informative and had received answers to their questions. Some of the last group added that they were happy to correct earlier misinformation they had had about the Catholic Church.

We asked those who disliked all or parts of the classes which were the worst parts. The two main kinds of comments were that the classes were uninteresting and superficial, and that they lacked discussion of rules and moral issues.

For many people, the decision whether or not to become a baptized Catholic is left unmade when one begins to attend the inquiry class. This is proper, since no obligation is entailed in attending such a class. Some drop out. The priests we interviewed made estimates of how many drop out, and the collective judgment was about one in six. The dropping out occurs early in the class, and is partly predictable from the nature of the motivation of the persons coming (for example, were they under pressure from other persons) and from the interpersonal dynamics in the class.

From our research we have no estimate on how many drop out of inquiry classes, but we do know how many decided during the course of the class to finish it and be baptized. We asked all the converts, "When you first came to the instruction class, were you certain that you would go through with it, or were you just giving it a try to see if you liked it?" Sixty-eight percent were certain they would go through with it, and 32% were giving it a try. We asked the 32% what made them decide to continue. Four main answers were given. Thirty percent found the classes informative and had many of their questions answered; 20% liked the instructors, 16% liked the openness and the good atmosphere; and 8% said they realized their need for religion during the classes and hence decided to be baptized.

In summary, the inquiry class should be seen as an agent of evangelization, since one third of the converts make decisions about conversion while attending the classes. Successful classes have solid information, instructors whom the students like, and an atmosphere of openness and friendliness.

The Rite of Christian Initiation of Adults (RCIA) is being used in more and more parishes in the early 1980s, but in the parishes where we worked, it had not yet been used. From our findings one could begin to predict which features of the RCIA will prove most beneficial. For example, the building of genuine supportive relationships, which the RCIA encourages, is important to both catechumens and parishes.

Switchers and Inner Converts

Early on we learned that converts vary widely in terms of the personal impact of the converting experience. For some, converting from one denomination to another is seen almost like switching brands of merchandise or transferring schools—a person who formerly swore by

Fords switches to Chevrolets, or a person who formerly attended one college transfers to another in hopes of a better experience.

Other converts have an inner conversion almost as dramatic as the Apostle Paul's Damascus Road experience. Many talked of changes in their entire life-style. We use the term inner converts to designate this latter group and the word switchers for the former group. We continue to use the word convert in an institutional sense, for example, adult convert.

For a researcher, inner converts are easy to recognize and a joy to talk with. They are usually happy, expansive persons whose recent conversion experiences—both inner and institutional—brought them new vitality, faith, and spiritual gifts.

How many switchers and how many inner converts are in our sample of Catholic converts? The question is, in principle, difficult to answer precisely, because these two types are abstract ideal types, and in the empirical world, people fall on a spectrum from one pure type to the other. No obvious cutting point is available for dividing them into two groups. The most defensible way to differentiate between the two is to ask questions about the results of becoming a baptized Catholic. We asked eight questions.

1. "As a result of your becoming a baptized Catholic, has there been any change in your family life?" Fifty-seven percent responded yes. "What were the changes?" Ninety-nine percent told of positive changes and improvements, and only 1% told of negative changes (more tension or friction with parents, in-laws, or relatives). The three main changes were more family unity, better family life and more closeness (45%), better family spiritual or religious life (27%), and more peace, calm, and contentment (18%).

2. "As a result of your becoming a baptized Catholic, has there been any change in your personal outlook or attitude toward life?" Seventy-seven percent replied yes. All were positive—more optimism, happiness, and calm (50%), more acceptance and tolerance of others (18%), more religious involvement or spiritual fulfillment (18%), and more giving of oneself to others (4%).

3. "As a result of your becoming a baptized Catholic, has there been any change in your personal life practices or your personal habits?" (If people asked us to explain, we mentioned such things as use of time and money, eating and drinking habits, or leisure activities.) Forty-five percent answered yes. The main changes were more time spent in churchgoing and religious activity (39%), more time spent in prayer or Bible study (15%), stopped smoking, drinking, or drug use (11%), and better personal morality in such matters as honesty, use of language, or sex behavior (7%).

4. "Has there been any change in your selection of friends or in

the group of people you socialize with?" For 29% the response was yes.

5. "In recent months how often have you attended Mass?" Eighty-one percent said weekly or more often, 11% said two or three times a month, and 7% said once a month or less. This is a much higher rate of Mass attendance than occurs among all American Catholics. A 1978 Gallup poll found that 44% of all Catholics reported that they had attended church weekly in the past few months.

6. "Are you active in any group or committee in the parish, such as the ushers, the school committee, the altar guild, or any other?" Thirty-two percent said yes. The main groups were the ushers, the CCD staff, and committees to sponsor festivals, bazaars, athletics, and Boy Scouts.

7. "Are you active in any other Catholic organizations, action groups, or movements other than those in the parish?" Nine percent responded yes. The main ones were the Cursillo movement, Marriage Encounter, the charismatic movement, and social service organizations.

8. "How important would you say religion is in your life—would you say it is very important, fairly important, or not very important?" Eighty-five percent said very important, 15% said fairly important, and none said not very important. (In a 1978 Gallup survey this question was asked of Catholics who attended church weekly, and they responded with lower levels of importance—75% said very important, 23% said fairly important, and 2% said not very important.)

To check if religion has taken on more importance for converts since becoming baptized Catholics, we asked them: "Think back about five years. How important was religion in your life at that time—would you say it was very important, fairly important, or not very important?" Thirty-nine percent said very important, 37% said fairly important, and 24% said not very important. By comparing their estimates of the situation five years ago with the situation now, we see that religion has greatly increased in importance for these persons. Even if we make allowance for some selective recall among these converts, there is still a major increase.

To sum up, well over half the converts had experienced some inner change as a result of becoming baptized Catholics.

In a separate attempt to discern how many were inner converts, we asked about their religious experiences. First, "Have you ever had a personal conversion'experience, that is, an identifiable turning point in your religious life? Was this in the past three or four years?" Twenty-five percent answered yes to both questions. "Did this have an influence on your decision to become a Catholic? How important an influence?" Eighteen percent of the total sample thought the influence was very important.

41

In a second attempt to identify religious experiences, we asked, "Was there a definite time in the past three or four years when you had an important religious experience and made a new personal religious commitment?" This was asked only of those persons who responded no to the first question. An additional 20% said yes—besides the 25% who replied yes to the first question. Did this influence their decisions to become Catholics? Ten percent of the sample said yes, very important; this is in addition to the 18% on the first question.

Thus we estimate that 45% of the converts had religious experiences momentous enough so that they would say yes to one of our two questions, and 28% found the experiences very important.

ATTITUDES ABOUT RELIGION AND MORAL ISSUES

We asked eleven attitude questions that had been used in nationwide polls during 1977 and 1978, so that we could compare the converts with active Catholics. The results are shown in Table A.3 in Appendix A. In brief, the converts' attitudes are closer to the doctrinal teachings of the church than the active Catholics' attitudes. Religion is more important in the lives of the converts than in the lives of the actives. Converts are less critical of the church for lack of spiritual life, they are less inclined to say individuals should arrive at their own religious beliefs independent of the church, and they believe more strongly that a person must attend church to be a good Christian.

On issues facing the Catholic Church today, the converts are slightly more liberal than active Catholics. Seventy-seven percent feel Catholics should be allowed to practice artificial means of birth control (70% of actives say this), and 84% generally approve of the changes in the Catholic Church since Vatican II (73% of actives say this). On the questions of premarital sex, abortion, and remarriage after divorce the converts have views similar to the actives.

To summarize, the converts adhere to church teachings more strongly than do active Catholics, except on the question of birth control. Also, they like the changes since Vatican II more than the actives do.

Chapter 3

THREE TYPES OF CONVERTS

In chapter 2 we described the 210 converts. Here we divide them into three types and discuss each type.

The most defensible way of letting the cases group themselves into types, rather than our forcing them into preset categories, is to identify the main predispositions leading individuals to convert and to see how the sample divides itself on their terms. We reviewed all the cases and recognized four main predispositions. Since one of the four usually occurred in combination with others, we ended up with three types.

The first type is the *intermarriage convert*. This is someone married to a Catholic or about to marry a Catholic, who feels concern for the marriage or experiences influence from the spouse or relatives. The second type is the *family life convert*—someone who has children being reared Catholic and who feels concern for their religious training or for family religious unity. The third type, the *seeker convert*, is a person coming to the Catholic Church through a sense of personal or spiritual need. Ninety-five percent of the cases fall into these three types; the remaining 5% are persons whose interviews were so uninformative that we could not categorize them. If anything, they are closest to the *seeker* type. Table 3.1 (page 44) summarizes the types.

These three types are defined by three of the four main predispositions we identified. The fourth, that of being dissatisfied with another church and having recently withdrawn from it, occurred alone in only two cases out of 210; the other nineteen persons for whom this seemed an important predisposition fit better with the seeker converts or the family life converts.[1]

A typology is inevitably an oversimplification of rich and varied

43

TABLE 3.1

THREE TYPES OF CONVERTS

	Percent
1. Intermarriage Converts. These persons are married to Catholics or about to marry Catholics, who feel concern for the marriage or are influenced by their spouses and relatives. About one fourth of these persons have spiritual motivations as well.	38
2. Family Life Converts. These persons are usually married to Catholics, but more important than the marriage is their concern for children who are being reared Catholic. These converts want to aid in the children's training and desire family religious unity. About half of these persons have spiritual motivations as well.	45
3. Seeker Converts. These persons are seldom married to Catholics, and if so, the marriages are unrelated to the conversions. They come to the Catholic Church in search of an answer to spiritual need or a sense of void or meaninglessness.	12
Inadequate data	5
	100

human reality. It must be justified by its usefulness, theoretically and practically. We believe our threefold typology will prove useful. In presenting it we will look at each of the three as ideal types and will stress what they typically look like. Of course there is much variation within each type.

Intermarriage is clearly very important, and we will look at intermarriage at some length. As mentioned earlier, 82% of the sample are currently married to Catholics and an additional 3% are engaged to marry Catholics. But 2% (four persons) seemed to convert for reasons entirely unrelated to their marriages. By deleting these four, we get 83% for whom intermarriage or family life is a primary motivation.

Intermarriage Converts

About 38% of the converts make the change out of concern for their marriages to Catholics. Some of their important characteristics, in comparison with the other two types, can be seen in Table 3.2. Fifty-five percent were females, and the median age at baptism was 28 years. Only about 6% converted prior to marriage; most did so afterward—

44

TABLE 3.2

COMPARISON OF THREE TYPES OF CONVERTS

	Inter-marriage Converts	Family Life Converts	Seeker Converts
Age when baptized Catholic (median)	28	31	34
Percent female	55	64	77
Percent with college degree or more education	25	23	12
Percent black	6	6	23
Percent single	6	0	38
If married, how long married before baptism (median years)	4	8	21
Percent with children 0 to 6 years old	19	61	15
Percent with children 6 to 18 years old	26	77	19
Percent with children over 18 years old	22	10	35
If children of school age, percent in Catholic school	17	36	*
Percent who took part in charismatic prayer group	14	11	19
Percent who took part in Marriage Encounter	14	11	0
Percent influenced by radio or television	14	10	21
Percent for whom dissatisfaction with their former churches was an important predisposition in their decision to convert	4	11	23
Percent for whom a feeling of void or of spiritual need or emptiness was an important predisposition in their decision to convert	24	47	100
Percent who had a personal conversion experience	33	39	54
If currently married, percent who were influenced by their spouses to convert	84	55	*
Percent for whom a friend or neighbor was an important facilitator	5	4	23
Percent for whom a priest was an important facilitator	15	13	27

*Too few to percentage.

sometimes years afterward. The length of time they had been married when baptized varied greatly. The median was 3.9 years, but 24% had been married over ten years. The majority of priests today recommend to non-Catholic fiancés and fiancées that they wait until after the

45

wedding to make a decision about converting. The reason is that a later conversion is usually done for more mature reasons and thus produces stronger church commitment.

We should note that 35% of those married were in their second or third marriages. The children were of all ages; some were from former marriages.

Eighty-six percent of the intermarriage converts had received religious training in their childhood, the largest numbers being former Lutherans, Methodists, and Baptists; only 3% were former Jews. Seventy-one percent had been active in other churches prior to becoming baptized Catholics. But most had dropped out of these other churches; 63% of this group reported that they had done so sometime before becoming Catholics. In summary, about three tenths of the intermarriage converts had never been active in any church, and seven tenths had. Of the latter group, two thirds had dropped out of these other churches some years earlier, while one third were active until they began attending Catholic churches. Of those who had dropped out earlier, most had done so during the late teenage years.

We asked the intermarriage converts if they had participated in the Catholic parishes for a time before becoming baptized Catholics, and 85% responded yes; most had done so for one or two years, primarily because of the influence of their spouses. Eighty-four percent had been influenced by their spouses to convert, and 18% had been influenced by in-laws; some mentioned both spouses and in-laws. The Catholic faith is important to their spouses; 81% of the intermarriage converts said that religion is very important in their spouses' lives.

An important finding of our research is that intermarriage converts very often come to the Catholic Church when a second motivation is added to the primary one of improving the marriage or pleasing in-laws. The second motivations may arise from personal or family problems, from feelings of spiritual need, or from new personal relationships. We asked if the intermarriage converts had experienced personal or family problems in recent years that had influenced their religious viewpoints, and 33% said yes; these were mostly marital or family crises, personal illness, or the death of loved ones. Six percent of the intermarriage converts stated that these had been very important influences. We also asked if they had recently experienced a sense of need or void in their feelings about life, and 47% said yes—21% of the total group said this feeling had been very important in their decisions to convert. Finally, we asked if they had experienced dissatisfaction in the churches (if any) in which they had been active. Of all the intermarriage converts, 44% said yes, and 10% said this had been very important.

Some of the experiences leading to conversion of intermarriage converts were very influential. Thirty-three percent had had personal conversion experiences that were turning points in their religious lives, and 9% said such experiences had been very important in their decisions to convert.

How many of the intermarriage converts are inner converts, and how many are switchers? The obvious interpersonal pressure would lead one to expect that many are switchers. To look at this we compared all three kinds of converts on the items asked about the results of converting. The findings are shown in Table A.3 in Appendix A. The differences among the three types of converts regarding how many are inner converts and how many are switchers are small. Yet it appears that intermarriage converts have a slightly higher percentage of switchers.

An example of an intermarriage convert is Sheila. She is quite typical in that she dropped out of Protestant church life some years before she married a Catholic. She made the decision to become a Catholic mostly because of the influence of her husband, his family, and an approachable priest.

Sheila: Just Married to a Catholic

Sheila came into the Catholic Church at age 22, just one year after marrying Steve. They live in a medium-sized city in New England.

She is the second of three children but is not very close to her siblings. Her childhood was filled with Sunday school, churchgoing, and youth activities in the Baptist church. As she looks back, she realizes she wasn't very close to anyone during her high school years.

"It was the time when everybody was looking for themselves, and I was kind of unhappy with the whole idea. I didn't have any close friends; I think that was part of the problem. And at the time I was growing up there was a searching, kind of—you know, everybody was into transcendental meditation and sensitivity groups, and they used to almost force you into saying things you really didn't want to say (laugh). I started going to the Baptist youth camp they have up in Maine. And that was a fun experience because it wasn't all Baptist. It was just people who were deeply religious. And that whole time, all through senior high school, I felt myself searching for something. You know, I used to go on the beach and talk to God and try to straighten myself out. And I never really found anything."

"How about your parents? Were your parents what you would call committed Christians, or not?"

"They were committed anti-Catholics. They weren't *for* this, but *against* this. My father's Italian and my mother's Irish. Somewhere back in each of their backgrounds I think that they were both Catholics at one time, and didn't want it. . . . Our family had the typical New England staunch Baptist—you could almost call it anti-Catholic—atmosphere. Really. When I was a kid my neighborhood friends used to get on their buses to go to catechism, and I used to want to go with them (laugh), but nobody would let me. What I grew up with was, you go to church on Sundays and they tell you to be good, and they tell you not to do this and not to do that, but they never really worried about your soul. They're too busy worrying about the financial statement and what hat is proper to wear the first week after Easter.

"My parents were definitely missing something, because I could see it in the way they lived. They're not pleased with themselves or their lives. And it probably comes from never questioning anything, just living it the way they were supposed to."

"How about your own religious training? Do you think it was good or not good?"

"Factualwise, you know, the stories they teach you and all that stuff, they did a good job. They taught me all the things I should have been taught, the Ten Commandments, the Golden Rule, all that. I think because of my activity I probably learned more than most kids who went through it did."

"Would you want the same training for your own children?"

"I'd like the same basic training in a different atmosphere."

"What would be the different atmosphere?"

"The home atmosphere. There was no home religious atmosphere when I grew up. I never got the feeling that my parents were that interested. You just were supposed to go to church every Sunday, and you went, and when things were happening, sometimes they went, sometimes they didn't, depending on how they felt. And that's the part that was lacking, was the home atmosphere. . . . And then the social activities, well, they were fun. The part that was lacking was in the actual worship service. In fact, I remember skipping out on that most of the time and sitting in the library, because it was so irrelevant. It was—I mean, they were relevant to today's issues, even when they were—if I went tomorrow, they'd probably talk

48

about the trouble with the hostages and all that stuff. They stuck close to the issues, but there was no spiritualness to the service at all."

"Would you identify your high school years as a time when you rebelled against the church or against God?"

"No, I never rebelled against God. I used to talk to him all the time. I rebelled against—against the church per se, but I didn't want to. I didn't want to be the kind of person who would say, 'Well, I don't need church, I have religion of my own,' because I think that's a cop-out, too. I have a sister-in-law like that, who doesn't feel she should have to go to church because that's not her scene. To me, you need to go with other people and worship. . . . And going to the church I went to, I didn't feel that they were all worshiping the same way I was. And that's what bothered me. But when I found people who were worshiping the way I was—like up in Maine—I was happy. I would go to the little chapel and everybody would really get into the spirit of being Christian, and that's what I was looking for."

Sheila went on to tell how she gradually felt farther and farther removed from her parents. But she had plenty of friends, since she was active and popular in high school. Two girlfriends were Catholics; one of them was in Confraternity of Christian Doctrine (CCD) programs and sometimes took Sheila along. Because of this friend, Sheila was, for a while, in a folk music group that performed folk Masses.

After high school Sheila drifted away from her friends and stopped going to church. She commuted to a state college nearby. This is where she met Steve.

"He was very, very religious. It was sort of like he had been brought up a Catholic, and it was just so much a part of him that you couldn't separate it. He never questioned any-thing, which is really weird, because he's very inquisitive and he just really liked himself. He had a lot of confidence, which is something I never had. I think that's one thing that—that attracted me, and it got me into the whole thing. I found that I could *like* myself. I learned enough about myself and about my God going to the classes and meeting Steve and starting to get some confidence that I really started to feel good about me."

"Did Steve have an effect on your religious and spiritual life?"

"Yeah. Once we really started dating, I remember thinking to myself the first time we went out, 'If I get involved with this guy, he's going to want to stay a Catholic. Do I want that?

49

Yeah. I can live with that.' And the more I got to know him, the more I *knew* that he was a Catholic and wanted to be one, and even though he wasn't the type of person to go around saying 'I'm Catholic,' and 'God this' and 'God that,' he was a good man. And it was his upbringing that made him that way."

Soon they were engaged. She left college at this time, and before long they were married. It was an ecumenical service, with both the minister of her church and the priest of Steve's parish officiating.

"Were you thinking about becoming a Catholic at the time of your marriage, or did you see this as a decision to be made later on?"

"It was always something I knew I would have to look at. I mean, once I started really seriously dating Steve, I knew that whatever happened to me, our family was going to be Catholic. And that never bothered me. A decision I did have to make was whether *I* was willing to be a Catholic too."

"What made you decide to do it when you did? Was there something specific that made you decide?"

"Well—I didn't want to dissent while I was in my parents' house. They would have felt terrible. My beliefs and feelings inside were okay, as long as I didn't flaunt them in front of them, you know, make them look bad in front of their friends or anything. And I also knew that they would be very hurt if I didn't get married in my church. . . . And what I did with my life once I'm married is my decision and will be for my family. But until I am married, my family is with my parents. I have to think of them before I do anything."

For a while Sheila had not been sure how to handle the problem of which church to belong to. She put off making a decision. She and Steve went to pre-Cana class at Sacred Heart, the parish in that area. This is where they met Father Don.

"And he seemed like a really nice guy. He knew Steve's friends because they were both from the same area, and then we got an apartment and moved into the Heights, which is about a mile down the street. The church there was an older church, and we didn't want to go there. So we started driving to Sacred Heart. . . . There's an awful lot of people in this area that do that. And I think what happened, we approached Father Don about my wanting to be a Catholic. And he said he would be glad to do it. Sure, OK. So we started setting up times, and the more we came, the more I wanted to be there, because he gave us a good book, and . . . "

"Did both you and Steve go?"

"Both of us. Right. The thing is, my husband is not talkative much about his religion, but coming home in the car every day we used to, you know, talk about it a little bit. And he learned as much as I did, because it was a lot of the Vatican II stuff, you know, explaining the changes in the Catholic Church. And it helped me because I was brought up with the before-Vatican II-type things. And that's all the stuff that my mother said, 'Oh, you can't do that because they believe in that. Those lousy Catholics, they do this.' It was sort of a spiritual explanation for the stuff that I had grown up with from afar."

Another influence was the good rapport she quickly developed with Steve's family.

"His folks had a big influence, because they're a very loving family. I mean they're not the huggy-kissy type, but they've got a respect for each other that's just unbelievable. You know, my folks have fire between them, because I don't think they've ever learned to respect one another. And Steve's parents are both deeply religious the same way *he* is. They're low-keyed. They're into it, and it's their life. But they don't go telling everybody at tables that they're into it. And I like that. I like the warmth that I felt within their family."

As noted earlier, Sheila was received into the church one year after the marriage. Now she works in a bank, and she and Steve are expecting their first child.

"How about the prospect of having a child? Does this have any effect on your spiritual life, do you think?"

"The only effect it has on my spiritual life is the worry that I have, what's going to happen at the christening?"

"What do you mean by that?"

"Well, a christening is a time for family, and I'm close to both families, and the only time the friction really gets bad with my folks is when there's something religious that pops up, and I'm just—I'm just afraid of hurting them, because they mean a lot to me. And I don't want to go out of my way to hurt them (pause). But this is my child, and I want to bring it up the way I want to bring it up. And Steve's family really get into christenings and birthdays, and they're all going to want to be here, and I'm going to want them here, and I'm going to want my folks here, too, but I don't want them to feel bad about it. I want them to be as happy as I am. And that worries me. They're going to let their pride stand in the way of enjoying their grandchild and the experience of bringing him into the world, and to present him to God, because to me it doesn't matter what church you're standing in. You know, a christening or a baptism, it's all the same thing. It's the same God. It's all your outlook towards him."

"You just happen to have a different community of people who are present with you."

"Right. Right. And the way I do it may be a little different, but I'm not a different person than what I was before I was a Catholic. I'm the same me, and I've got the same feelings inside of me. And I just want everybody to be as happy as I am!"

Sheila is a person for whom strong ties—with her husband and his family—were pulling her to the Catholic Church, and no strong countervailing ties were present. In the interview she did not affirm her home life as an adolescent, and she told how her ties with her parents, siblings, and friends had slowly weakened. Yet she had some concern for her parents' feelings, for she had arranged for an ecumenical wedding, and now she is worried about how to handle a christening that will offend neither family.

Apparently, Father Don was important in her decision to become a baptized Catholic. The relationship Sheila and Steve had with Father Don was a typical facilitating relationship, shown by their decision to drive across town to his parish and to be instructed by him.

FAMILY LIFE CONVERTS

The numerically largest type of convert is the family life convert, comprising 45% of our sample. These persons have children being reared Catholic, and they are concerned about the children's religious upbringing. Usually, they believe in family religious unity. For some, personal spiritual needs are also important in deciding to become baptized Catholics.

In our sample most family life converts were currently married, but a few were divorced. Sixty-four percent were females, and the median age at the time of baptism was 31 years. The median time between marriage and baptism was 7.6 years, but this varied greatly; 14% had been married longer than fifteen years. All had children under age 18.

Table 3.2 tells us that 58% had an additional predisposition—47% had experienced feelings of void or spiritual need, and 11% had felt dissatisfaction with their former churches and now were looking for different church homes.[2] Over half the family life converts came into the Catholic Church as a result of an additional motivation, combined with the primary motivation of family life and child-rearing. The decision was made when other factors also came into play.

In many respects the family life converts are similar to the intermarriage converts. Eighty-eight percent of the family life converts (compared with 86% of the first type) had received religious training as a child. Their denominations were similar. Sixty-nine percent stated that the influence of other people was very important in their decisions to convert (compared with 68% of the first type). The key persons were spouses, relatives, and their own children—the last in 12% of the cases. Priests were facilitators in 13% of the cases (compared with 15% for the intermarriage converts).

An example of a family life convert with several motivations for converting is Sid. He began the inquiry class only after several facilitating events occurred, and he had a good relationship with a priest.

SID: THINKING ABOUT WIFE AND FAMILY

Sid, a construction supervisor, lives in a residential suburb in the East. He came into the Catholic Church at age 30. He grew up as a Presbyterian in the South, but in looking back he had little good to say about the church he attended.

"The biggest thing I didn't like about the particular church I went to, was the fact that it was more of a fashion contest than a church. People wouldn't be caught dead in the same hat two weeks in a row, or if you bought a new suit, that would be the first place you'd wear it—the church. And people seemed to always be competing—see and be seen. And the same people you'd see drinking Saturday night would be at church Sunday morning. And the first part of my life I got a bad feeling about the church."

"Did you feel comfortable around the Presbyterians? Did you feel at home?"

"I always felt very uncomfortable. Basically because my family didn't have the money to buy the real rich clothes and everything. I always felt kind of out of place. Self-conscious I guess you would say."

Sid's home life was rocky; since his mother was ailing, his father began drinking, and Sid and his brother were involved in endless rivalry. During his teenage years Sid came to resent his brother, whom he saw as more favored—"Whatever he did was just perfect." So he began to rebel against his home life. He stopped church attendance and in other ways tried to emancipate himself from his family.

After high school Sid went to college. He was glad to get

53

away from home. But college was difficult, and he lacked good study habits. He began falling behind and felt discouraged. So he joined the army. Soon he found himself in a construction unit in Vietnam.

The army time was an emotional void. He found military life boring, but he was in no hurry to get home, since home did not beckon him either. He did a lot of reading and thinking. During this time he attended both Protestant and Catholic services occasionally—the latter out of curiosity.

After a short while he decided to get out of the army, go home, and finish college. He reentered college but did poorly because he couldn't concentrate. At this point he met Louise.

"I met Louise, and she was Catholic, so I started going to the Catholic Church with her. And then we got married. And the biggest agreement we made when we got married was that the children would be baptized Catholic. And then there wasn't any real pressure on me about coming into the church. It was something I decided to do later on."

Louise is the daughter of first-generation Polish immigrants, in Pennsylvania. When Sid met her she had been living away from her parents for several years.

"She grew up in Pennsylvania where the church was—even though it was Catholic—it was very, very formal. The priest was almost in a palace, and he spoke down to the congregation. The congregation didn't participate at all. They just kind of sat there. And her parents are still part of that. They go to Mass here, and they don't say a word. They don't participate at all—I mean even the responsive readings or anything. They just sit there! And I went to their church, and that's the way it is. And she was very turned off to that. So she was forced to go, as much as I was. So when we got married, she kind of of—she took a little leave too. And now she's starting to go back. And Father Al was instrumental in that. Plus the girls are getting older."

"Had your wife been an active churchgoer all those years?"

"Well, while she was home she was active in the church in Pennsylvania. But when she came down here, she was here for like four years on her own. When she went home for a weekend or something she'd go to church. But as far as I could tell, when she was here by herself she wouldn't go."

Sid found it interesting how Louise's parents reacted to the modern-style parish where Sid and Louise now attend.

"I don't really think they feel comfortable here. They feel that they're satisfying requirements, and they're going to church. But I don't really think they feel comfortable, because a lot of things here are a lot more leisurely than where they are. They go out of obligation, and when they're here they go out of obligation also."

After Sid and Louise were married, Sid had no interest in going back to the Presbyterian Church and in fact never visited a Presbyterian church. Sid and Louise first went to the same parish as Louise's sister in the town they lived in; then when they moved, they went to a parish in the next town. When they bought a house in Woodlawn they started going to the local parish, St. Michael's.

"As you compare the three parishes, what appeals to you or doesn't appeal to you about them?"

"Well, the other two we never really got too involved with. I guess because we just felt we didn't have any roots. We just more or less went. You know, we were just living in an apartment and didn't really feel associated with the town like we do here in Woodlawn. So St. Michael's appealed to me as being very open and friendly. The one in ―――― was friendlier than the one in ――――, but I think this one is the best of all. We've visited the other parish in Woodlawn, but we like St. Michael's the best."

Several times Sid mentioned the informality of the Catholic church.

"And another thing that really fascinated me about the Catholic church in this area was the fact that it was less formal. That a person could go to church in shirt and pants without having to wear a tie and suit. It was totally unheard of down there (in the Presbyterian church in his hometown) for somebody to go to church without a vest and a suit, a coat and a tie. And here, of course you don't see shorts and everything, but you do see people a good deal less formal."

Soon Sid and Louise had two children. Sid had a good job in heavy construction, and Louise was an elementary schoolteacher. They attended St. Michael's parish occasionally, although Louise still felt ambivalence about the Catholic Church and avoided going to confession for many years.

"I'm interested in the whole process by which you came into the Catholic Church. There were years when you were thinking about it, and then you actually went to the inquiry class. What was the train of events that brought this?"

"Well, it was becoming more attached to the parish, for one thing."

"You and your wife both?"

"Right. And being attached to Father Al."

"How did you get to know him?"

"Well, just through his services and everything."

"Were you in a group or something?"

"No. We just—we would try to pick his Mass. They had a schedule, you know. You could plan ahead."

"Did he ever come and call on you?"

"You mean as far as coming to the house?"

"Yes."

"No. He was supposed to a couple of times. He never did. But—you know, the parish always has a printed program, what you get at the end of services, and it always listed the basic inquiry class. And I thought about it and thought about it, and I figured, you know, why not? So I called the number, and Father Al answered the phone, and I said I was interested in starting a basic instruction class. So he told me, he said, 'Come on over. If you don't like it, you can leave. There's no pressure. It's strictly a voluntary thing. We're already into it a couple weeks, but there's no problem there. It's going to last a long time. You're welcome to start.' And just the openness that everybody extended just impressed me to no end. At first I was a little bit leery. I don't know why, but I was a little leery about going. I guess it was something new. But once I got there I was really happy. I went to it, and I think I only missed one class the whole time."

"Did your wife want you to do it, or didn't she care?"

"Well, she wanted me to do it, but she didn't want to pressure me. She always said, 'If you want to, you can. It would make me feel good if you did it, but I'm not going to force you to do it.' And she always said that it would make her parents glad if I did it. So they were really happy when I joined the church."

"Was there any event in your life, something good or something bad or something different that had an impact on your religious views?"

"Well, possibly my mother dying did. Well—my mother and my grandmother died, and I more or less decided I should go ahead and do it for them, because Grandmother always said that 'it's better for you to be a Catholic than not to be anything at all.' You know, she wanted me to be a Presbyterian, but at least she was happy I was going to some church."

Sid came to admire Father Al. The interviewer asked about this. "Did you already know Father Al before you started the class?"

"Right. I liked his ideas and the way that he related to young people. . . . Father Al is the kind of person you can relate to, and if you have a problem you can talk it over with him, and he's pretty good about it."

"So Father Al, you knew him at a distance, but you didn't know him personally?"

"Right."

"So this was probably a factor in choosing the parish then."

"Right."

"Would you classify Father Al as an unusual priest?"

"Yes, I would. Yes, I really think he's an exceptional person as well as a priest."

"What are his exceptional qualities?"

"Well, the fact that he's able to bring out the best in everybody. Like I think he could get anybody to do anything for him. He just almost has a magnetism about him. And he's a very open person and talks about his own family life and his childhood and things like that. You feel like you're part of it, when he goes into it. And the fact that he's willing to communicate with everybody on such a personal level impressed me more than anything. Because it's the first priest I've ever—well, the first religious man of any time I've really gotten close to. Because you know, the congregation of the Presbyterian church is probably seven, eight hundred people. You just see the guy once a week. You can't relate to somebody like that."

Sid also talked at length about a restlessness he was feeling in his life.

"Twenty-nine to me was what thirty is to a lot of people. That's when I was really going through a lot of questions and answers. And so I was trying to really solve a lot of things in my mind. I started the turning point—the year I was halfway through my work life, I guess you could say, because in another thirty I would be sixty, and I was asking myself a lot of questions about my job, questions about my marriage. Did I want to stay in this, did I want to do that? So, finally, what led me to the church was, I needed something to hang on to."

At another point he elaborated: "I guess I had my 'passages' at age twenty-nine instead of thirty-nine like the book says. There were a lot of uncertainties at that point. I really—I went through a lot of questions. Why am I doing this? Do I want to stay with this company? ·Am I happy with my job, my marriage, everything. I figured if I was going to get out, I better do it then. Because after thirty you can't be doing a whole lot of jumping around."

The inquiry class was a good experience.

"It was really a good group of people. It ranged from—there were some people in their fifties and the majority of people were in their thirties. And I'd say ninety-five percent of the people in the class were fallen-away Catholics who grew up in the church, and they were gradually coming back."

"So why were they in the inquiry class?"

"Just to be reindoctrinated and things like that. There were two or three other people interested in joining the church. And one guy was a Ph.D. and a scientist. His wife was a Catholic, and he joined I think more out of curiosity than anything. It was one of those deals where, when they got married, she dropped out of the church because he was against it. And gradually he came to the church with her out of curiosity, and I think he finally joined later on. But he was a very scientific person that had to have everything explained to the nth degree. It had to be shown to him in black and white. He couldn't accept just anybody's word for anything. There were a lot of women in the class who had married somebody and fallen out of the church. And they just dropped their religion and took their husbands', more or less. And now they were establishing their independence and coming back into the church."

"What brought these people back?"

"I think the biggest thing that brought them back was that they were just the same way I was—they were just looking. They didn't feel comfortable in other churches. They did it more out of obligation than desire when they left originally, and then I think they found the courage to say to their husbands, 'Look, I'm going to start going back to my church. If you don't want to go, you stay where you are, but I'm going back.' And I think that was representative of just about all the women in the class."

"What was the best thing the class did for you?"

"It gave me a lot in common with other people. We had some pretty frank discussions. People would ask—you know, would really talk openly. And it was really amazing, here people would walk into the group and had never seen each other, and they'd be your friends when you walked out of it. It's kind of funny though. Socially, it would never work, it'd never click. They tried a couple of get-togethers, and it just didn't work. But as long as we had that class in common, it all worked out real well, where we were in class. Of course, Father Al was a big catalyst to all of us."

The interviewer tried to get some feeling for the various influences on Sid: "Do you and your wife agree or disagree on religious matters now?"

"Well, originally the only agreement we had was about the baptism of the children. And that was basically an agreement before we got married. And we agree pretty much now, you know—like the First Communion (of the daughter) she wanted to be more traditional. She wanted the veil, and a lot of things to be exactly like they used to be. So I said 'OK,' you know. 'It's really important to you and your family. You do it the way you want to do it.' "

"So her parents came down for that?"

"Right. They were here for all that. So we had a big to-do with that."

"Did having children affect your religious life or your spiritual life?"

"Well, I think it made me more conscious of my responsibility as far as getting them started, I guess you could say, right, in the church. I figured it wouldn't be a very good example if I did what my parents did—fell away from the church altogether. I wanted the children to have a strong structure. And then later on let them make their own choice as to what they wanted to do. But having children—it made me want to join the church. It made me want to get established somewhere. So that's what we did."

"If there were no children, would you be in the church today?"

"I think so. Because like I was telling you, when I was—at age twenty-nine a lot of questions were going through my mind, and it helped me an awful lot. So I think I would have done it then. Because I felt more comfortable with this church here than I've ever felt before anywhere."

After Sid was confirmed Catholic, Louise went to her first confession for a decade, with Father Al. She received Communion on the same day as her older daughter had First Communion. Now Sid is thinking about how his daughters are doing in CCD. He feels happy as a member of his parish, and he sees the other members of his inquiry class at church. But he doesn't like confession and in fact doesn't believe in it, since he is convinced people won't be honest in confession. He put off his own confession as long as he could, then he had face-to-face confession with Father Al.

Sid's experience shows clearly the power of a facilitating person,

59

and it also exemplifies how several predispositions can combine to form a strong enough motivation to evoke new behavior—in Sid's case, to call Father Al about the inquiry class and take the personal risk to try it out.

There is one last point to be discussed about family life converts: Do they tend to be inner converts or switchers? The number of inner converts in this group appears to be higher than in the intermarriage convert group. Thirty-nine percent told of a recent conversion experience (versus 33% for the intermarriage converts), and 19% said that it was very important in influencing them to convert. And the conversion had a bit more personal influence on them than was the case with the intermarriage converts (see Table A.4 in Appendix A).

Catholic schools were facilitators in many of these conversions. Of the family life converts with children of school age, 36% have their children in Catholic schools. Also, 24% told us that concern for their children's education was a very important influence in their decisions to convert.

SEEKER CONVERTS

The seeker convert is the type that best fits past social science research on religious recruitment. No intermarriage is involved. The individual has needs that impel him or her to an interest in religious groups and religious study, and sometime during the seeking he or she finds a person or group who is genuinely helpful. This person or group facilitates the individual's joining the church through the influence of affective relationships. Outside relationships that would keep the individual tied to another church or that would oppose his or her joining the new church progressively weaken. Often a decisive event during the seeking-and-trying-out phase accelerates the decision.

In our sample, 12% of the converts are seeker converts. Possibly a few more should be added to this type, but in these cases our data is too sketchy to be sure. Seeker converts are relatively older than other converts; in our sample the median age at baptism was 34 years. Seventy-seven percent were females, and 38% were single. The high number of single persons probably occurs because single persons sometimes feel ill at ease in family-oriented churches, and because single persons have fewer social ties preventing them from moving from one church to another.

The high percentage of blacks (23%) in this group is because certain types of parishes in recent years have been successful in evangelizing blacks, and several such parishes were in our study. Black

60

persons who desire to attend integrated churches befitting middle-class life-style often find themselves in Catholic parishes in their neighborhoods, when the Protestant churches are less racially integrated or less appealing. Black families moving out of inner cities to middle-class suburban areas are often inclined toward Catholicism, if the parishes are friendly and religiously nourishing. For some blacks, the Catholic schools are an attractive alternative to other available schools. One often hears today that blacks are easier to evangelize than whites, and we believe it is true. It is also true, however, that blacks are harder to evangelize in the early 1980s than they were in the middle 1960s, before black self-determination became strong and Catholic schools declined.

Seeker converts have had, on the average, less religious training during childhood than other converts; in our sample, 73% had received some religious training (versus about 87% for the others). They came from various Protestant denominations—like other converts—except that few are former Lutherans. A lower percentage of seeker converts were active formerly in other churches, compared with other converts (50% versus 66% of the others). But among those who were active in other churches, a higher percentage had been active till recently, and fewer had dropped out some years earlier.

As Table 3.2 shows, the seeker converts have experienced much in their recent religious lives. Nineteen percent have been active in charismatic prayer groups, and 21% have had their religious lives influenced by radio or television. For 23%, dissatisfaction with earlier churches was an important reason for making the change. We asked what the main dissatisfaction was, and although the descriptions varied greatly, interpersonal difficulties were most commonly mentioned. Some persons had been through unpleasant episodes in other churches, some no longer felt welcome, and some were offended by certain teachings or practices.

Fifty-eight percent said they had experienced personal or family problems recently that affected their religious viewpoints. This is a higher percentage than among the other types of converts. We asked what kinds of problems they were, and most common were the death of a loved one and personal conflicts involving sex, drugs, or the like. Twenty-seven percent said that these problems were very important to their decisions to become Catholics.

Sixty-two percent said they had experienced a sense of need or void in their feelings about life, and 23% of the seeker converts said this was very important in their decisions. Fifty-four percent had had personal conversion experiences, and for 38% of the seeker converts this was a very important influence.

Most of these persons had been seekers for a time, some quite consciously so. Forty-two percent had been seeking religious truth in various places and looking into various kinds of teachings. (Twenty-eight percent of the other converts said this.) But like the other converts, they found their way to Catholic parishes through facilitating persons and relationships. For 23%, friends or neighbors were main facilitators; for 27%, priests were important. Spouses and other relatives were much less important.

We asked how they had chosen the particular Catholic parish where they were baptized, and the answers were similar to the answers given by other converts. This was surprising, since we expected the seeker converts to have found new church homes after some searching, and to have their choices determined by particular priests or friends. But apparently, not a great deal of church shopping had taken place—60% said the parishes they had chosen were the closest ones, 8% said their friends belong there, 8% chose the parishes because of the priests, and the rest had various reasons.

Laura is an instructive example of a seeker convert with strong personal needs who found her way to the Catholic Church through the timely influence of friends. After a difficult period in early adulthood she began reconstructing her personal and family life, and the inspiration of her Catholic friends plus the support of a nearby parish persuaded her to become a Catholic.

Laura: in Search of Stability

Laura, 34, lives in a large city in the Midwest. She had been a confirmed Catholic for two years when we interviewed her. Laura was reared in a Missouri Synod Lutheran home in the area, and the whole family attended church weekly. She received two years of confirmation training and was confirmed during junior high school. She had good relations with her parents.

At age 17, Laura married a man in the armed forces who "had no religion." She attended college for a time and then had two daughters. Not too long after this, the marriage was in trouble, which caused her much anguish.

"The Missouri Synod Lutherans have an attitude, I think similar to the Catholics, that divorce isn't the way to go. Marriage is a Sacrament. And really, the Lutherans don't consider it a Sacrament, but it is. And I was kind of the oddball when I got my divorce. My church wasn't much for divorce, even in the early 70s—not in the background I was raised in. It was the first divorce in my family, which made it more painful."

62

She talked about her Lutheran faith and her dislike of divorce.

"Well, I think my faith up to a point kept the marriage together for a long time. I really think it did because, well, number one, I had children with him, and I felt that divorce was wrong, and I still believe it's wrong in most cases, and I think that without my faith probably I'd have taken the easy way out, which would be just to walk out and leave. And I think I stuck along longer than I should have, but in the end I think that I really didn't have a choice in the matter. It was either get a divorce or—I was losing my mind."

The marriage was going badly. "There was a lot of things wrong with my life at that time. I was raised that drinking was wrong. My husband drank a lot at that time. But I also was raised that divorce was wrong. I had called home, and my mother supported me as much as she could without telling me just flat out to get a divorce, come home, whatever."

Laura and her husband, John, went to the Lutheran minister for marriage counseling. It led to a blowup, about which she still has strong feelings.

"I don't think if I ever had a friend who needed any type of counseling I would send them to minister, a priest, or a rabbi, for that matter. I would suggest they go to a professional counselor. . . . If a minister's trained in this area, or a priest is trained in this area, fine. This particular one I don't think had had any counseling experience, and I think possibly he let his own emotions get too involved when he was listening to all these stories, because first of all, my husband went separately and I went separately to counseling sessions for a long time. Then we both went together. And of course my husband would say the exact opposite, but I would think—and I still think—it was a thing of a man taking a man's point of view, and I was furious. Boy! My husband told him first of all he had never run around during his married life, he did not have a drinking problem, I mistreated my children, just a bunch of crap. Like this guy was a judge, instead of a counselor. And boy, he told me I better just beat a path home to my husband's door, and I better quit my job, and do right by my family. I was losing my mind! I think I was ready for the loony bin, really. And I got the idea from the whole counseling session that he believed him, he really believed my husband. And this man *knew* me! I had taught Sunday school there. And you know, when you work in a church that much, you get to know the people, and all of a sudden, why, 'Your poor husband, you've been running

63

around, you're just something else.' And I was furious. I had had it. And boy, that was it."

Laura left the church and initiated divorce proceedings. She never talked to the minister again, and he never called her. John grabbed the children and drove off to another military base to which he was transferred, and he got the divorce in another state. Since Laura did not go there to contest the divorce, the court awarded him custody of the children. Laura was devastated. In the interview she went on and on about it all.

"Did you feel the Lutheran Church had thrown you out, or somehow rejected you as being less, somehow, than they had expected?"

"Yes, I did. Yes."

"Did you feel that of the Lutheran Church, or of the Lutheran minister?"

"I think it was the minister, number one. Because I think that a church owes a little support to a person that's going through any kind of an emotional experience, whether it be divorce, death—there's a lot of things that happen. And I just felt a total feeling of rejection all the way around. . . . Plus, my husband really gave me a bad time during the divorce! He stirred up a lot of trouble in the neighborhood and among our friends, as to what was going on during the divorce. I had just had enough! I mean—there was years of this stuff. The drinking, carousing, the constant threat of—'I don't know why I ever married you.' He accused me—at one time he made the comment, the second child was *no way* his. . . . And he brought up a lot of doubt in a lot of people's minds. . . . Because I don't know of anybody that went through a divorce but that they have a great feeling of inferiority when they're going through it. It's a bad time, frankly."

She went to her mother to help, and her mother tried to support her.

"In the end, I really didn't ask my mother's opinion. I just got the divorce. And when my husband got custody of the children, that was when I started punishing myself. I thought everything was wrong. Maybe the way I had lived was wrong, and maybe he was right, maybe just have a good time, live for the minute, forget the world. Well, I tried that. It didn't work *at all*. I went through a really bad time for about six months. I tried to drink. I could last for about two drinks, and I was absolutely silly. It just didn't work. Had a lot of bad feelings about myself. I didn't like myself too much. I did go to a

64

counselor, for six sessions. I came out with a lot of good feelings. That helped me a lot. And I think, too, the fact that maybe I was growing up. Then I started thinking about, well, you know, you've got to feed yourself, you've got to put a roof over your head."

The divorce was finalized when Laura was 25. Her mother lent her money and convinced her to start legal action to get the children back; after much time and expense, Laura succeeded. It was a new day. She had proven to all that she wasn't such a bad mother after all. She transferred her membership to another Lutheran church in the city.

"But I just never was active there. They didn't really have any programs that sparked my interest, and I think, like I said, I was just terribly bitter. I was a Girl Scout leader for about three years over there, and that was really the only contact I had with any of them."

"So you weren't against Lutheranism in general."

"That's really hard to say, it's been so long ago. There's nothing wrong with the Lutheran religion. I think it's just a matter of my finding *my* place in it—from what my viewpoints were on religion."

"Would you say that a lot of it was based on that minister."

"Oh, you better believe it!"

"And it carried over into your whole feeling with Lutheranism. Is this correct?"

"Right. I mean, I have nothing against my mother being Lutheran, or anything like that. But *I* would never join the Lutheran Church again."

Laura's daughters came to live with her. For several years she hadn't gone to any church, but now she started thinking about the girls' religious training.

"When they came to live with me permanently, I thought, 'Well, it's about time they did get religion.' I think probably it was about time I got some too. And the fact that I got my kids back had a lot to do with it. Really, it made a difference in my life."

The babysitter offered to take the girls to her church, and Laura accepted the offer. After several months of this, Laura went too.

"I went to the church. And I did not agree with what they were getting in the way of religion."

"What church was this?"

"It was nondenominational. This was just too unreal. I was raised in a rigid, I'd say formal church, and this 'Hallelujah' and 'Amen' business was just for the birds! So I thought, well—and at that time I was going once and a while with the girls at work, on holy days, to a Catholic church. I thought, well, it's too bad the Catholic Church doesn't have a religious program for kids, because that's really why I'm going to go anyway. And I thought, oh, well, I'll try Mass a few times. . . . And the lady across the street saw me, and she said, 'You know there's some religious programs for the kids at St. Mark's. You ought to check into this sort of thing.' And I did, and we started going to Mass there, fairly regularly, and it definitely helped the kids."

"Were there any other influential people that made a difference as far as your moving into the Catholic Church?"

"Yes, I have a neighbor who is an amazing person. He's been divorced for a number of years. I didn't even really realize he was Catholic. I knew he went to church every Sunday, but I didn't know what religion he was. We've become real good friends; in fact, he is working on my porch today. He's just a friend, and boy, at that point in my life, I needed all the friends I could get. And he's just always been around. I think his inner strength, too, came from the same thing. And I think that made an influence on my life. I might mention, too, five years ago, when I changed jobs, I work at an all-Catholic office. Everybody is Catholic."

"Did that have an influence on . . . ?"

"Naturally. Well, not the fact that I just worked with Catholics, but also, you see, these people practice their faith every day. And I mean, one woman is really struggling to pay for tuition for girls' high school for her three teenaged kids. And I mean, people self-sacrifice to get these things. You know, that takes a lot."

"That does something to you."

"Sure it does. Just everyday life. And you work with these people probably as much as you're awake and at home, and it really makes an influence. . . . It made me think."

The other women at the office were the main influence on Laura's decision. She started taking private instructions at St. Mark's, where the girls were in CCD. It was not the parish nearest her house, but her girls liked it and soon had friends there.

"So I started going to religious instructions, and I went privately. I went for quite a while. Let's see, it started in August, and I was confirmed in March. I had ample time to make my decision, and I think I learned enough about the teachings of the church to see that they coincided with a lot of what I believed, and I learned a lot. Good educational experience. It's been a long time since I'd had any religious education. And I joined the Catholic Church!

"I never said anything to anybody at work for a long time, because I didn't know how they'd react. You know, it's kind of unusual for someone who's divorced to convert. I have not seen it happen too many times. And I was not too sure how they would react, because I knew that especially one lady I worked with was absolutely against divorce. And in fact she and I have had a few run-ins in the past over divorce, because I still don't think it's right, but I think there are reasons behind it. When it came time for my confirmation, I invited almost everybody in the office to the confirmation. Most of them came too. Of course, one lady talks about the parish where I go as being 'that divorced parish,' but I think she's accepted me."

"Did your parents have any problems with your changing?"

"No, my mother had none at all. She told me that she does feel, though, that when it comes time for Debbie to be confirmed that it's got to be her decision. Now listen, I wouldn't have had that choice when I was in eighth grade. No way. I would have been confirmed, and that was it! And I still don't think she needs that much of a choice. I mean, you know, if she was just adamantly refusing to do it, that would be one thing."

"Did you ever think about joining any other religion?"

"No."

"You just started going with Catholic friends and kind of moved in this direction?"

"Uh-huh."

"What are some of the things in the Catholic Church that appeal to you?"

"For one thing, the fact that things don't change. You know, they're against abortion, it's not right, will never be right, it's a sin, and that's it. I think that was a big factor—a lot of stability there, and believe me, that's one thing I needed in my life at that point, was stability. I realize now, you know, from being more involved with the Catholic Church, there *have* been a lot of changes, but I think a lot of them are for the better. Some things I don't even like. I mean, all of a sudden everybody charges up to the front of the church and stands around the altar. I'm still not used to that."

The interviewer then checked out Laura's views of the special nature of Catholicism.

"Was the stability and solidity of Catholicism a major influence attracting you, or was it an accidental thing due to your Catholic friends? What if your friends had been Methodists and not Catholics. Would you be a Methodist today?"

"I'll tell you the truth, I doubt it. I *do* think it is the solidity, and it is a stability factor. No, I don't think I would be a Methodist today. Or whatever. I think my friends helped me find the solidity of the Catholic faith, and I think it was the inner strength they had. I'll tell you the truth, I had never found that kind of strength in a, say, Methodist (laugh). Sounds like I'm militant religious. No, I'm not. No, I think the stability of my friends—they have a very deep faith, a lot of them."

The interviewer also checked out whether Laura is thinking of remarriage. Her reply was, no, not for the present; maybe later when the girls are grown.

There had been a religious turning point, a profound experience, in the midst of Laura's worst times. She told of a time in church.

"I went to church with several of my friends, on lunch hours and things, like there'd be a holy day. And it was so peaceful, so serene, the one place I would go—no demands were made on me, where I felt there weren't. . . . It was quiet. I could just sit there and think. Pretty soon I started to pray. And boy, I'll tell you, I look back now at how much worse things could have turned out in my life than did happen. . . . God was always watching over me the whole time, face it, because I tell you, I could have really hit a low. You know, there's all kinds of things that could have entered my mind, and they probably did, I just don't remember it. You know, a lot of people don't pull through, but I did."

"God was with you, even in the depths."

"That's what I say."

Laura's experience demonstrates the role of the facilitating persons. The women at the office won her respect and then took her along to noontime Masses. She admired their faith and their way of life, and she felt affirmed by them, as was shown by the "surprise" confirmation event. Probably the decisive event causing her to begin inquiry class was the coming of her daughters to live permanently with her, with the added sense of responsibility she then felt. In a way, her daughters were also facilitating persons, since they liked CCD at St. Mark's and soon had friends there.

Our second example of a seeker convert is Rhonda. She is a bit unusual in that her reasons for becoming a Catholic are quite utilitarian. She is clearly a switcher, and her commitment to the Catholic Church is still unsteady.

RHONDA: FOR CATHOLIC SCHOOLING

Rhonda, 28, is black and has recently converted in a suburban parish near a large eastern city. She had been reared in the inner city by her mother, a strong Baptist, who insisted Rhonda go to Sunday school and church every week. Rhonda and her mother went to one Baptist church for some time, then to a different one. During her teenage years she grew restless and stopped going. She joined her girlfriends in visiting various churches.

"Did anyone have an influence on your religious life during your teenage years?"

"Well, my friends. They were taking me from church to church even though I couldn't join."

"You couldn't join because of your mother?"

"That's right."

"But she would let you visit?"

"Yes, I could visit. I had several friends I would go to church with."

"And one or two of them were Catholic?"

"No, there was a few of us in the neighborhood that wanted to become Catholic."

"So there were several girls who were dissatisfied and you went together?"

"We went to Catholic. And one of my friends went to Holiness, and I would go to that church, the Holiness Church."

"Did your religious or spiritual life change during your teenage years?"

"Yes. My religious life changed because I was going constantly to a different church. And it was like a man without a home, searching. Trying to find something that I could really latch on to, and it was just difficult."

"Did you rebel against your religious training or against God?"

"Just from church—Baptist Church. I wanted something different."

At age 17, Rhonda married a Baptist. He wanted her to stay a Baptist, and she went with him to the Baptist church. But the marriage was short-lived; within two years Rhonda and her husband were separated. She had a daughter who was aged 10 when we talked. Three years earlier she had moved from the city to the suburbs. Her daughter had been in a special school in the inner city, but in the new suburban area there was no such school.

"When I moved to Glen Acres I had to put her in the public school. I wasn't acquainted with what Catholic schools or religious schools were in the area. And I found that the public school really didn't care. When I speak with other parents who have kids in the school, they say I just ran into a bad teacher. They say they haven't had the same experience, but I found that the teacher wasn't interested in what my child knew. She was just interested in getting through the day. And when I tried to tell her my child was in a test school and showed her letters from other teachers saying what my child knew, she just wasn't interested. Anything to keep me out of the school. So I became very upset and when I did find Holy Redeemer was in the neighborhood, I took my daughter up for a test, and as everyone knows, once you come out of public school going into Catholic school, it's difficult to adjust, and after the testing they generally put you back a grade. Well, they said that she tested very well and she would have no problem fitting in, and it was December when she started."

"What were the circumstances leading up to your decision to convert? Why did you do this now and not some time earlier?"

"It was when my daughter entered school. She had been at Holy Redeemer I guess a few months. And she came to me and she said that she wanted to become Catholic, because she felt left out when they went to Mass, and everyone received Communion but her, and she couldn't. I was still going to a Baptist church, and I told her, I said, 'Well, this is something that you're going to have to think about because once you make the switch, then this is what you're going to be.' "

"How old was she?"

"I guess she was eight. And I told her that I had wanted to become a Catholic anyway, but because of her father—he was really unhappy with the decision—I had to think about it. And we started taking classes and we spoke with the priest."

Rhonda went on to tell how she had established a good relationship with Father Kennedy, who conducted the inquiry class, and she felt she could go to him at any time. Her mother didn't approve of her becoming a Catholic, but by this time her relationship with her mother was weak, so she didn't care.

70

Rhonda occasionally still goes to the Baptist church. She said, in response to a question, that her becoming a Catholic did not have an influence on her family life, her attitudes about life, or her personal habits.

She had mixed feelings about the parish school because of some bad experiences there. Her daughter had gotten into trouble several times for fighting, and neither Rhonda nor Father Kennedy seemed to be able to straighten out matters with the principal. After a time Rhonda's daughter was expelled from the school. This angered Rhonda, who blamed the problem on the "unfeeling" principal. She put her daughter into the public school.

Rhonda's feelings have not subsided. She told us how unapproachable and unfeeling most of the priests and nuns were—with the one exception of Father Kennedy. She complained about the high tuition cost and the mandatory Sunday offering envelopes for parents of children in the school. She told us how much money she had paid during that first year—when she was a non-Catholic—since she had to pay non-Catholic tuition at first. Now that her daughter was out of the school, she had cut back on her contributions drastically.

Someone suggested she and her daughter go to Catholic Charities for counseling, and this is now in process. It is a big help, and she appreciates it. She stills attends Mass at Holy Redeemer with her daughter, and she is trying to avoid creating bad feelings with the priests and nuns there. Her experiences have not weakened her belief in the Catholic Church in general, but they have weakened her enthusiasm for Holy Redeemer parish.

Rhonda's motivations for becoming a Catholic are probably related to her love for her daughter, the desire to save some of the school tuition money, and her desire to change her own life in some ways. Perhaps a desire for greater autonomy was present, since she became a Catholic even though both her mother and her husband disapproved. Later, when her daughter was expelled from the Catholic school, Rhonda's church commitment quickly weakened, indicating how much this church commitment was related to her daughter's upbringing.

Are there more inner converts and fewer switchers among the seeker converts than among the other types? Table A.4 tells us no. They do not seem to become more committed church members than the other types of converts. As Rhonda teaches us, some have weak commitment.

71

Chapter
4

INTERFAITH MARRIAGE IN AMERICA

INTERMARRIAGE BETWEEN Catholics and Protestants is the greatest single source of new Catholic converts. It is also the greatest single source of disidentification from Catholicism.[1] Since intermarriage is so crucial to the field of evangelization, we look at it in detail, sociologically, in this chapter.

Some church leaders who heard us say that 83% of new Catholic converts came through intermarriage inferred that evangelization is concerned with only the other 17%, and that convert-making through intermarriage is a kind of automatic, or mechanical, process. This conclusion is wrong. It is true that interfaith marriage is common in America and is the product of underlying strong social forces not easily changed by institutions or leaders. It is not true, however, that the religious outcome of interfaith marriage is somehow automatic. On the contrary, the religious outcome depends on the experiences of the couple and their relatives, and it sometimes hangs in the balance for as long as ten years. After intermarriage, some Catholics convert to Protestant churches and some Protestants convert to the Catholic Church, for reasons discussed in earlier chapters. Intermarriage is a mission field.

Sociologists have uncovered numerous facts about patterns of interfaith marriage, and this chapter reviews the most important ones. The chapter is organized around four questions: What are the trends and patterns in interfaith marriage? Who intermarries? What happens to the religious faith and commitment of the intermarried? Are interfaith marriages less stable than single-faith marriages? Since the best research is on Catholic-Protestant and Catholic–no-religion intermarriages, we stress them most.

About 40% of the Catholics who married in the 1970s married non-Catholics. This is an estimate based on several studies.[2] The majority married Protestants, but a few married Jews, persons of other religions, and persons with no religious preference. The percentage of those marrying non-Catholics has been inching upward for decades, and it will probably move higher in the future. Between 1935 and 1965 the rate moved upward about ten to fifteen percentage points. In Canada, where census data include information on religion, more precise figures are available on intermarriage; there the percentage of brides and grooms marrying spouses of different faiths rose from 10% in 1947 to 16% in 1967.[3] Rates in the United States have always been higher than in Canada, but the upward trends are similar.

One way to understand intermarriage rates is to compare the actual rates to a mathematical model assuming random matchmaking. According to such a model, matches are arrived at randomly, and if, for example, 50% of the young males living in an area were non-Catholic, then a young Catholic female would have a 50% probability of intermarriage across religious lines. If 90% of the males were non-Catholic, her probability of intermarriage would be 90%. At the end of the 1960s the actual number of intermarriages in the United States was roughly *half* of that predicted by the random model.

One strong predictor of the number of intermarriages entered into by Catholics is the percentage of non-Catholics in the state or region. That is, the fewer the eligible Catholic marriage partners in the area, the more intermarriage occurs. The random matchmaking model would predict it, and empirically, it is true. The highest rates of intermarriage by Catholics occur in the south Atlantic and the east south central regions, exactly where Catholics are the lowest percentage of the population. For instance, already in 1950 the intermarriage rate for the diocese of Savannah-Atlanta was 70%.

Another strong predictor of intermarriage rates is whether ethnic or social class barriers exist in the locality, impeding mixing of young people across religious lines. Where the barriers exist, intermarriage rates are low. For example, in 1950 the intermarriage rate in the diocese of San Antonio was only half of that in the diocese of Syracuse, even though the percentage of Catholics in the population was the same for both. The reason is that the Hispanic community comprised most of the Catholics in San Antonio, and strong ethnic and socioeconomic barriers reduced the kinds of contacts across religious lines that produce marriage.[4] Partly for this reason, the intermarriage rates in the United States are lowest in New England and in the west north central region.

Why are interfaith marriages increasing? The answer to this question follows from the above. If the absence of ethnic or socioeconomic barriers produces higher rates of intermarriage, one would expect that the gradual trends of weakening ethnic barriers in American society would produce more intermarriage. Urban youths, who formerly seldom ventured outside their Italian, German, or Anglo-Saxon neighborhoods, today are less conscious of their ethnic differences, and in addition, they probably live in ethnically indifferent suburbs. They are now in close contact with other youth of all religions and ethnicities.

A second factor is the upward social mobility of American Catholics. Overall class differences between Protestants and Catholics are a thing of the past in the United States. In the 1960s Catholics attained a socioeconomic status equal to the average of Protestants. Some ethnic differences in class remain, but an overall class difference along religious lines does not.[5]

In a nationwide study of college students Albert Gordon concluded that the increasing rate of college attendance is one source of higher rates of interfaith marriage. "Young people of varying backgrounds who attend college together have this education and environment in common, and are less likely to concern themselves with differences in family background, origin, or religion." [6] In America much freedom is given to young people to choose their own marriage partners, based on the view that love rather than parents' wishes is most important in choosing husbands or wives.

A final factor probably having an effect on intermarriage rates is a general weakening of the influence of churches in our society, so that church-related considerations are weaker in affecting actions of young people than they were several decades ago. And many denominations are more ecumenical in attitude in the 1970s and 1980s than they were earlier.

Several researchers have charted changes in attitudes toward interfaith marriage. All found a trend toward greater acceptance. For example, the Gallup poll found that 63% approved of Protestant-Catholic intermarriage in 1968; by 1978 the figure had risen to 73%. Approval is greater among the Catholic population than among the Protestant population.[7]

The changing attitudes of society are reflected in changing positions of the Catholic Church regarding mixed marriage. In 1917 the Codex Iuris Canonicis instructed the clergy to deter the faithful from mixed marriage to the best of their power. By 1966 the Decree on Ecumenism suggested that "the rigor of the present legislation be mitigated regarding mixed marriages . . . in regard to certain norms of ecclesiastical law by which the separated brethren often feel offended." [8] By 1970 the non-Catholic partner was no longer required to make a written promise to raise children of the marriage as Catholics. Now the official attitude of U.S. bishops stresses the potential benefits for the ecumenical movement that mixed marriage affords.

What types of people intermarry across religious lines? Definite patterns have been found. With regard to religion, Catholics intermarry out of their faith at a higher rate than Protestants (when one defines an interfaith marriage as crossing any of five lines: Protestant/Catholic/Jew/no religion/other religion). Within Protestantism, rates of intermarriage out of the Protestant religion are lowest for Baptists and Methodists, partly because they constitute majority religions in certain parts of the nation. Lutherans have the highest rate, approaching that of Catholics. Catholics who marry outside the denomination marry Lutherans more than any others.[9] One study in Pennsylvania looked into which factor influenced intermarriage rates between groups more—the congruence of churchlike or sectlike religious institutions, or the sizes and similarity in social classes of the religious groups. The conclusion was that the latter has more influence.[10]

WHO INTERMARRIES?

Interfaith marriage is usually considered to be a deviant form of behavior, since all religious groups prefer intrafaith marriage over interfaith marriage. Much research has been done to try to discover which conditions motivate a young person to surmount the barriers of religious training, parental expectations, and social norms to contract an interfaith marriage. One might expect that young persons whose parents are less committed to religious norms would be more likely to depart from these norms when choosing marriage partners. This is so; in every study young persons from homes rated as not religiously devout or church-involved were found to be more willing to marry outside their faiths.[11]

Even if the homes were religiously devout, family discord or parent-child tensions may weaken the effect of the parents, thus giving way to more interfaith marriage. This has also been found. Intermarried persons, more so than intramarried persons, are likely to have felt dissatisfaction with parents and with family relationships, to have had strifeful family life, and to have been emancipated from their parents at the time of marriage. Also, children of mixed marriages are more likely to enter mixed marriages themselves.[12]

75

Most striking is the research finding that many more second marriages are religiously mixed than first marriages. This has been found repeatedly, but no study has clearly shown why.[13] One leading possibility is that certain characteristics lie behind both divorce and interreligious second marriage—the factors that make a person likely to divorce, contrary to religious and social norms, are the same as those that make this person likely to intermarry in the second marriage.

The age of persons at marriage is another predictor of rates of intermarriage. Teenage marriages are especially likely to be religiously mixed, partly because teenage marriages often represent broken social norms. Generally, schools, churches, parents, and community groups oppose young marriages. For any teenager to go ahead with a young marriage requires that he or she feel little constraint from adults or from community opinion. Youth culture emphasis on romance and the purity of young love strengthens teenagers' attitudes that the views of adults in the community should be ignored. In short, if particular teenagers go ahead with early marriage against adults' wishes, they will similarly go ahead with intermarriage against adults' wishes.[14]

Data from Iowa in the 1950s showed that for brides aged 17 or younger, 41% of the marriages were religiously mixed. For brides aged 18, the rate was 35%. For brides between ages 19 and 22, it was 19%; for brides between ages 23 and 29, 21%. And for brides aged 30 or older, it was 24%. In a separate study of college students in Iowa, 25% more freshmen than seniors were willing to marry out of their faiths.[15]

Older than average age at marriage is also associated with a higher rate of intermarriage, although to a lesser degree and for different reasons. Perhaps the limited supply of marriage partners for persons over age 30 makes for decreased concern about norms against religious intermarriage. Or perhaps parental norms are almost nonexistent for persons in their late 20s, or 30s. Whatever the reason, we judge that the uniqueness of marriages contracted after age 30 is diminishing in American society. The divorce rate is high, and nowadays matches are made for marriages or remarriages at all ages.

Several other factors influence who intermarries. The incidence of intermarriage is higher among Catholics who have had more education than the average of their ethnic groups. The amount of religious education seems to predict lower rates of intermarriage, but the patterns in the research are not consistent. Paul H. Besanceney discovered in the 1960s that intermarriage rates did not differ between those who had attended Catholic schools and those who had not. Yet a study of college students determined that attendance at Catholic high schools or colleges predicted lower rates of interfaith marriage. This could have been because religious education later in one's upbringing has relatively more deterrent power, or because some Catholic young people met their future mates in their high schools and colleges.[16] At any rate, research has not been able to distinguish the influence of Catholic schooling from the religious motivation of the parents who send their children through this educational system.

We might expect that persons with strong religious orientation would have low rates of intermarriage. In a cross-denomination study this pattern was found in those denominations that are antiecumenical—such as the Mormons and the Seventh-Day Adventists. In ecumenically minded denominations, such as the United Methodist Church and the United Church of Christ, the opposite pattern obtained—that there was more, not less, intermarriage among the more religiously committed.[17] Apparently, a strong religious motivation encourages intermarriage for youth in ecumenical denominations but discourages such coupling in antiecumenical organizations. Among Catholics and Lutherans in this study there was no pattern at all.

Strength of ethnic identification seems to inhibit intermarriage, according to research findings, and one study of intermarriage among Catholics in New York City found different rates for different ethnic groups—highest rates were among Germans, Russians, and "Americans" (those in the United States at least four generations). In a nationwide study, Andrew Greeley found that intermarriage occurs less for Irish, Italian, and Hispanic Catholics than for other Catholics.[18]

What Happens to the Religious Faith and Commitment of the Intermarried?

When a Catholic marries a non-Catholic, the couple has five religious options: (1) The non-Catholic can convert to the Catholic Church. (2) The Catholic can convert to the other church. (3) Both can convert to a different but mutually acceptable church. (4) Both can remain as they are. (5) Both can drop out of church life entirely to escape the problem. Which solution is the most common? Research provides some rough guesses. Two studies in the 1960s estimated that 50% or 60% of interfaith marriages involved a conversion in one direction or the other. J. Milton Yinger, in a 1968 review of the research, concluded that in half the interreligious marriages, conversions take place at or near the time of marriage, and in the other half the couples opt for solutions 4 and 5 above.[19]

When conversion did occur during the 1950s and 1960s, more Protestant spouses converted to Catholicism than vice versa. The ratio of Protestants-who-converted to Catholics-who-converted during these decades was found to be 2:1, or 3:1, or more, depending on the study. The ratio has shifted between then and the early 1980s, so that it is about 1:1 today. We lack recent studies showing this precisely, but Greeley made estimates based on the best nationwide data of the 1970s. He stated that about 40% of Catholics intermarry, and of them, about 23% of the Catholic spouses disidentify due to the intermarriage and about 7% do so for other reasons. About 20% of the non-Catholic spouses convert to Catholicism. And about 50% of the marriages remain mixed, with no conversion over many years.[20] That is, the ratio of non-Catholics-who-convert to Catholics-who-convert has dropped to about 1:1. The data used by Greeley do not tell us about frequency of church attendance, but only about religious self-identification.

Is there a trend toward a higher or lower rate of unification of mixed marriages through conversion, either one way or the other? The research is unclear on this point, but persons we spoke to recently seemed to agree that young people feel less pressure today to unify a mixed marriage than they did a decade or two ago. This sounds plausible.

If one of the spouses converts, which one will it be? All research agrees that the relative devoutness of the two spouses is crucial—the less devout spouse usually converts to the church of the more devout. Attitudes of families and in-laws are usually involved in the decision.

There is also some evidence that conversions tend to be in the direction of the spouse with the higher social status. In a study in New York State, W. Seward Salisbury found that Catholic wives converted to the churches of their Protestant husbands more readily if the husbands were professional men.[21] The social status factor in conversions was often discussed by intermarriage researchers in decades past, when it was probably more salient. But today, when overall Protestant-Catholic social status differences are gone, it is probably weak.

When conversions do occur, past research indicates that they usually occur near the time of the marriage or when the first child is less than age 10. The marriage itself and the question of how to educate the first child provide the two occasions producing most conversions.

Finally, the religious involvement of intermarried couples who decide not to unify their marriages religiously is substantially lower than for other couples. Nationwide data in the mid-1970s showed that "half (51%) of Catholics with Catholic spouses said they attended church services once a week or more; the corresponding figure for Catholics with non-Catholic spouses was twenty-six percent." [22] A religiously mixed home tends to reduce the involvement of the spouses in any church. Church attendance by one spouse without the other is less meaningful, and the problems of children's education are always potential sources of tension.

Research has looked both at marital satisfaction of interfaith marriages and at survival rates. With regard to marital satisfaction, several studies agree that mixed marriages are less satisfying than single-faith marriages. In nationwide surveys in the 1970s, respondents whose spouses were now of the same faith said they were very happy in their marriages to a greater extent than those whose marriages were religiously mixed.[23] The surveys did not identify persons whose marriages were initially mixed but later unified through conversion of one spouse. But they suggested that, in general, to unify a religiously mixed marriage through conversion of one spouse (or both spouses) would increase marital satisfaction. We have seen the same result in our study of intermarriage converts, in chapter 3.

A Manhattan survey in the 1950s compared Catholics married to other Catholics with Catholics married to non-Catholics; the findings showed that the intermarried Catholics had slightly less marital satisfaction and slightly poorer mental health.[24]

A number of studies have looked at problems in interfaith marriages. Couples who maintain their own separate religions tend to have less marital happiness, partly because companionship is reduced, and in modern marriage, companionship is the most valued aspect. A major problem is how to handle the religious training of children. Birth control, family size, and interference from in-laws regarding religious matters can also be troublesome.[25]

Controversy abounds on the topic of survival rates, but the best studies show a higher survival rate for single-faith marriages than for interfaith marriages. The best study, which uses a nationwide sample and investigates many factors, is Larry Bumpass and James Sweet's analysis of marital instability. Data from a 1970 survey of white, ever-married women under age 45 showed that "in intrafaith marriages, Jewish couples have the lowest levels of instability, Protestant couples the highest, with Catholics intermediate. . . . Mixed Protestant-Catholic marriages are less stable than religiously homogamous marriages."[26] Mixed marriages are five percentage points less stable than Protestant-Protestant marriages and eleven points less stable than Catholic-Catholic marriages. This difference occurs even when other factors, such as age at marriage, are controlled.

A study in Iowa came to the same conclusion. Catholic-Catholic marriages in this study had a 96.2% survival rate. Survival rates of interfaith marriages depended partly on the religions involved. Catholic-Lutheran marriages had a 90.5% survival rate; Catholic-Baptist marriages had a 81.6% rate, and Catholic–"unspecified-Protestant" marriages the lowest of all (the exact figure was not known). Obviously, social class factors influenced these survival rates but probably not enough to account for the pattern.[27]

The most reliable conclusion seems to be that interfaith marriages generally have lower marital satisfaction and lower survival rates even if all other factors are controlled. One should remember that other factors are very powerful. Other important predictors of marriage survival are older age at marriage, more education, no premarital pregnancy, upbringing in the southern states, and no former marriage by the spouses. Taken together, these have much more impact on marriage survival than religious factors.

Research on intermarriage demonstrates how much intermarriage decisions are influenced by broad social forces, some church-related and some not. Also, it depicts the close relationships between family life and church. Each supports the other, and when one weakens, the other suffers.

Chapter

5

WHO ARE THE DROPOUTS?

In this study a dropout is a baptized Catholic who no longer attends Mass as often as twice a year (apart from Christmas, Easter, weddings, and funerals) and who has stopped within the past three years. We interviewed 182 such persons.

Dropouts are more difficult to interview than converts. Many feel uncomfortable when the church is discussed, and they do not want to talk about it. Whereas most converts are happier now than before, many dropouts are not. Some feel conflicted or guilty about the church. In some cases, young people whose parents have been badgering them to go to church seemed to hear us as being church authorities trying to discover wayward youth and force them back to church. It took much talking to convince them that we were academic researchers from out of town, sincerely interested in their views regardless of whether they liked or disliked the church, and that they could talk to us at their convenience and in confidence.

Many refused to be interviewed, even though they clearly fit the definition. The refusal rate was high among young persons aged 18 to 22—an estimated 45% to 55%. More men refused than women. Typically, young men in the wild oats syndrome refused to talk to us. Quite a few told us they had to go work on their cars or were leaving to go out with friends. Some parents told us that their 18- to 20-year-old sons were indeed inactive, and that they were sorry about it—but their sons would not listen to them, and anyway they were seldom at home. The sons came in to eat and then went out again with the boys. We came to understand how young men with a freedom-loving, roaming life-style would stay away from us and indeed from any researcher.

The problem was more intense among working-class young men than middle-class. Some observers told us it would be worse in the Italian and the Hispanic populations than in others. We could not keep records on this and do not know.

Another bias occurred in our study of dropouts. As our work progressed we saw that the interviews included very few persons who had dropped out after marrying a non-Catholic and switching to the other religion. Many such persons exist, but our method of research missed most of them. If we hit the family of one of them in our random calling, we always asked for the person's phone number and requested permission to call them and ask for an interview. Many parents declined to give us the numbers, since they did not want to be meddling, and since sometimes there was family tension over the matter. A few parents asked for a day to talk with their children about the study before they gave us their children's numbers. We gladly consented to this, and occasionally, it did result in an interview with the son or daughter. (If the son or daughter lived hundreds of miles away, we could not follow them up.) As a result of these conditions we missed most of the young adults who switched churches after intermarriage.[1]

CHARACTERISTICS OF DROPOUTS

The dropouts tend to be young. Figure 5.1 shows two estimates of their ages. The top of the figure portrays the age of dropping out for those in our sample. Broken lines have been added to correct the bias from the higher refusal rates among young persons; these lines are more accurate than the uncorrected data. The bottom of the figure shows the age of dropping out among the 198 persons in our sample of returnees. We asked all the returnees at what age they had stopped Mass attendance. Since the returnees tended to be young adults, it follows that few could have dropped out at the higher ages. (Their median age was only 31.5 years, and only 12% were age 50 or older.) Hence, the bottom of Figure 5.1 has a built-in bias toward younger ages of dropping out.

We believe the most reliable estimate of age of dropping out is the corrected version at the top of the figure. But it has limitations. Since our lower age limit for interviewing persons was 18, no one could have dropped out prior to 15, even though, in fact, some persons drop out earlier, as the bottom of the figure proves. Also, as noted earlier, we almost entirely missed persons out-converting after intermarriage.

Within these limitations, we estimate that about 35% of those dropping out did so by age 20, and 54% did so by age 25. Then about

FIGURE 5.1

AGE OF DROPPING OUT

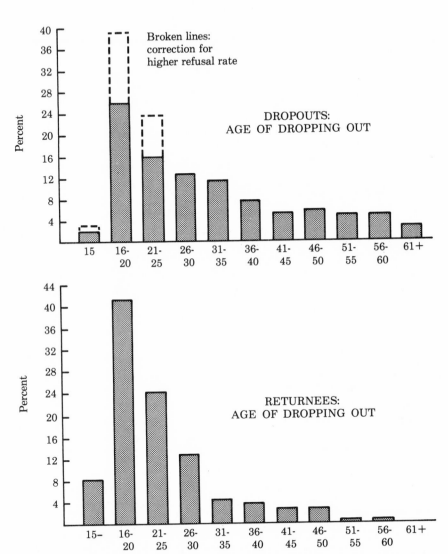

20% more dropped out between ages 25 and 35, about 16% did so between ages 35 and 50, and the other 10% did so after age 50.

What percent of all baptized Catholics, let us say, between ages 15 and 20 or between ages 25 and 30 drop out? Our study provides no estimates. The only research providing information is the Roozen study mentioned in chapter 1, which found that about 42% of all

Catholics drop out sometime during their lives. A majority return.[2]

Of the dropouts we interviewed, 40% were males and 60% were females. But we know that males refused more often than females, so probably a majority of the dropouts are males. With regard to race and ethnicity, 84% were whites, 3% were blacks, and 13% were Hispanics. The largest ethnic groups were Italians, Irish, Germans, and Mexican-Americans—but 23% said they were of mixed ethnicity.

The large dropout during the teenage years and the early 20s is a phenomenon best studied separately, since it often occurs for reasons specific to this age-group. Teenage dropout, or teenage turnoff, is a problem facing all Christian churches; it begins in seventh, eighth, and ninth grades.[3] Therefore, in this chapter we first look at young dropouts, then older dropouts. Young dropouts are persons who stopped Mass attendance at age 22 or younger (a total of 64 persons); older dropouts are persons who dropped out at age 23 or older (118 persons). The cutting point between ages 22 and 23 was selected because persons aged 22 or younger have typically not yet assumed adult roles such as marriage, establishment of a household, parenthood, and long-term employment. When they reach age 23, 24, or 25, many more assume such roles, and this affects their church involvement.

We estimate that young dropouts—using our definition—account for about 45% of all the dropping out prior to old age (based on data corrected for refusals in our study). Dropping out by teenagers is so common nowadays that some religious educators wonder if it should not be seen as normal and expected. Such dropping out results from broad social forces in the society. Parents of youth who drop out evidently do not always recognize this, for during the data collection we talked with some parents who felt terrible that their 16- or 18-year-olds had stopped going to Mass even though they, the parents, had faithfully put the children through years of Catholic school, or catechism and C.C.D. Many mothers told us how badly they felt and how they could not understand where they had gone wrong.

Guilt feelings such as these are largely undeserved, and they call for a clear discussion of the problem in several quarters. First, the magnitude of the phenomenon needs to be explained, then the naturalness of a high-schooler's urge for detachment from the church should be discussed. John Westerhoff, a leading religious educator, holds that the high-school years represent a distinct stage of faith development—"searching faith." It is a time characterized by doubt, critical judgment of the tradition, and a desire for experimentation with other kinds of life-styles and commitments. The church should recognize this natural stage and not try to extinguish it. Westerhoff suggests we ask the parents of such youth how old they themselves were

84

when their religion "came together." In particular, Westerhoff indicates that this stage be recognized publicly by an adolescent rite of transition, celebrated perhaps on St. Thomas Day, according the young person the privilege to doubt and to study and to embark on his or her own "vision quest." Confirmation would be postponed until the 20s, when the young person is into the next faith stage, "owned faith." [4]

Alvin Illig reports the suggestion of a Catholic educator that the church hold a "de-commissioning ceremony" for parents of youth who are about age 18, in which it is openly stated that the parents are now de-commissioned from their obligation to bring up the child in the faith, and the child is now on his or her own. The ceremony would acknowledge what is sociologically true today, that parental influence on children's religious faith by age 18 is weak, and parents cannot be reasonably held responsible for their children's decisions. Probably the main benefit of such a ceremony would be for the parents.

Young Dropouts

The outcome of the global coding for dropouts is shown in Table 5.1 (pages 86-87). The predispositions for stopping Mass attendance are diverse and sometimes elusive. We coded eight kinds. The first one in the table—"tension in parental family; rejection of family pressure once the pressure is off"—is clearly the most common for young dropouts. It is rare among older dropouts, but in our sample several cases were of persons in their 20s.

Another main predisposition, present in about 27% of young dropouts, is objection to confession, fear of confession, or a problem of a life practice being in conflict with the church's moral teachings. These are usually aspects of a single problem and hence are grouped together. Very often a fear of confession among young adults is due to a fear of confessing some practice that is contrary to the church's moral teaching, or to an avoidance of the confessor because he may be condemnatory. The problems occur most often in the realm of sexuality, where, for example, a person engaging in premarital sex, cohabitation, or masturbation feels too guilty or fearful to go to confession.

A third main predisposition is either a feeling that the church is boring or a loss of interest in the church. In the interviews the term lazy is used often, but laziness should be seen as a lack of positive motivation or a motivation blocked by conflict. The question must be asked why there is no motivation, or why the motivation is blocked. In many cases this predisposition is a reflection of a lack of any internalized faith. In

TABLE 5.1

PREDISPOSITIONS AND FACILITATORS FOR DROPOUTS

	Percent	
	Young	Older

Predispositions

Tension in parental family; rejection of family pressure once the pressure is off	52	2
Objection to Catholic moral teachings	16	26
Objection to confession or fear of confession, or present life practices conflict with church's moral teachings	27	15
Objection to changes in Mass or other recent changes	3	19
Other objection to Catholic Church--not biblical enough, too cold, too much talk of money, or other	9	11
Feels that the Catholic Church is boring; lazy; has lost interest; or an earlier motivation has been taken away	27	24
No support from family or spouse, or struggle with family or children	5	6
Feels a void or spiritual need in life; feels emptiness or lack of meaning or emotional depression	6	22
Other	5	4
Total	150	129

Facilitating Persons or Relationships

Spouse, fiancé, or fiancée	16	11
Relative or in-law	9	3
Children (if children took a conscious role or consciously opposed the church)	0	6
Friend or neighbor	16	8
Peer group	19	1
Took part in charismatic group--mixed-denomination or unspecified-denomination	2	3
Took part in non-Catholic religious group--mainline Protestant	0	3
Took part in non-Catholic religious group--fundamental, Baptist, Mormon, or Pentecostal	13	15
Television program or reading	3	3
Other	0	3
Total	78	56

(continued)

TABLE 5.1 CONTINUED

	Young	Older
Facilitating Events		
Moved to new parish or community	3	8
Left home or school	27	1
Marriage, remarriage, or upcoming marriage	8	3
Conflict with priest	14	19
Conflict with other parishioners	6	5
Divorce	2	7
Small children to care for	3	1
Disabled, or need to care for disabled person	0	4*
Conversion experience or religious experience	0	3
Children have left home	0	8
Other	9	13
Total	72	72

*This figure is undoubtedly too low. The true figure is unknown because most older disabled persons refused interviews (see note 1, chapter 5).

others it is closely related to the predisposition discussed previously, that of conflict over life practices disallowed by the church's moral teachings. But in some cases it may be motivational in its own right. Since liturgies and parish programs vary greatly from parish to parish, the feeling that the church is boring may arise after a person experiences meaningful worship in one parish, then moves to another and finds it deadly dull. Or a person may experience a letdown when a beloved priest leaves and he or she cannot relate to the replacement. This person drops out of Mass attendance and says the church is too boring to sustain interest.

A fourth predisposition, present in 17% of the cases, is objection to Catholic moral teachings. This is a predisposition for older dropouts more so than for young dropouts, but it exists for both. The objections usually have to do with teachings in the general area of sexuality, including premarital sex, birth control, and abortion. Besides these four, other predispositions occur less often for young dropouts.

In some cases two or more predispositions are present. The most prevalent combination involves the first predisposition in the table (rejection of family pressure) and the third or the sixth (fear of confession or the feeling that the church is boring). This pattern is common, because the first predisposition provides an occasion for dropping out, but the motivations often arise from the third or the sixth.

The analysis of dropouts' attitudes leads to the conclusion that, for most people, moral teachings are more consequential than doctrinal teachings. When we asked the dropouts to give us their views about Catholic teachings, they usually began to discuss moral concerns. When

87

we asked them about changes they would like to see in the church, they talked about moral teachings. And within this realm the most consequential topic is sexuality, broadly considered. In the early 1980s the crucial issues are moral theology, and the battlegrounds are birth control, abortion, sexual freedom, divorce, and sex roles.

The middle of Table 5.1 outlines the persons facilitating the decision to stop Mass attendance. Persons were visible in 47% of the cases of young dropouts. The main ones were peer groups, spouses, fiancés or fiancees, friends, neighbors, and non-Catholic religious groups.

The bottom of the table outlines events that facilitated the decision to stop Mass attendance. They were visible in 72% of the cases. By far the most common was leaving home or school; the second, having a conflict with a priest. Many inactive Catholics told us stories of conflicts with priests. But we found the information difficult to interpret, since hearing one side of a conflict gives little reliable information about what really happened. We cannot know who was blameworthy, if anyone. Some conflicts apparently occurred when priests denied requests not allowable under church law. Some opposition arose over changes in the liturgy or in parish practices. An unknown number resulted from personal differences. Interviewees also told us of conflicts with other parishioners, but they were less frequent.

Religious Training and Family Life

Every young dropout had had Catholic religious training as a child. Seventy-five percent had attended Catholic school, in most cases for five or more years. The majority said they had liked the religious training. Ninety-one percent had attended church every week as children. We asked, "When you were growing up, did your parents insist that you go to religious training and attend church?" and 86% answered yes. We then asked those persons, "Would you say they pressured you too strongly?" and 46% replied yes. Fifty percent reported that they had rebelled against their religious training at some point, and the most common ages were 14 to 16. We asked why, and the main reasons given were that they had disagreed with the ideas and practices in church, or they were bored, or they were rebelling against their parents.

Since family rebellion is a factor for many youthful dropouts from church, we asked several questions about family relations. "When you were in high school, how close did you feel to your parents?"; 59% were extremely or quite close, while 41% were somewhat close or not at all close. "When you were in high school, how much of the time did you feel you could discuss your problems with your parents—would you say always, usually, sometimes, or never?" Fifty-five percent said always or usually, and 45% said sometimes or never. Over half had attended college, but only a few said that college had influenced them regarding religion and the church.

Most of the young dropouts were single—67%. Forty-two percent were living apart from their parents.

What Influenced Them to Drop Out?

To help understand why they dropped out, we asked several questions in the telephone interviews. Then we reviewed all the information given when we made the global codes, and we included some clinical and pastoral judgment when doing so. The resulting global codes are, in our view, more reliable depictions of the motivations and facilitators of the dropping out. They were shown in Table 5.1. The raw data are also interesting, and they are depicted in Table A.2 in Appendix A. We can summarize the main patterns.

The most important reason given for dropping out was dissatisfaction with the Catholic Church or its teachings; for 42% this was very important. What were the dissatisfactions? Most common was a dissatisfaction with doctrines or practices, usually with the perceived inadequate Bible study and the lack of relevance of religion for daily life. Some were unhappy with the excessive emphasis on money, and some found the Mass and the sermons boring.

Seventeen percent stated that an important reason for dropping out was that they had found spiritual help or religious truth in other religious groups, 16% said that personal conversion experiences had led them out of the Catholic Church, 14% had experienced a sense of need or void in their feelings about life that had influenced them to drop out, 13% told of conflict or tension with priests or nuns, and 13% were influenced by other people (mostly friends, parents, and siblings).

Some possible influences turned out to be unimportant—impact of personal or family problems; influence of participation in charismatic prayer groups, Marriage Encounter, or cursillo weekends; influence of radio, television, or reading; and experiences of conflict between themselves and other parishioners. None of these had much influence on the decision to drop out.

Twenty percent of the young dropouts are now participating in other religious groups—a large variety of Protestant denominations plus (in the case of one person) Judaism. We cannot accurately depict the forces leading some of the dropouts to other religious groups, mainly because our sample is so deficient in young dropouts who

89

married outside the Catholic faith and switched to other churches. It is a safe estimate that the majority of Catholic dropouts now attending other religious groups do so as a result of intermarriage or of anticipated intermarriage. Others are pulled away by friends, relatives, and sweethearts devoted to other religions. But past research supports the conclusion that sheer force of theological argument seldom can induce a switch of religious allegiances, and interpersonal ties can do it only when the person's ties to his or her religious group are already weak. Many preachers and missionaries in America are actively seeking to attract Catholic young people to other religions. By and large they succeed only when the personal ties of a Catholic young person to family and parish are already weak for other reasons.

Results of Stopping Mass Attendance

How do the young dropouts feel about their decisions? Are they happier? To see, we asked five questions. First, we asked if there had been any change in their family life, and 21% said yes; the majority of them reported more tension with relatives and more tension within the nuclear family. The changes are clearly more negative than positive.

Second, we asked if there had been any change in their personal outlooks or attitudes toward life, and 41% said yes. Most of these spoke of positive changes, especially more optimism and happiness, more autonomy and freedom from restrictions and rules, and more spiritual fulfillment.

Third, we asked if they had made any changes in their personal life practices or personal habits, and 30% said yes—mainly, less time spent in churchgoing and religious activity, and stopping smoking, drinking, or drug use. The latter changes were probably part of commitment to other religious groups.

Fourth, we asked if there had been any change in their selection of friends or the groups of people with whom they socialize. Twenty-five percent said yes.

Fifth, we asked how important religion is in their lives now, and in a separate question we asked how important it had been five years ago. Now religion is very important to 38% of the young dropouts, whereas it had been very important to only 28% five years ago. For the majority, the act of dropping out of Mass attendance was not a matter of turning their backs on religion. They argued that they are as religious as ever, and they insisted that no one really needs the church to be religious; people can relate directly to God on their own. The act of dropping out of Mass attendance was a personal change in their own spiritual lives, more in response to their feelings about the church than their feelings about God.

Attitudes on Religion and Moral Issues

The attitudes of the young dropouts concerning religious and moral questions were comparable to those of the older dropouts, except on two issues. The young dropouts are more individualistic in their religious quest, agree more often that an individual should arrive at his or her own religious beliefs apart from any church, and are more tolerant of premarital sex.[5] These attitudes are common to young American adults in general.

OLDER DROPOUTS

All persons who dropped out at age 23 or older we call older dropouts. In racial and ethnic composition they are similar to the young dropouts. In educational level they are slightly higher than the young dropouts but lower than new converts. The sex ratio is unknown due to biases in our data.

Table 5.1 summarizes the predispositions, facilitating persons, and facilitating events leading the older dropouts to stop Mass attendance. Five predispositions predominate. First, about 25% had serious objections to Catholic moral teachings. The main problems had to do with the church's teachings in the overall areas of sexuality, divorce, and sex roles. Second, about 24% told of feelings of void or spiritual need that were not dealt with effectively in their Catholic situation. Third, about 23% said the church is boring, that they are simply lazy, or that they had had reasons for church participation earlier (such as an active spouse, or children to bring up) but recently these influences were removed (they were divorced, or the children left home), and the motivation was now gone. Fourth, about 19% objected to changes in the Mass or other recent changes in the Catholic Church. Many parishes we studied were in the midst of changes in liturgical music, liturgical architecture, lay participation in the Eucharist, and the like. Some persons disliked the changes intensely and stopped Mass attendance. Fifth, about 15% objected to or feared confession.

In some cases two predispositions were visible. The most common combination was the second in the table (objection to Catholic moral teachings) plus one of the others, generally the sixth (feeling that the church is boring). Also, the sixth and eighth tended to combine with the others.

Table 5.1 also summarizes which persons or relationships facilitated the decisions to stop Mass attendance. Less than half had obvious facilitating persons—although all facilitating persons add up to 54%, since some persons had two. The most common were

91

participation in a fundamentalist, Baptist, Mormon, or Pentecostal church; influence of a spouse, fiancé, or fiancée, and influence of a friend or neighbor.

It is important that one facilitating relationship for dropouts is participation in a charismatic group (mixed-denomination or unspecified-denomination). Participation in a charismatic group is also a facilitator for conversion to the Catholic Church; it is also a facilitator for returning after being inactive. That is, it serves as a catalyst both ways. Several cases of dropouts depict a definite sequence whereby a Catholic drops out of Mass attendance via charismatic group involvement. The sequence has two steps: first an involvement in a mixed-denomination or unspecified-denomination prayer group, then a series of new influences from non-Catholic persons in the groups, followed by a switch to a fundamentalist, Baptist, or Pentecostal church. Non-Catholic teachings about the Bible and New Testament images of the church seem to influence Catholics in these groups.

The number of converts and returnees whose change is facilitated by charismatic prayer groups is larger than the number of dropouts who leave via them. In our estimation, about 5% of the converts and 9% of the returnees had their religious change facilitated by charismatic groups, compared with 2% or 3% of the dropouts who stopped Mass attendance because of charismatic groups.

Events leading to the decision to drop out are summarized in the bottom of the table. Primarily, they were a conflict with a priest, movement to a new parish or community, the life change after one's children had left home, and divorce. The cases under "other" include death of loved ones, breakups with fiancés or fiancées, marital crises, and occupational changes.

Religious Training

Ninety-eight percent of the older dropouts had received religious training as children, and 59% had attended Catholic schools. Sixty-two percent of their mothers and 32% of their fathers had attended church frequently when the dropouts were children; this is lower than for the young dropouts (84% and 58%, respectively). Among the older dropouts the factor of rebellion against their parents is virtually absent. It appears that parents who are strongly church committed may have some of their children drop out of the church during adolescence as a form of rebellion. By contrast, parents with less church commitment do not induce frequent adolescent rebellion, but their children often drift away from church during adulthood.

92

What Influenced Them to Drop Out?

We asked sixteen questions in search of factors influencing these persons to stop Mass attendance. As noted earlier, the raw data given us is less reliable than the global codings, but it is still useful. (See Table A.2 in Appendix A for the figures.) In short, the most important factor cited by the interviewees was a dissatisfaction with the Catholic Church or its teachings, reported by 47%. We asked them what their main dissatisfactions were, and four main themes predominated. First, many were dissatisfied with the changes in the church since Vatican II (20% of all older dropouts). Second, some were dissatisfied with specific doctrines or practices, especially inadequate emphasis on the Bible (14%). Third, some were dissatisfied with the church's stand on birth control (14%). Fourth, 10% disliked the church's stand on divorce and remarriage of divorcees. One could say that dissatisfactions with the church took two forms: "it's moving too fast" and "it's moving too slow." Of the two, the latter is numerically the more common.

Other influences were also reported to have had an effect. Nineteen percent said that a personal or family problem had had a very important influence on their decisions to drop out; 18% had found spiritual help or religious truth in other religious groups; 17% had been strongly influenced by conflicts with priests or nuns; 15% told of a sense of need or void that the church was not able to address; 14% were strongly influenced by the difference between Catholic teachings about sexuality and their own viewpoints.

There was no important influence from participation in charismatic groups, Marriage Encounter, cursillos, or from radio, television, or reading. Conflicts or tensions with other parishioners were also unimportant.

Nineteen percent of the older dropouts are now participating in other religious groups. Most are in Pentecostal, Assemblies of God, Baptist, or nondenominational churches, and a disproportionate number of these live in the West or the Southwest. Only four out of twenty-three are now in mainline Protestant denominations, such as United Methodist, Lutheran, Presbyterian, or Episcopalian.

The two main avenues into other religious groups are intermarriage and evangelization by other groups. On the former, our sample is very weak, and we can say little. On the latter, persons who followed this avenue had their first contacts with the new religious groups mainly through friends or neighbors; some were influenced by their spouses or said they had visited other churches. Evangelization by other groups succeeded only if their ties to Catholic parishes were already weak.

Of the older dropouts, 86% are currently married, and 22% married non-Catholics. However, in most cases the spouses were not

93

important in the decision to stop Mass attendance; only 6% of the married older dropouts said their spouses were very important influences.

Children were a more important factor than spouses. Of the older dropouts, 15% said their children were a factor, and the reasons varied greatly. Some children had left the Catholic Church or were rebelling against it, and this influenced the parents. A small number of the parents disliked the religious education in their parishes or had had unpleasant experiences with regard to parish schools, Confraternity of Christian Doctrine (CCD), or First Communion.

Results of Dropping Out

What life impact did the dropping out have on the older dropouts? We asked five questions. First, we asked if there had been any change in their family life, and 28% said yes. The most frequent changes were increased family unity and better family religious life. Several said the dropping out had increased tensions in the immediate family and had weakened the children's religious education. Apparently, some changes were positive and some were negative, with the majority clearly being positive—partly because of new religious meaning some dropouts found in other religious groups.

Second, we asked if there had been any change in their personal outlook or attitude toward life, and 34% said yes. The main changes were a more positive outlook on life and self (reported by eleven persons), a more negative outlook and feeling of emptiness (reported by nine persons), and more religious fulfillment (reported by four).

Third, we asked if they had made any changes in their personal life practices or personal habits, and 22% said yes. The main change was that some had stopped drinking, smoking, or using drugs. Also, a few were spending more time in prayer or Bible study or were spending less time in churchgoing.

Fourth, we asked if there had been any change in their selection of friends or in the groups of people with whom they socialize. Fourteen percent said yes.

Fifth, we asked how important religion is in their lives now, and in a separate question we asked how important it was five years ago. Now it was seen as very important by 52%, whereas five years ago it was reported as very important by 32%. Thus, for most, the act of dropping out of the Catholic Church was not a rejection of God, but a personal change in religious stance—one that intensified their personal religious commitment. This finding is the same as occurred among the young dropouts, but the pattern is stronger here. For the older dropouts, stopping Mass attendance was more consequential for their lives.

Chapter

6

FIVE TYPES OF DROPOUTS

DROPOUTS ARE diverse, and to understand them best, one needs to classify them and to look at each type. As with the converts, we based our typology on the predispositions for the change. Since our global code of predispositions included eight categories, we looked first to see if certain categories occurred together and if certain groups were closely related. From our coding experience we knew the second and third in the global code (shown in Table 5.1) were similar and, for simplification, could be lumped together. The fifth, sixth, and seventh also could be combined, since persons voicing criticisms of the Catholic Church frequently were those with weak motivation to participate. These two combinations left us a total of five types, which appeared to provide a useful typology with least loss of detail.

The problem of how to handle cases coded as having multiple predispositions was solved by reviewing all the cases, one by one, and making judgments about which predispositions most often seemed causally prior. Thus we ordered the five as shown in Table 6.1 (page 96). Each case was assigned to the first type it fit, beginning with the family-tension dropouts.

A sixth type of dropout, about which we have no information, is included at the bottom of the table. Undoubtedly, many of this type exist in the population, but we succeeded in interviewing only three. It seemed preferable to claim no information, rather than venture some statements based on the three cases plus indirect information. Hence, we deleted the three cases of out-conversion after intermarriage (in addition to the three cases of old-age disability) before constructing the typology.

95

TABLE 6.1

FIVE TYPES OF DROPOUTS

	Percent* of Dropouts 22–	Percent* of Dropouts 23+	Percent* of All Dropouts
1. Family-tension Dropouts. These persons experienced tensions in their parental families, and as soon as possible they rebelled against both the family and the church. Often this took place when they left home or when parents reduced their pressure.	52	2	24
2. Weary Dropouts. These persons found the church boring and uninteresting. Motivation for Mass attendance was lacking. In some cases an earlier motivation for attending had been taken away, for example, loss of a churchgoing fiancé or fiancée, or grown children had left home.	23	39	31
3. Life-style Dropouts. These persons objected to Catholic moral teachings and feared going to confession. Some were divorced; some had life-styles in conflict with the church's moral teachings.	19	25	23
4. Spiritual-need Dropouts. These persons experienced strong feelings of spiritual need or void that were not met by the Catholic Church. In their distress some stayed away; others gravitated to non-Catholic religious groups.	2	11	7
5. Anti-change Dropouts. These persons objected to changes in the Mass and other recent changes in their parishes. They usually preferred the old-style Latin Mass and felt uneasy with liturgical innovations.	0	12	7
Other or inadequate data	5	11	8
Total	101	100	100
6. Out-converts After Intermarriage. These persons married non-Catholics and converted to the churches of their spouses.	unknown	unknown	unknown

*The percentages are based on data weighted to overcome the bias from higher refusals among the young. They are percentages of the cases in our interview data, after the six cases of out-conversion after inter-marriage and dropping out due to old-age disability were removed. Percentages may not add up to 100 due to rounding.

Table 6.1 shows the percentage of each of the five types of dropouts. These percentages are based solely *on our interview data.* The last column on the right lists the estimated size of each type, after weighting the data to correct for the higher number of refusals among young persons. Our data on dropouts is less reliable than our data on converts and returnees, and should be interpreted with this limitation in mind.

Of the five types of dropouts, two are, in effect, defined by age. One type, family-tension dropouts, is composed almost totally of persons aged 22 or younger; these individuals rebelled against parental pressure the first chance they had, usually during or after high school years. The other, the antichange dropouts, is made up entirely of persons aged 23 or older; their ages range from the 30s to the 60s.

Table 6.2 (page 98) outlines some characteristics of the dropouts.

Family-tension Dropouts

Many young persons drop out of church life for reasons other than church life. They drop out because they are in rebellion against family pressure. This phenomenon takes two forms. In one type of situation these young persons have received religious education and have attended Mass during childhood and early adolescence yet for various reasons have never internalized or "owned" their faith. They do not identify with the faith or with the Catholic Church. As they grow older, they feel no motivation to go to church, and as soon as family pressure is off, they drop out. Parents do not strongly object, since they have defined their duty as exposing their child adequately to the faith and tradition, and if the child wants to walk away from it, it is the child's business.

The other form comprises a general rebellion by the youth against their families and all their families stand for. This situation is laden with emotion; when one talks with the youth one hears long histories of bad feelings, most of which are unrelated to churchgoing or religion. The youths may charge the church with faults and weaknesses, but these charges are not explanations for their behavior; they are rationalizations. We heard three criticisms of the church from such persons—that the church is full of hypocrites, that it is unbearably boring, and that the priests are always asking for money. (We agree that in some cases these arguments, when based on specific experiences, may have their own motivational power, but usually, when they are stated in general terms and put forth as principles, they do not.) This second type of family-tension dropout entails a frontal attack on the parents, whereas the first does not. Although both forms of family-tension dropping out were visible in our experience, we were

97

TABLE 6.2

COMPARISON OF FIVE TYPES OF DROPOUTS

	Family-tension Dropouts	Weary Dropouts	Life-style Dropouts	Spiritual-need Dropouts[a]	Anti-change Dropouts[a]
Age when dropped out (median)[b]	18	26	26	34	40
Percent with college degree or higher education	12	12	12	7	14
Percent currently married	29	81	63	64	100
Percent black or Hispanic	12	9	20	36	7
Percent for whom dissatisfaction with the Catholic Church was very important in the decision to drop out	44	43	49	36	71
Percent for whom the influence of another person was very important in the decision to drop out	12	10	5	7	14
Percent for whom a recent sense of need or void in life was very important in the decision to drop out	21	10	15	29	21
Percent for whom a personal problem or a problem in the family was very important in the decision to drop out	6	7	27	29	0
Percent for whom recent conflict or tension with priests or nuns was very important in the decision to drop out	6	12	29	7	21
Percent for whom different views held by the Catholic Church and themselves about sexual values and practices were very important in the decision to drop out	6	12	29	0	0
Percent for whom spouse's influence was very important in the decision to drop out	3	5	5	0	14
Percent now participating in another church or religious group	15	24	12	29	0

[a] Because of a low number of cases, percentages in the last two columns are rough estimates.

[b] The median ages of dropping out are computed using data weighted to overcome biases from the many refusals among young dropouts. All other information in the table is based on unweighted data.

not able to distinguish them clearly in the interview data and hence have lumped together all family-tension dropouts.

Of all dropouts aged 22 or younger, half are family-tension dropouts. This finding is worthy of reflection, since it reminds us to what extent dropping out of church is precipitated by factors outside the church itself. The ratio of males to females is unknown, but probably more males drop out than females. These family-tension dropouts grew up in strongly churched families. When they were children, 94% attended church weekly, and 85% of their mothers attended frequently or regularly. Ninety-seven percent of the youth said their parents insisted they go to religious training and attend church. We asked them if their parents pressured them too strongly; 73% answered yes.

Next we asked, "Was there ever a time during your youth when you wished to be out of your parents' house and on your own, so you could live as you wished?" and 74% replied yes. Did these feelings influence them regarding religion and the church? Forty-eight percent felt this was true.

The family-tension dropouts often criticized the Catholic Church. We asked if they had ever felt dissatisfaction with the Catholic Church or its teachings; 79% answered yes. What dissatisfactions? Primarily, they gave these three responses: (1) Some felt uncertain about the Catholic faith as a whole and did not trust church authority. (2) Some felt the church was too impersonal and too formal. (3) Some said the church put too much emphasis on money.

Seventy-one percent of the family-tension dropouts were single; 29% were married. Of those who were married, only 40% had Catholic spouses. We asked these married dropouts if their spouses influenced their decision to stop Mass attendance; only 10% answered yes.

Bill is a fairly typical example of a family-tension dropout. His account illustrates how church-committed parents can alienate their children from the church if they themselves do not communicate their own faith to the children and accept the children's feelings.

BILL: FINALLY ON HIS OWN

Bill is 22 years old and lives in a midwestern suburb. During his elementary and high school years, he was enrolled in Catholic schools. He attended a university in another part of the state for two years, then dropped out after breaking up with his fiancée and wearying of studies. Now he is back in the metropolitan area where he grew up, working as a store

99

manager and living in an apartment. He is single but thinking of marriage.

Bill looks back on his Catholic schooling with mixed feelings, but they are more positive than negative.

"I enjoyed the fact that my parents sent me to private, parochial schools, because it gave me a little bit better values or quality of morals and a better education. I think I got a lot better education in a private school than I ever would have in a public school. I was sick a lot, and I don't think public school would have allowed me to catch up."

But he thought the nuns in elementary school were a bit tough.

"It was a pretty rigid school system. I was taught by nuns—half by nuns, half by lay people. You can't get much more fundamental Catholic than a nun. I even remember some of the names of some of my teachers from first grade, and they were very firm and very rigid. The first thing we did at St. Paul was, before we went to class, we went to Mass."

"How did you feel about going to Mass?"

"I really didn't think about it. It was something I was supposed to do, so I did it. When I was small, I didn't question as to why. You got up in the morning and you went to Mass, then you went to school, and then on Sundays you got up and you went to Mass."

"Was there a time later when you did think about it?"

"When I got into high school. I didn't like going someplace because somebody was making me go. I never really skipped Mass; I very rarely, if ever, did that. When somebody was making me go, that would start me off going with a negative attitude. So, if Mass started at ten-forty-five, you'd be waiting for eleven-forty-five to roll around. A lot of times I just daydreamed, played mental games. From going to Mass so often, I have every prayer memorized practically through repetition. I probably can't even remember a sermon; I never paid much attention.

"I didn't enjoy Mass since it's too set, it's down pat. I can sleep through a sermon better than most people, I like to think. I'm good at it. I can sit perfectly upright, not remember a word of it, and be completely rested when it comes time for the creed. I've got it so down pat that as soon as the priest says the beginning lines of the creed, I'm up on my feet. Even though I'm not awake, I can still say the first few lines."

"Were there important people who had an effect on you during your schooling?"

"I can't really think of anybody specifically. There were times when somebody would say something to influence me positively and just the same with people who would say something and I'd think negatively of what they said. . . . I suppose negatively it could be my parents, because I could ask them, 'Why go to Mass?' and they would say, 'Because you're supposed to.' That sort of logic didn't work after I was old enough to reason. There were some positive influences—some priests where I went to high school. I suppose I actually did sit down and listen to a sermon occasionally there, because they talked to you as a more specific group. So therefore they could be a little bit more specific in what they were saying."

Bill's parents were active Catholics. His father was a member of the parish council. They did not include religious discussion or devotions in home life but, more or less, relied on school to provide Bill's religious training.

"Could you talk to your parents about your questions about God?"

"No. Mom would usually walk out of the room. Dad would yell at me and tell me to shut up, and that was about the end of it. If I didn't accept their point of view, they really didn't want to hear about it. It isn't right, but I always felt they should have been responsible for keeping communication lines open. That's how I felt. I know it wasn't right. I guess those lines never really got established. I don't know where it should have started or where it could have started, but lines of communication in the sensitive areas, personal emotional areas of my life, were never established."

"Did anyone else influence you one way or the other?"

"Sometimes I could talk with my friends; they would sympathize with my feelings. That never really resolved anything as far as how I felt or how I believed."

"How about an older person?"

"I suppose there were people that I could have talked to, if I'd ever sought after them, but at the time I was unsure of my own emotions, so I wasn't really able to express them. It might have helped to have somebody around to help me express them, but I don't know if it could have helped, because I couldn't."

"Did your religious life and your spiritual life change during these teenage years?"

"I felt I'd received an overdose of the Catholic Church, every day. It wasn't so much God; it was the church. Going to theology five days a week. When I was younger it didn't dawn

101

on me, then it just built up. I was going to Mass every day. I
got into fights because I was a Catholic. It dawned on me—why
was I defending being a Catholic, when I really didn't like
being a Catholic all that much? I was a Catholic; I wasn't going
to deny it, but I was willing to accept other viewpoints. I really
didn't like somebody else's viewpoint being forced on me. I
thought that I was old enough and knowledgeable enough that
I should be allowed to choose which viewpoint I desired. That
was the cause of great conflict, and it still is to this day."

When Bill entered college, he found a new freedom. He
was also exposed to different kinds of people and different
styles of life.

"College was basically a moral decline—drinking, girls, not
living a very exemplary life-style. I saw other people doing it
and thought, 'That looks like fun, I'll do it,' but nobody ever
forced me to do it. . . . There was pressure on me from home
to go to Mass, and I didn't want to go. I really didn't want to
let anybody down, but it was a matter of obeying myself rather
than somebody else.

"I can't remember any one specific week, month, or day
that I suddenly saw things in a different light as far as not
going to church. At first it was a newfound freedom, not
having to get up and go to Mass on Sundays, and then when I
did go, I realized that I wasn't serving myself any purpose and
serving the people around me any purpose. There were times I
had my doubts as to even whether God existed. But they were
minor times and relatively short. . . . The only time I went to a
Mass was when I came home on a weekend or during the
summer."

"In your workaday world do you find any influence spiritually?"

"The people I work with are not too helpful in trying to
lead a Christian life-style. They're not really bad people, but
they just don't lead a very moral life-style. I don't enjoy their
language, and they go out and get drunk and high, and those
are the things I'm trying to get away from. During college it
was not an uncommon thing to go and find a bar and get
drunk along with the rest of everybody there. There wasn't too
much else to do. I had a girlfriend down there. She and I
almost got married. We weren't exactly leading a Christian
relationship. The job I had in the summer was very downgrad-
ing—actually two jobs. I sold cars for a grand total of two
weeks. I really don't see how any real Christian can condone
the way I was taught to sell cars. And then another job I

had—I just said nuts to people-contact jobs, and I got another job driving a forklift for the summer. The people you meet working in a warehouse, aside from the summertime college students like myself, aren't too morally inclined, and they aren't too mentally inclined. It wasn't too beneficial in the atmosphere there."

Bill now attends a nondenominational church affiliated with the Assemblies of God. His present girlfriend took him to this church. She was reared in the Christian Science tradition but had been a religious seeker for some time before joining the church.

"She and I started dating, and there was something different about her. Then she and I got to talking, and she explained that she was a born-again Christian, and why she did certain things, why she didn't do certain things. And I thought I liked her. The first time I went to pick her up after one of her services, I walked into the place and I just about had a heart attack—hand-clapping and hollering and the whole bit, just like the things in the Southern Baptist Church. I stood for a couple minutes and watched. I thought, 'Oh boy!' A couple weeks later she asked me to come along and I said no. She didn't push it. Another time she asked me and I said yeah. I was kind of curious. I had taken a class in high school on charismatic groups and all sorts of born-again Christian groups. I went and watched, and I thought it was kind of nice, and then eventually I got involved. It just kind of happened. There *was* one day a certain specific decision I made got me involved in it. It's not like when I sort of drew away from the Catholic Church—on that there wasn't any specific time or decision or event. But when I became involved in this church, it was a specific day and event. I said, 'If I don't do it now, I'm never gonna do it.' So I did it."

"Does your family know about this, and if so, what do they think?"

"My father has always pretty well respected my decisions in that he's not going to downgrade them. He's always said, 'Why not. You're free and you're twenty-one, and you do what you please. You can come to me and ask what I think, and I'm gonna tell you.' That's one thing that I always have liked about him. Mother wasn't too thrilled. . . . Once after I'd accepted Christ and been that way for a while, she heard [that my girlfriend and I were going to church]. When I came home, I was queried quite severely about it. I explained it. Sometimes I don't know whether my mother believes it. I know she doesn't

103

approve of it. I wish there was some way I could change her train of thought or thinking to at least accept it. I really prefer if she came over to my way of thinking, but then again she really prefers that I come over to her way of thinking. I do wish that she would at least accept it. She tolerates it at the moment, because she can't do anything about it, but I wish she would accept what I'm doing."

Since finding his new religious commitment and his new serious girlfriend, Bill is thinking about his life more earnestly. He is giving up his habits of partying and is thinking through what Christian life-style should be. He spoke critically of his old buddies who went to Mass on Sundays but never practiced their religion the rest of the week. And as he thinks of possible marriage he is deciding what a Christian marriage and a Christian household should be. He still thinks of himself as a Catholic, but as a born-again Catholic who goes a little farther than others in taking the whole Bible seriously and being a Christian every day.

With regard to the church, Bill's history is similar to that of many family-tension dropouts. He did not communicate with his parents about his views of God and the church, and when he left home he stopped going to church. But he felt a bit uneasy about it. And he felt uneasy about his "not very Christian" relationship with his first girlfriend and about his partying friends and dishonest associates. Later, when he met the girl with the serious Christian life-style, he was impressed. In effect, she represented his family's values but without the onerous obligation of Mass attendance. If he marries this girl, they will have to make some decisions about church loyalty; the most likely short-term solution is that they will be active in the Catholic charismatic renewal.

Bill's story is unusual in that he found religious satisfaction in another religious group. As noted earlier, only about 15% of family-tension dropouts are active in any religious group.

We asked the family-tension dropouts if their family life had changed as a result of their ending church affiliation; 27% replied yes. The majority of these persons reported that it had increased tensions both within their own nuclear family and in the extended family. Apparently, feelings in the families were still high.

Such situations of family tension are likely to change, when conditions change. Because the rebellion is not aimed directly against the church, we expect that many family-tension dropouts will return to the church. When adolescent problems subside and these persons enter into stable adult roles, more than half this group will find their way to parishes of their liking, for personal and family reasons. They will then heave a sigh of relief over the improved family relations.

WEARY DROPOUTS

The weary dropouts form the largest single type. They are diverse. Their ages range from the teens to the 60s, but the main concentration is in the 20s; the median age is 26. The percentage men and women is not clear; in our sample 53% were women, but due to many refusals of interviewees our data are imprecise.

What defines this type is that, for some reason, these persons had no motivation for Mass attendance and thus stopped going. The question must be raised, why didn't they stop earlier, if they lacked motivation to go? We asked why they had dropped out at *this* time and received a variety of answers: (1) They had recently become disenchanted with the church or had found it meaningless, in some cases because they had learned more about other religions. (2) Their children were now grown and had moved away from home, and they no longer felt the need to go to church. (3) They were working at a new job or for more hours and no longer had time. (4) They were separated from their spouses or from their fiancés or fiancées, who had encouraged them to attend earlier. (5) They felt no support from their spouses or children and finally decided that the struggle to get them to go, or to go alone was too hard. (6) They had recently experienced an unpleasant conflict with a priest or with others in the parish. In short, something had happened to remove an earlier extrinsic motivation, and no intrinsic motivation remained. Or an unhappy incident or ongoing struggle had overpowered their weak intrinsic motivation.

The word weary applies to many in this group but not all. Another term might be "bored dropouts." Some are "no longer obligated" or "free to do as they please." But the general sense of saying to oneself, "It's not worth it!" applies to all. An inner faith and spiritual life is lacking, hence motivation is weak.

Like the other dropouts, the weary dropouts voiced a number of criticisms of the Catholic Church. They stated that it did not follow the Bible enough, that it was too rigid in its rules and restrictions, that there was too much emphasis on money, and that the rules regarding birth control needed to be changed. The extent to which these criticisms motivated them to drop out is not clear, but we suspect that in most cases they were not the main motivation.

Twenty-four percent of weary dropouts are now participating in other religious groups—mostly Pentecostal churches or nondenominational Protestant groups. We asked what had attracted them to other groups, and they answered doctrine, their experience that other churches met their needs, and the personal enthusiasm in other churches. Primarily, their initial contacts with the other churches were through friends or neighbors. Some of these persons have found nourishment in the new groups, for they report improvement in family life and personal outlook.

An example of a weary dropout is Ken.

KEN: COULDN'T RELATE TO THE PARISH

Ken is 21, single, and lives with his family in a residential suburb in New England. He is the fourth of seven children and has lived in the same house all his life. When he was younger his parents went to church weekly, but about ten years ago his father stopped going.

Ken attended the parish school at St. Matthew's for five years. Then, because his parents were dissatisfied with the way the parish school handled his brother, Ken and his brothers and sisters were transferred to public school.

"Was this changeover to the public school important in your life religiously?"

"Well, all my friends from the neighborhood went to public school, so I just did too. Most of my family was out of St. Matthew's at the time. . . . Well, another thing. We had a very old pastor, and his pride and joy was to build big gorgeous churches. And he built one here, and all of a sudden the parish went from a little chapel and a school to this big million-dollar church. But every week the sermon was 'struggling to meet the mortgage,' 'so much a month for heat.' And I'm not the only one that feels like this. I know it. A lot of my friends felt the same way, and they stopped going. And it was just his way. He was very old-fashioned. He'd think nothing in the middle of a Mass, if somebody was making noise, to stop the whole Mass and chastise you. That's a very uncomfortable feeling, I'm sure."

"Do you think that could have had anything to do with your gradually growing away from the church? Say, if the pastor had been a young man and a real relevant guy, would that have made it different?"

"I don't know, it's hard to say. I think there might have been a good chance that I could still be active right now. As a matter of a fact, when my sister Bev got married—my last sister to get married—the priest grew up with her husband. He's a young guy, twenty-four, twenty-five. A real nice guy, got up there and talked. I never enjoyed a Mass so much in my life. He wasn't like somebody up there, some stranger. He was like someone you knew. It was very nice. I really enjoyed the Mass."

After leaving the parish school, Ken attended CCD (Confraternity of Christian Doctrine) every Monday afternoon for three years. The interviewer asked him about his experiences in CCD. Ken had nothing good to say about the nuns.

"I know nobody likes the nuns. Nobody. So *discipline*-oriented. I went there for CCD, and the playyard, after the new church was built, was the parking lot of the church. And there was the yellow lines for the parking. And right up through eighth grade, when I was there, the center line, the girls were on one side, the boys were on the other side. If you crossed, it was two nights after school. Now in the eighth grade, you're starting to socialize. In the public school, by this time they're having social dances and things like this. And here they are, *boom*! You can't cross the yellow line or it's two nights after school. Nobody likes that. And there were nuns that stood on that line the whole break period. There was this one little nun, she had this clicker thing—it was a piece of wood with an elastic and another piece of wood. And if she saw you crossing, she clicked this thing, and boy, you better respond."

Ken talked about adolescent rebellion and about how he and his friends rebelled against school authorities, police, church authorities, and family restrictions.

"I remember going to CCD classes in the ninth grade. By this time I was old enough, at least I thought I was old enough—you're rebelling against everything in the ninth grade. Your parents say you have to be in by ten, you stay out till midnight just for the fact that they said to be in by ten. And I remember going to CCD class, and the nuns came in—I'll never forget—one night, the expressions on their faces. We were watching a movie that was getting us ready for Confirmation. And the nuns came in and started treating us like two-year-olds. And some of these kids were almost old enough to vote! And they said, 'Look, if you people don't want to take this thing seriously, if you want to act like little babies, you all know where the door is.' And the whole class got up and walked out.

"We used to go around and get in trouble just to be chased. Nothing serious. If we saw a cop coming down the street, we'd pop the street light just to run. It was just a basic teenage phase you go through. You want to be on your own. With the CCD, I just said to myself, 'These people aren't going to tell me what to do anymore.' As far as 'Sit there, sit here, sit there,' I had had it. I went through five years of it in school, three years of it on Monday afternoons. I had had it."

Ken felt ill at ease as a public school student around the parish school. Earlier he had been an altar boy; then his family was proud of him. But when he left the parish school he was phased out of that. When he was in sixth or seventh grade his father stopped Mass attendance because of his dissatisfaction with the parish. Ken stopped going to church after he was confirmed. Later, when he got his driver's license, he went again, since his grandmother needed to be driven to church. He liked to drive and drove every opportunity he got. But three years ago he fell away from church again.

"Have you gotten any feedback from your brothers and sisters or your parents?"

"I wouldn't call it feedback as in 'You must be some kind of weirdo. You don't go to church.' But my mother says to me always when she goes to church, 'I'm going to pray that you'll get back into the church.' 'All right, pray for me. Thanks, I need it.' But it's not a feedback; she says it like, 'I hope you get back.' Because every Sunday she goes to church."

"So you sense that she would like you to if you want to?"

"Yes. But nobody says, 'Go to church or get out of the house.' "

"So there hasn't been any pressure at all. Your brothers and sisters don't have any opinion on this?"

"My sisters all go to church. They just don't say anything. I don't bother them, and they don't say anything to me. I don't turn around and say, 'You're a dope going to church.' It's a respect. Who am I to tell them, and who are they to tell me?"

"Has there ever been any sense in your family that it's more acceptable for the men not to go to church than the women?"

"I never thought of it, but now that I do think back, my mother, I think she pressured the girls a little more. 'Come to church, come to church, come to church.' I never thought of it like that, but now that I sit back, kind of, yes."

The interviewer went on to ask about family relationships and about the influence of Ken's buddies and girlfriends. Ken said family relationships were good, and that he could talk over anything with his father. His buddies were mostly away from the church but not opposed to it in principle. Recently he had

108

gone with a girl for a while, and he told of the time he went with her to a Christmas midnight Mass. He went out of respect to her and to the church, but he was shocked to see people who were drunk at the Mass. Some were sleeping and some were laughing. This disgusted him.

"The girl that you were going with, was she religious?"

"Well, I don't know if it was a religious concern. I work in a disco, and it has a pretty bad reputation. Little kids get drinks in there, and they fight. And she always tells me, she'd joke and say, 'Keep up working there, you're going to go to Hell!' "

"Do you think it's a concern of yours if you go with another girl, that she be a religious person?"

"No. It doesn't make a difference at all."

Ken, too, is a bit embarrassed at being a bartender in a disco. His mother thinks he should find another job, and he agrees. He hopes to get into a sales training program in his father's firm. He is working toward an associate degree in business, and he wants to get a start in sales. Despite his not going to Mass, Ken still thinks of himself as a Catholic.

"Have you become active in any other religious group?"

"No."

"Have you looked for any other religious affiliation?"

"No, because I feel as though, if I want to talk to God, I can just sit back and talk. I don't have to go to church. I can be sitting listening to the radio if I want, when I'm driving sometime, any place. I don't have to go in 'that building' to pray and talk to God, who I *do* believe in. So I've never felt any need to have to look for another religion, or any other outlet."

"Do you still consider yourself Catholic?"

"Yes."

"When you were in Catholic school, what would you say you learned of value that you've incorporated, that's become part of you?"

"I don't go to church on Sunday, but I think I've got pretty strong morals. I know a lot of people that, for them, 'moral' is just a word in a dictionary. I think I've got pretty high morals. That's basically my religious background. For instance, the big issue right now is abortion. I deal with people, guys that have paid for their girls to have abortions, and I know girls that have had them. It's disgusting to me, personally. And I just feel it's killing. And my parents never taught me that. That came from one place: religious training. And they just shun it off—'It beats having a kid running around.' I don't believe that."

But Ken disagrees with the church's teaching about birth control. "The church is totally against birth control, but then they are totally against abortion. That to me is off balance right there. We're a society where sex is fairly out in the open, and it's just that to eliminate one, you have to have the other. And I for one am in favor of birth control. They say, 'It's bad, it's bad, stay away, stay away.' Being a young guy, I'm going to tell you. It just can't be, as far as I'm concerned. One or the other. This is the twentieth century. This isn't 1844, where if you kiss a girl you're going to die."

"Anything else about the church's teaching?"

"Well, this is an old thing. . . . Millions of people are dying here and there. 'Pitch in that extra effort and put that extra quarter in the basket.' And then I look around and I see all these gorgeous churches. My parents just came back from Italy, and my mother told me about all these gorgeous churches. There is one called 'Church of a Hundred Steeples.' And she said it's just gorgeous. And instead of using gold paint on the walls, they used actual gold. And I look around, and I say that if the Catholic Church could be a little more timid, sell some of their assets, they could probably feed the world. That's just my view."

"Do you have any relationships with priests and nuns, generally?"

"Well, there's Father George. He's serving over in Belmont now. And I think if he said Mass in my parish, I'm sure that I'd go. I'm not saying I'd go every Sunday, but I'd give it a shot. Just to see what it was like. You can see him and you wouldn't know he's a priest. When he goes out he doesn't wear his collar all over, and he's the first one at the bachelor party to sit down and have a beer with you, if he's going to do a marriage. Someone started telling dirty jokes at a bachelor party, and then they realized he was there, and he said, 'That's all right. I'll forgive!' And he's a real nice guy, and he's almost like one of the guys, but he's still a priest and everybody respects that, but they still treat him like they did ten years ago."

"Would you ever talk with him about your own religious convictions and feelings?"

"Sure, if anybody. I've never so far yet wished for someone to talk to, but if anybody, he would be the one that I would

110

turn to as a priest. Because I have a couple of friends that I work with, and he knows them, and he says all the time, 'Oh, in that environment, the girls, the booze. If you ever want to talk, I'll straighten you out.' He tells it joking, but I'm sure there's meaning in it. I could pick up the phone right now and say, 'Can I talk to you?' And he'd make time."

Ken went on to tell about his friends, about the bachelor parties and weddings they had had, about his perplexity with the draft and with war, and about his future. He mentioned that he had attended church on impulse about six months ago. He went with his mother and came back feeling good.

"A church is supposed to supply a sense of community, a family experience. Do you think that when you leave the family, you might seek out a very small, personal church community?"

"I don't know that. It's funny that you should ask that, because the guy that my sister Bev married was an inactive member, and now he goes to church every Sunday. They moved out of the city, and they're in a nice little neighborhood, down by the water, and the church is like an old barn. And he goes to church every single Sunday, and I don't know, maybe that'll happen. He also comes from a close-knit family. One for all and all for one. And here is he. He didn't go to church for four years. Every Sunday now he doesn't miss it."

Ken's objections are not against the Catholic faith, but against the people in his parish. At present he cannot relate to any of the priests, nuns, or staff, and he finds the Mass meaningless. But if a new facilitating person would appear on the scene—such as Father George from Belmont—or if he would move to a different parish—such as the one where Bev's husband goes—he may find himself in active church life again.

Ken's story also exemplifies the tension in some subcultures between young adult masculine behavior ideals and church attendance. In his family none of the men attends church, but all the women do. The last two times Ken attended was when his mother and his girlfriend asked him. Ken himself is somewhat ambivalent about the carousing life-style of his buddies, as shown by his indignation at the drunks sitting in the Christmas midnight Mass and his embarrassment about being a disco bartender. He is apparently ambivalent about the church, too, for similar reasons. His male friends tend to pull him away from the church, but he has second thoughts about them, and other persons pull him toward the church.

Life-style dropouts discontinued Mass attendance for reasons related to moral problems, usually in the realm of sex and marriage. Their present attitudes and life-styles were in conflict with the church at this point, and when faced with the choice of changing life-styles or dropping out of the church, they left the church. In the interviews they criticized Catholic teachings about sex and marriage, and they objected to the obligation of confession. Most life-style dropouts were in their teens, 20s, or early 30s; the median age was 26.

Sixty-three percent of life-style dropouts were currently married when interviewed. Thirty-two percent were single. Of those married, 36% were in second or third marriages, and 32% were married to non-Catholic spouses.

The religious training and upbringing of these persons corresponded to that of other Catholics. When we asked if they were ever displeased with the church or its teachings, they expressed a similar level of dissatisfaction as we found among other dropouts, but their specific complaints were unique. Primarily, their unhappiness was caused by the rules governing birth control, the church's stand on divorce and remarriage, and the changes since Vatican II.

Not many life-style dropouts are now involved in other churches—only 12% in our sample; these churches are mainline Protestant, not Pentecostal or fundamentalist. The dropouts were invited by friends to attend church, or they joined after "shopping" various places. Yet, we should not conclude they are happily involved in these other churches, for when we asked them the results of their decision to drop out, many expressed personal emptiness. Also, they stated that religion is not very important in their lives—their estimate was the lowest of the five types of dropouts.

Although their religious attitudes are similar to those of other dropouts, on issues like abortion, birth control, and remarriage in the church after divorce they advocate more liberalization than the other types of dropouts. For example, 88% feel divorced Catholics should be permitted to remarry in the church, and 95% believe Catholics should be allowed to use artificial methods of birth control.

Of all the dropouts this type reported the most conflict with priests. Indications are that the conflicts had more to do with church authority and law than with personal differences. Life-style dropouts were sometimes angry at the church and at the priests when the priests refused their requests—sacramental remarriage after divorce, approval for artificial birth control, approval for premarital cohabitation, and so on.

Wanda clearly represents the life-style dropout.

Wanda, 29, is single and lives in a large mid-Atlantic city, where she is a municipal official. She grew up in this city and followed her older sister all the way through Catholic schools. Then she attended a Catholic women's college. She liked the experience, and it seemed to her as though the Catholic schools were almost like families. She felt close to the nuns and admired them. After college she returned to her neighborhood and started working.

"So I was back in my own parish. I went there fairly regularly until a lot of the people changed in the parish. They changed the pastor, they changed most of the priests in the parish, and it wasn't really home anymore, and I didn't really relate to the people that came in. They were like a whole different kind of people. I think that's when I started losing interest.

"We had one excellent priest who was from Ireland, and he had a very good background in terms of public speaking. He was excellent and his education was very good. He was one of the ones who I really enjoyed listening to. He was the last one that I could really relate to. The others—their public speaking was very poor. I don't think they're really in touch with today's world. The church is their world, and they don't really have much of a view of the outside and what it's like on the outside. I can't relate to them at all. I don't think they can understand me at all. They're not somebody you would really approach to speak to."

"Would you say there were any sudden or abrupt changes in your religious life?"

"No. I would say it was more like drifting away from the church. Like I said, when I came back from college and came back to my own home parish and found that I didn't really feel comfortable there anymore, I physically moved away from home—out of that parish to this location. I did go to another church on one occasion, but I didn't feel comfortable there either. I've never gone on a regular basis to another parish. I would say there were other things in my personal life that affected my being active in the church."

Wanda's mother thinks she should be going to church. Her mother has always been a steady churchgoer. Her father, however, has been off and on with the church. Several years ago he went through a struggle with alcoholism and fell away. But now he is coping and has returned to church. Wanda's sister stopped churchgoing after she married.

Wanda expressed displeasure with her own feelings about life.

"My spiritual life—I wish there was something more there. But I don't know how or where I'm going to find what I'm looking for. There should be more to my spiritual life and there isn't. In terms of my personal life, not being married, I feel there's an emptiness there. I think my *work* has a great deal of meaning for me. It was something that I really wanted to do and at one point I never really thought that I would be working in this particular field. It was just through determination and persistence that I was able to get this job. I've been satisfied with it."

"Any personal friends that you are close to—any of them involved or uninvolved in church life?"

"Well, I think we're all about in the same boat, really. I don't see any who are active. Most of us are fairly inactive religiously."

"Just to check this, there was nobody that was particularly influential in your decision to become inactive in the church?"

"Well, there was one area of my personal life that I think affected it, looking back on it. It wasn't really a conscious decision. I had a personal involvement with someone that was married. I would say that affected my attendance at church, and the Sacraments. So I would probably agree, that that was probably a guilt feeling . . . (pause)."

"I would think that that would probably have an influence on your decision to become inactive—not feeling that it was OK for you to be there."

"I think that was probably true. I didn't really think of it that way at the time. I know that there were periods when I *would* go back to church occasionally. That was when I wasn't actually involved with this person. It's been an on and off thing for a long time. . . . Like I said, it wasn't really conscious, but there was always this idea that what you're doing wasn't right. So I would say that had a good deal of influence."

"Was that a recent awareness? How recent?"

"I would say I started thinking about it when this interview . . . (pause) I don't really want to get too deeply into it. But I still don't know what to do. . . . I still don't know how to deal with it."

The interviewer and Wanda talked a bit with the tape recorder off, then Wanda made a general statement for the tape.

114

"Like I say, I don't think it was a conscious decision, that I really thought about, that I was gonna leave the church because of this relationship. But I found that I didn't feel comfortable in church when this relationship was active. There were times when it was inactive, and it was broken off *because* of guilt. But it always re-started. And . . . sometimes I would attend church when I was not actively involved in the relationship. But there was always the guilt. I would not receive Sacraments usually, while the relationship was active. And I didn't feel that I could break the relationship, and I didn't really feel comfortable in the church. I felt it was not something that the church would approve of. It was something that was wrong in terms of the church. But—the relationship was too deep to break off."

"And you felt that you didn't have a place to fit into the church as long as this relationship was continuing?"

"No. For the most part, no. And then there were other factors involved—that I didn't really feel comfortable in my own parish. That was another thing. Probably if I had felt more comfortable there, I would have continued to go to church. Probably not receiving Sacraments."

"Did you feel a loss when you felt no longer able to participate actively? Was that a loss to you?"

"No, not really consciously. I don't really see anything that would go on in the church right now that would make that much difference in my life. I would *like* to go and participate, because I think you should offer some kind of worship. I don't see any place that I would really feel comfortable going to at this time."

Wanda went on to say that in years past her religion had not been a source of strength or comfort to her, but was something she knew she should have faith in. She believes in most of the traditional teachings of the Catholic church and has no interest in any other church, but she is troubled by the idea of penance.

"I always had a problem with penance in terms of going in and actually telling somebody else all your faults and what your sins were. It was all right when you were a child and you only had these petty little things. Even when I was a child I felt things that I wouldn't consider really a sin now, but just a mistake or a fault; but the idea of sin was *engraved* in my religious education. You used to bring things into the confessional that today I wouldn't even mention. They were so—so minor. You know, like you dislike someone. There's nothing wrong with that, as long as you don't hurt them. So I think *I* matured a lot in those terms. But you still have a kind of repressive idea of sin, and what you can do with your life and can't do with your life in terms of the Catholic Church—what's acceptable to them and what's not acceptable. . . . Now I feel like, as far as the church is concerned, I'm an outsider. I'm on the outside."

"So you feel the church has kind of shut *you* out in a sense, too. Even if you *wanted* to be more involved in the church at this point, you wonder whether you fit in?"

"Right. . . . I didn't really consciously think about this— where my religious life is today. It's not something I think about. It's just something that happened, and something that's there. You know, it's like when it rains—it happens."

"And so if you don't dissolve this relationship, you feel there's no room for you in the church. That's what you mean?"

"Right. Uh-huh. Like, I have to live a certain way in order to be in the church. I can't really live that way. . . . The church is—and I realize that—many people, many things, and these policies have been in effect for hundreds of years."

Wanda's story is poignant and a bit sad. She feels guilty because of the affair, and she cannot break it off. Hence she feels she cannot go to church and cannot discuss her spiritual needs with a priest. Nor can she relate openly to her family. She feels powerless to overcome her problems.

She would be helped by a trusting relationship with a spiritual adviser or counselor. Even our interviewer for this study helped her gain insight during a single interview. If somehow she could be reconciled with the church, it would be an occasion of great joy.

SPIRITUAL-NEED DROPOUTS

The spiritual-need dropouts comprise a small group of persons—only 7% of the dropouts we interviewed—so our information is limited. All age-groups are represented, but the median age is 34. Thus, they are somewhat older than the life-style dropouts, although they are similar to this type. And they left for different reasons.

It is interesting to note that 79% of the spiritual-need dropouts are females and 36% are blacks or Hispanics. All of them told of personal problems or recent experiences that deeply troubled them. Five persons had just gone through divorces which left them with a strong sense of need, but they did not feel they could go to a Catholic parish

116

for help. Some were depressed. One dropout said, "I couldn't understand why God would let this happen. I felt that God had let me down, so to speak." One woman had just lost a baby after moving to a new town. She did not like the parish in the new town and did not want to go there in her time of personal need. Others were in situations of marital crisis, menopause, or long-term recurring emotional problems. Two persons recently had confrontations with priests and felt they could not go back to their parishes.

In short, the spiritual-need dropouts left in a time of spiritual need or personal crisis when they felt they could not go to the church for help. Their needs persisted after they dropped out. We might expect that many have found their way to other churches. Indeed, 29% are now associated with Baptist, Pentecostal, or Mormon churches. Others are ripe for out-conversion, since their predispositions for change are strong, and when facilitating persons appear, they will join other groups.

A high percentage of the spiritual-need dropouts in our sample were women. Also 29% were divorced and 7% were single. As shown in chapter 3, currently unmarried women tend to be religious seekers more often than other adults. The seeker converts included a large number of such persons; the spiritual-need dropouts do also.

The case of Ron exemplifies the person with a deep spiritual need who found no nourishment in the Catholic Church and looked elsewhere. But Ron is atypical of this kind of dropout in that he is quite young and is still working out early adult identity questions.

RON: SPIRITUAL SEEKER

Ron is 23, single, and lives in a suburb in an eastern state. He is the oldest of five children in an Italian family; his grandparents on both sides were immigrants. During his childhood he attended church and CCD regularly. His family life was good, and all the family members continue to have good relations with one another. One of his brothers is a seminary student.

Recently Ron earned a degree at a state college and returned to his hometown, where he now lives in a house with two other men. When the interviewer asked about religious life in the family, Ron spoke of a special grandmother.

"I have a grandmother who is a very, very devout Catholic. She just is so Catholic I can't get over it! But I believe she really loves the Lord also. And I believe that my coming to know Jesus in a personal way is because of her prayers. Somehow I feel very close to her."

117

"How would you describe her?"

"Very faithful. Faithful to what she knows. All she knows is the Catholic religion. I don't know how to describe her relationship with Jesus. It's hard! She only knows Jesus in the church. And that's all she's ever been taught, and that's all she knows. But yet she's so faithful to those things, and you can tell by her spirit that she touches God regularly, on a regular basis. And when you touch God you come off with a sweet, sweet, sweet spirit."

Ron's spiritual journey took an important turn in high school, when he rebelled against the family yet outwardly conformed.

"When I was in high school, I was living under a self-deception. I was very sly, in other words; on one side I was being obedient to my parents, but at the same time I was very heavily involved in drugs, and I separated the two. I said, 'Well, I can do this when I'm with the family, and I won't tell them about this half, and then I'll do this half and won't tell the people I'm with here about my family life.' And it was very disastrous! At the time there was no outward sign that said, 'Hey, this guy's schizophrenic,' or 'This guy's just gonna fall apart,' or 'He's crazy,' or anything like that. It was just natural. It's just that because of my personality, I can't really live that way. I'm not a very stable person. I need—encouragement, I need strength, and I need other people around me. What I was doing, I was surrounding myself in two worlds. My parents picked it up, and they tried to say 'Hey, don't be with those friends, because this is what's happening.' But I don't think they had a full grasp of it.

"My convictions about the church were, you go to church once a Sunday and you're holy. Big deal. I don't see any difference in the people that are going to church once a week and the people that aren't. I was not involved in church, because I didn't see anything there. There was no life. It just wasn't there."

"Was there ever a time you rebelled against the church or against Jesus Christ?"

"Yes. There was a period when I wanted to be my own man. I wanted to be God. I felt I had to be independent, free-spirited. . . . So there was a period, right in middle high school it started to blossom; early college it came out in full force. I was there, and I could do whatever I wanted. Nobody put a hand on me! And so it came out.

"Now, because my parents obeyed the principles of God in

118

raising me in a disciplined way of life, I knew in my spirit that I was doing the wrong thing. You see, that's what guilt is. Guilt is like the light on the dashboard. The light is not broken; that's not the problem. The problem is, something under the hood is wrong, and the light is just showing you that it's wrong. See? When you raise a child up in the ways of God, he gets that in his spirit, so that when he does things that are wrong, the light starts blinking, and alarms start to go off. The rebelliousness was always there, until finally I gave in and said, 'You're right, God, I'll do it your way.' "

The interviewer asked Ron about his college years, and Ron replied that he spent the first two years goofing off and partying. He joined a fraternity and had some wild friends. He started out studying business but found that too boring, so he switched to psychology. He was troubled by the clash between his Catholic training and the "humanistic" psychology espoused by some of the teachers. At the same time he started to reflect on his own life.

"What happened so that you said to yourself, 'Gosh, I'm just wasting my time'?"

"I cried out to God. I believed firmly there was a God— since I was raised a Catholic—there was never any doubt in my mind. There had to be a creator. . . . So I just said, 'God, you're out there. You show yourself to me. You make yourself real to me. I want to know!' So I began checking into different sources. I began reading the Bible, I got into Buddhism fairly heavily, a couple of Eastern religions, meditation, and thought of being a vegetarian, and (laugh) ran the gamut. But God's voice rang the loudest and the clearest. He said, 'This is the way. This is what you need to do. Do it.' And I don't know how or why—I think it's my grandmother's prayer that struck me—but it paid off.

"And God allowed me to go through certain things; I think he ordained my footsteps. You know, there were a thousand times I could have been arrested and put in jail. And a thousand times I could have been in a car accident, driving home drunk. And he protected me through it all. And he said, 'The reason I'm doing this is so that you can come to the place where you see you have nothing. And when you come to that place, you'll cry out to me.' And when I cried out to him, he said, 'Allelujah, this is what I've been waiting for. I spent twenty years preparing you for this particular moment.' "

"Some people sort of come to themselves out a sense of guilt or something. Did you have that?"

119

"I think I went through a period of guilt. Guilt is of God. He said, 'If you do something wrong, I'm gonna put an alarm in you, so you know that it's wrong.' "

"You did have a real turning around, the way it sounds."

"The funny thing is, for people looking at me, it was a real turning around. For me, it was the most commonsense thing to do (laugh). For me, God raised me up and showed me I was walking the wrong direction and said, 'Now turn around and walk back to me.' And it wasn't that drastic."

"Then did you shift to a new group of friends and a new social group?"

"No, I stayed with the same friends. It happened eventually that I evolved to a new group—over a two-year period. But I was in a fraternity, and I was very active in it, so I was pretty close to them. A lot of things changed, like the amount of time I spent partying changed, and I started studying. And so I didn't go out as much or as often."

"You haven't mentioned the academic part of college, the teachers. Were there any important teachers?"

"There were some very, very important teachers. One in specific was the head of my department, philosophy. He was a Christian. He was also probably one of the more admirable people I've ever met. He had that sweet spirit that I've mentioned. He also spoke about six languages. He's done almost everything. He spoke so eloquently that you could just sit and listen to him talking about anything, because he was fun to listen to. I admired him greatly. I went to him frequently to become—anybody who has a handle on a language like that I admire, because they're taking what's in their minds and putting it in presentable form, so others can understand. I admire people who can get it out. I wanted to be able to do that. And he was probably the most constructive force in my mental discipline during college. He taught me how to think clearly. Now there were an array of other teachers, almost all philosophy teachers, who did the same thing for me. Philosophy is a good discipline."

The interviewer returned to Ron's college friends. "Were you with a group of people at this time who were in similar situations?"

"Probably not. As a matter of fact, most of my friends thought I had lost it. They thought I went off the deep end. After I started getting interested in God, God led me to people who were in the same circumstances. And then I began associating with people who had common interests, as opposed to

120

people who didn't. And that's what fellowship is all about."

"Were there religious leaders who were important in this period of your life?"

"Not that I really recall. There was one guy, Father Leonard, kind of after the fact. I said to myself, where should I go? I was raised a Catholic, so I went to the Catholic Church. He kinda helped me. He was very intellectual—extremely intellectual. The spirit of God was vague. I believe that this priest loved the Lord, and he was desirous of serving him, and that was his way. His way was intellectual. He understood God in intellectual terms, so he portrayed that to the people. But I don't believe that was the life they needed. And so I kinda . . . I was looking for life. And when you know life, it's kinda like fresh air. When you're in a place where there's no fresh air, then when you smell it, you know it. It doesn't look any different, but you know it! And so I started hitting different places. And I hit some fresh-air places."

"So at that time you were like a seeker?"

"That is a good way to put it. I was looking for something. I found some friends—Bill and Tim—the people I'm living with now. They had been into this for a little while, and they were willing to take the time to show me what I needed to learn and help me study and teach me things. And so I kinda bonded up with them. I continued going to the Catholic Church, and I continued looking for other fresh air. . . .

"I went through a flurry of fellowships. I didn't know what I was looking for. I was looking for that *life*. That life flow. I hit a couple of places. I was out in California for a while on my own—it was just a thing I wanted to do. I was into a couple of fellowships out there. I never really saw that life anywhere.

"This is where I started going to TAG—the spirit-filled church in _____. The spirit of God *flows* in that place. At the time, I was at a Baptist church. And the preachers at TAG came out with a teaching that was contrary to what I was hearing in this Baptist church. One group is telling me that baptism of the spirit is of the devil, and the other says, 'Hey, this is of God.' And I was torn. I said, 'Lord, if it's you, I want it, and if it's not you, I just want to get away from it!' And God used the same kind of thing—where do you sense the fresh air? Where is the purity? So I went to TAG. The teachers started this whole story about what God's purpose is today in the earth. They helped me come into an understanding that God is doing something! And they brought that home to my spirit, and they said, 'You need to be plugged in with the body of believers.

121

You've got to have other people around you that are solid bricks for Christ.' "

Ron told of his spiritual experience in TAG (a charismatic interdenominational church). He felt the spirit and became dedicated to the church. He met with the leaders in special times of study and counseling. He has continuted in TAG until the present, although he is moving his spiritual life to the New Prophecy Church in his town.

"How did you get into contact with the New Prophecy Church?"

"You could say, I prayed about it, and God answered my prayer. I went around to different churches throughout the area, and I just couldn't find what I was looking for. Finally, at TAG, I asked, 'Do you know anything in the Stonehill area?' and they said to call this guy Ralph Durham. And I called him up, and *boom*, when I went there, I knew it! The fresh air, it was like, Allelujah! And so I found what I was looking for. Now I'm not saying they are pure, or were pure then and not pure now, but you see the willingness in their hearts. They want to go in with God. Now I'm in that church."

"What about your parents during this time? Were they all upset?"

"Extremely. Extremely upset. They didn't like me coming in and talking about these things. They kinda let me do it, because they saw the change in my life. Instead of being rebellious, I was submissive to them. And when they said to do something, I did it. My room was in order. I mean, little things like this that I wasn't doing to please them. I was doing them because God was calling me to be faithful."

"Your family must have been impressed."

"They have since said yes. They are happy. My mother continually jokes, 'Some day you're gonna be back in the Catholic Church.' It's a joke now, but she still says it. But I wasn't worried about it. The Catholic Church to me—Catholic, Baptist, I don't care! I do not even care."

Ron is praying his parents will come to know Jesus and experience what he has. He has talked to them about this many times, pointing out that outward religion is only a means to an end, and sometimes it gets in the way of a personal relationship with God. He thinks they are in a time of rethinking their spiritual lives, and he hopes they, too, will experience the spirit.

"You're a man of quite a spiritual pilgrimage. What's your view of the Catholic Church at this point?"

"I am very cautious, because sometimes I have a tendency

122

to be very zealous. Actually, I believe there are many, many Catholics who love the Lord. Father Lee here in town, he loves Jesus! But I believe the church is so religious, he can't escape it. The reason the Jews did not see Jesus as the Son of God was because they read the scriptures, and they commented on the scriptures and said, 'Jesus is going to be a king, therefore he's going to be powerful, with an army.' They were so religious they didn't recognize him! And I place the Catholic Church today to be exactly as I placed the Jewish Church then. They know God, but they're pharisaical, and they're hypocritical, in that they don't see God. Now, that's why I'm trying to be cautious, because it's not true of every individual. . . . But the biggest problem we have as humans—outside of the fact that we're rebellious towards God—is that we have a tendency to get religious. Religious is doing something over and over and over again because it makes you feel good. You know, you're justifying that guilt complex by—well, you know, I sinned yesterday, so today I'll wake up and read six verses in the Bible, and then I won't feel so bad. That's a wrong attitude!"

"Are there Catholics who have the spirit of the Lord? Are you in contact with any?"

"Yes. There are many. There are some right here in Stonehill that I am very close to. Some at St. Anthony's, as a matter of fact. They have a charismatic prayer group there, and—charismatic is not important, but you need to be hinged on the spirit of God."

"If others come to you and ask you about the Catholic Church, what do you say, in general?"

"If their family is Catholic, but they're not really practicing, you know—they just take on the name of Catholic, then I will send them to Catholic brothers and say, 'Would you take care of this guy? He's a Catholic, he wants to stay a Catholic, but I know you, I know your character, and I know you love the Lord. Would you raise him up in the ways of God?' That's what I would do."

"So the whole denominational thing is sort of secondary."

"Denominations disgust me. If people want to argue about it, I don't even want to talk to them. I can feel for them, because two years ago that was me. Six months ago, that was me. I was ready to cut anybody down. But more important to me now is, we're out to build the kingdom of God, to build the nation of Israel. I'm gonna bring the people together; I'm not going to dissent. That's what it's all about."

"Do you ever expect to be back in the Catholic Church, or

not?"

"Now I found my place in the Body. Right now I believe the will of God is for me to be where I am. He may turn around and say, 'Hey, you've got a Catholic background, I'd like to use you in the Catholic Church.' I'm open, whatever God wants me to do."

Several months after this interview we talked with Ron again, and he told us he was getting married soon to a girl he met when he started going to the New Prophecy Church. She is very active in the church too. Ron has had no more contact with the Catholic Church or even with members of the Catholic charismatic renewal.

Ron felt a strong spiritual need at the time he was answering the call of the Lord during college, and he sought out religious counsel from several priests, ministers, and professors. His spiritual quest was guided by his reaction to these leaders. He did not find Father Leonard helpful, since he was too intellectual. But he did respond to TAG, since "the spirit of God *flows* in that place," and he immediately followed the Reverend Durham; in Ron's words, "*Boom*, when I went there, I knew it!" His period of seekership has ended for a time, since he is about to marry a girl who is committed to the New Prophecy Church, as he is, and this will strengthen his ties there.

Ron exemplifies the Catholic who leaves the church via the charismatic movement. The typical sequence is a shift from traditional Catholic worship to a charismatic group (either Catholic or nondenominational), then a second shift to a Pentecostal church. Ron's path was more complex than this, yet the two shifts are clearly visible.

ANTICHANGE DROPOUTS

The rapid changes in the Catholic Church since the late 1960s have been welcomed by most laypersons but not all. Some people have bitterly opposed them, and some have dropped out of church life because of them. When we designed the Study of Religious Change, we preferred to exclude those persons who dropped out of the church during the late 1960s and 1970s—when change was the fastest—so we limited the study to those who dropped out within the past three years. However, we got some antichange dropouts anyway, partly because many parishes have been making changes in style and program, even up to the present.

As Table 5.1 shows, 3% of the young dropouts and 19% of the

older dropouts have as one of their predispositions for dropping out their dislike of the recent changes in the church. We were told by several priests that antichange dropouts often turn out, on examination, to have dropped out for other reasons, but publicly they give opposition to changes in the church as their reason. This hypothesis was tested during the interviewing, and we concluded that it is only partially true. Some people convinced us that opposition to the changes was their foremost motivation for dropping out. For others, whose commitment to the church was not very strong to start with, when changes in their parishes were introduced, they found these good occasions to pull out.

We inspected all cases in which two predispositions for dropping out were present—one of which was dislike of changes in the church—and we judged that normally the *other* predisposition was more motivational. Thus we categorized all such persons with the other predisposition when making our typology. After these were taken out, 7% were left as antichange dropouts. That is, for about 7%, opposition to change in the church seemed to be the primary predisposition for dropping out.

The antichange dropouts were in their 30s, 40s, and 50s, with a median age of 40, when they stopped Mass attendance. They had histories of less Catholic training than the other dropouts. Only 64% had attended church weekly as children, compared with 88% for all dropouts combined. Also, 21% were converted to Catholicism when they were in their 20s. These findings surprised us, since we tentatively theorized that the antichange dropouts would have histories of intense Catholic training, and that such persons would experience the most distress with the changes in the church during the 1960s and 1970s. The opposite proved to be true: The majority of antichange dropouts were not of this type, but were persons whose church commitment in the past decade was superficial. However, we found examples of both strongly committed and weakly committed persons among the antichange dropouts, as stated earlier.

All the antichange dropouts were married. Of the school age children of these dropouts, none was enrolled in a Catholic school. After dropping out, none of the antichange dropouts became active in another religious group. The most important persons to facilitate and encourage the dropping out were the spouses. In all cases there were indications that their relationships with the priests or nuns had been strained. Had there been better communications with the clergy and parish staff, their feelings about parish changes probably could have been heard and allayed.

When we asked about their dissatisfaction with the Catholic Church, most dropouts in this group talked about changes in the Mass.

125

The Mass was clearly the focal point of their feelings. Typically, they found the new liturgy too social, too modern, and not serene or quiet enough. Many disliked the new musical forms, such as folk music. A second theme was dissatisfaction with the priests or nuns: they were too socially oriented, too buddy-buddy, or, in the case of nuns, they should dress like they used to.

Greta is an example of an antichange dropout who had received intense Catholic religious training as a girl, then married and moved to a different type of community with a different type of parish.

Greta: It Isn't the Same Religion

Greta, 41, is married and has four children, ranging in age from 10 to 21 years. She lives in a new suburb outside a large northeastern seaport. Her grandparents were Lithuanian and Ukrainian immigrants, and she grew up in a Catholic city neighborhood that was mostly Irish. She attended Catholic schools for twelve years and then married someone from a nearby parish. Nine years later they moved to the suburb, where they have been for the past twelve years. She spoke of her religious background.

"I went to _____ School and _____ High School. So, I mean, religion was really drummed into me. And then, it seems like after my husband and I got married, you know, we went to all of the lenten services, we'd go to the stations every week and everything, and as the years went by, things changed."

The parish she lives in has a high concentration of relatively affluent young families, and the parish church is innovative. A modern sanctuary was built eight years ago, and the parish is quite experimental in liturgy and program.

"What do you think are the most important changes that have taken place in the parish since you moved here?"

"Well, aside from the changes in the Catholic Church itself, you know, how everything has changed from Latin into English, and everything, what I do not like in the church is this bit about shaking hands with people, and all the music that goes on during Mass. . . . When we still went, we went on Saturday evening, and it was like going to the theater. It was very dramatic. In different parts of the Mass all the lights would go out, then all the lights would go on, then there was a spotlight on this person or spotlight on that person. And you just didn't get a feeling—a peaceful feeling, you know, something to tide you over for the week. In other words, there was

126

no reason why I should go to church. It didn't make me feel good. It felt like a show to me. . . . That's just the feeling I got. I mean, I was raised that you go to church, and it's quiet, and you pray. But it seems like we did everything *but* pray."

The interviewer inquired further about the changes and asked which ones were the most disturbing.

"It may sound funny, but—I grew up with the thought that the priest was really taking God's place on earth, and that he was above reproach. And it seemed like the priest could do things that nobody else could do. But now we have all of the laity doing the same things that the priests do. To this day my husband and I will not take the Host in our hands and put it in our mouths."

"So it seems to be compromising."

"I guess, also, because when we were younger, I can remember things happening, like when the Host dropped on the floor by accident. Everyone was so upset, and the priest had to walk down the aisle. I mean, when you're raised in this for, let us say, twenty years, you just cannot change and all of a sudden everything is just so nonchalant. What was sacred before isn't sacred anymore. I mean, something has got to stay sacred, otherwise why have the religion? . . . You say you're still a Catholic, and it's the same religion, but it isn't!"

Interestingly, Greta's parents live in the area and go to the same parish. But their reaction to the changes was different. Whereas Greta and her husband stopped going out of disillusionment, her parents still go regularly. "They go every week. But it's just because they are afraid if they don't go to church and they die, they're going straight to Hell. And that's the only reason they're going to church. They will not even discuss the changes. They say, if that's the way it is, that's the way it is! And I can't be like that.

"But my mother and father won't take Communion except if it's from a priest. They will walk around to the other side of the church to take Communion. They only take it from a priest."

"So what's their attitude toward the changes?"

"They just grin and bear it, I guess you'd say."

Greta had moved from a Catholic city neighborhood and Catholic schools to a new pluralistic suburb with a modern parish, and she had done this at precisely the time when the American Catholic Church was undergoing the most change. It was a double dose, and she was aware of the difference between the two levels. The adjustment was made harder by her difficulties in child-rearing, since she found she could not rely on the parish for help in bringing up her children in the same way her parents had done.

"It was the same thing with raising my children. The world now is so different than when my husband and I grew up. And it's really difficult to raise children nowadays. It's impossible! (laugh) No matter what you teach them, there are so many influences out there on them, that—you just don't know, you just don't know. . . . When we first started, we would *never think* of missing Mass. And then it seemed to be, well, the kids going to the different Catholic high schools around were being taught that it wasn't really a sin to miss Mass. There was a time, I'd say maybe about five or ten years ago, a lot of the kids were being told that. And then it seemed like, sort of—well, if you miss Mass it was, well, OK—you sorta didn't feel right about it, but it really wasn't as wrong as it used to be. And I guess that's the attitude I have now, because I feel now that I go if I feel the need or want to, not because I have to. And before, you would never *dream* of missing Mass. It's just like—it seems like in our church here, anything goes. If something doesn't work right, well, then they just change it to fit somebody else."

"It makes you wonder what the true way is."

"That's right! So then you wonder, well, if the other way was wrong, what makes this way right? So you doubt it. . . . And the thing that really did it for my husband—the corker I think—was when my daughter was confirmed. In order to receive confirmation, all the children had to go on this week-end retreat. And when Anne came home, she said the first night—I don't know if they practiced or what they did—but she said, then they all went outside and had snowball battles and everything, and this was midnight till one and two o'clock in the morning! Now, if my daughter were at home, she would not be allowed to go out at that time. And my husband said, here she is in the custody of the priests and the nuns, and that's what they're letting her do. In other words, we always thought of the religion as being, you know, guidelines for us to lead our lives. Whereas they are now more liberal than we are! And it's hard to raise the kids (laugh), I'm telling you!"

Greta's children dropped out of CCD several years earlier. They were not interested, and Greta and her husband were not convinced the children were really learning much religion. Besides, taxiing them to the weekday CCD classes, which met at different times for different ages, got to be too much. Now Greta vaguely wishes that her family would return to church

128

life, but she has such strong feelings about her parish that she cannot go back. When asked if she had thought of going to other parishes, she answered that they had tried doing this, but they didn't like it. She talks a lot about the church with her sisters, and they, too, are shocked by all the changes.

The interviewer asked about the priests Greta knew. Were there any in the parish whom she felt she could talk to? "Well, there was but he left the priesthood. He baptized our youngest one, and we were fairly friendly with him. He was really a friend to everybody, especially the young people in the parish. But then, several years after that, he left. And of course that shocked us too."

This priest left about eight years ago, and since then Greta's ties with the parish have slowly weakened. "We would go, but not like we had to go to church all the time. And all these things were going on, and somehow—it didn't mean as much." Three years ago they stopped entirely.

Greta's decision to drop out of the church is understandable, in view of the pressures she faced in adjusting to the new suburban situation. Her rigid Catholic training left her unprepared for understanding changes in the church. The suburban parish did not have the familial and ethnic ties she had experienced as a girl, and in this respect was a failure for her personal life and family life. Perhaps most crucial was the fact that she did not feel free to talk openly with any of the priests at the parish during the past eight years. Given her vague feelings of need, she would probably respond well to a priest or parish staffperson who understands her background and wins her trust.

Chapter

7

WHO ARE THE RETURNEES?

A RETURNEE is a person who has returned to Mass attendance at least twice a year (apart from Christmas, Easter, weddings, and funerals) after having been away from it for a time. He or she must have returned within the past three years. The length of time he or she had been inactive was not clearly specified, but we did not interview anyone who had been inactive less than a year. Also, we did not interview anyone who had returned so recently that we couldn't be certain that he or she had in fact intentionally returned. In all, we interviewed 198 returnees.

Returnees are found in concentrations. They are not distributed evenly across all parishes. Rather, they are commonly found where two conditions exist. First, they are mostly in suburban parishes with neighborhood populations that range in age from 25 to 40 years, and are persons who are relatively well educated. Second, they are in parishes where the leadership and program relate effectively to them. Since educated persons aged 25 to 40 generally prefer post-Vatican Catholicism, with varied liturgical forms and a participatory leadership style, the parishes with the most returnees are indeed of this character.

By contrast, parishes with virtually no returnees were often older city parishes whose members tended to be old and, in some cases, to have a distinct ethnic identity. Also, small rural parishes in which there was virtually no movement of population—in or out—seldom had more than an occasional returnee. Where populations are constantly in a state of flux, opportunities exist for attracting new converts and reactivating persons who are now inactive. But where no one is moving in or out, patterns of human association tend to harden, precluding much religious movement by anyone.

130

How many returnees are there in the United States? No one knows. Our research does not provide an estimate. However, the number is lower than the number of dropouts, because all returnees are former dropouts. The study by Roozen, noted earlier, concluded that more than half the persons who stop attending Mass begin again, later on.[1]

Returnees are easy to interview. They are usually happy about their return to Mass attendance, so they do not exhibit the conflicts and negative feelings the dropouts do. They are willing to tell how they returned to church life and what their views of the church are. The rate of refusal was about 15% to 25%, and was higher in the Northeast than elsewhere in the United States. The reasons for refusal, when we could elicit them, often had little to do with our specific study. Many persons did not want to take the time, or said they refused all telephone interviews, or they had visitors, or the like.

A refusal rate of 15% to 25% introduces some bias, but we do not know what the bias is, except that more men refused to be interviewed than women, resulting in an unduly high representation of women (71%) in the data.

Some returnees have been inactive for more than one period in their lives. This occurred most commonly with people in their 40s, 50s, or 60s. A number of returnees told how they had been inactive when they lived in one town; became active again when they moved to another town, or had children of school age, or whatever; went inactive again; and then, due to some event, returned to Mass attendance. Some told of changes in work schedule or in health that induced them to drop out of church life or return to it. Roughly half the interviewees over age 40 told of more than one time of inactivity. (Since we could not keep records on the topic, this estimate is based on memory.) In such cases, for interview purposes, we asked the person to think only of the most recent time of inactivity and to answer the questions relative to this period.

CHARACTERISTICS OF THE RETURNEES

The ages of the returnees are shown in Figure 2.2, in chapter 2. Their ages are comparable to the ages of new converts to the Catholic Church; indeed, since the motivations for converting and for returning after inactivity are similar, returnees resemble new converts in several other respects as well.

Twenty-four percent returned at or before age 25, and 53% did so at or before age 30. Thirty-three percent returned between ages 31 and

131

40, and 15% returned after age 40. In sum, most returnees, like converts, are in their 20s or early 30s.

The ages at which these persons became inactive are indicated in Figure 5.1, in chapter 5. Fifty percent became inactive at age 20 or younger, and 74% became inactive at age 25 or younger. The median time they were inactive is 7.9 years. Most were inactive between 2 and 10 years, but a few were inactive for as long as 20 years.

All the returnees were once dropouts. For them, dropping out took place at about the same age and for the same reasons as for the young dropouts discussed in chapter 5. This is as we would expect. Therefore, studying the returnees helps us predict what will happen in the years ahead to some of the current young dropouts.

Eighty-six percent of returnees were whites, 4% were blacks, 10% were Hispanics, and 1% were other. The largest ethnic group was Irish, followed by Italian, German, and French; 18% stated they were of mixed nationality. Seventy-one percent were females and 29% were males. In terms of education, 50% had college degrees or at least some college or technical training. This compares with 67% among the new converts, 52% among the dropouts, and 28% among active Catholics. In brief, the educational level of returnees is similar to that of dropouts but lower than that of converts.

Our categorization of predispositions and of facilitating persons and events is shown in Table 7.1. The categories in this table are the same as those used for the converts, except that another predisposition has been added—"feels guilt for inactivity or for being away from the Sacraments"—as well as an additional facilitating event—divorce.

Three predispositions account for a majority of the returning. In about 55% of the cases, the returnee has children being reared Catholic and feels a concern for their religious training or for family religious unity. This motivation for returning to church life is currently the most common stereotype of the returning Catholic.

The second most important predisposition is that the person feels a void or spiritual need—an emptiness or lack of meaning, or depression; this factor is present in about 41% of the cases. This often occurs in combination with the first.

In the third condition the person feels guilt for inactivity or for being away from the Sacraments; this is true of about 30% of the cases. This feeling of guilt affects only inactive Catholics who have had a strong religious upbringing or whose past family ties have included close church associations. These persons sometimes feel nostalgic or have a sense of guilt that they are not living up to what they remember their lives were like in earlier, better times. In some cases events have occurred that have caused them to feel uncomfortable about being away from the church.

132

TABLE 7.1

PREDISPOSITIONS AND FACILITATORS FOR RETURNEES

	Percent
Predispositions	
Married to a Catholic or about to marry a Catholic; feels concern for the marriage (concern for children is secondary or absent)	8
Has children being reared Catholic and feels concern for their education or religious training, or for family religious unity	55
Dissatisfied with another church; recently withdrew from it, and the dissatisfaction is still significant; desires a new church	1
Feels a void or spiritual need in life; feels emptiness or lack of meaning or emotional depression	41
Feels guilt for inactivity or for being away from the Sacraments	30
Other	1
Total	136
Facilitating Persons or Relationships	
Catholic spouse, fiancé, or fiancée	29
Relative or in-law	17
Children (if children took a conscious role in facilitating)	7
Friend or neighbor	13
Priest	14
Other parish staff	3
Charismatic group	9
Marriage Encounter	4
Television programs or reading	6
Other	2
Total	104
Facilitating Events	
Marriage, remarriage, or upcoming marriage	5
Annulment of former marriage or death of former spouse	1
Death of loved one	9
Marital or family crisis	11
Divorce	3
Serious illness or personal crisis (including serious illness in the family)	17
Birth or baptism of child	12
Child entering Catholic school	6
Child entering CCD or making First Communion	5
Moved to new community or changed parishes in same community	10
Had religious experience	10
Other	5
Total	94

A fourth predisposition, present in about 8% of the cases, is that the person is married to a Catholic and in the context of marriage feels a need to become active again. It may be a response to pressure from the spouse or a response to difficulties in the marriage.

We were able to identify predispositions in 94% of the cases, and we coded one, two, or three for each person. Two combinations came up repeatedly—the second and fourth predispositions (concern for children and a feeling of void) and the second and fifth (concern for children and feeling of guilt for inactivity). These far outnumbered other combinations.

Table 7.1 also lists the facilitating persons or relationships that aided in the decision to return to the church. The most common persons were spouses, relatives or in-laws, priests, and friends or neighbors. Comparing facilitating persons for converts and for returnees, we see that spouses are much less important for returnees than for converts, but otherwise the relative importance of the various persons or relationships is similar.

The facilitating events listed at the bottom of Table 7.1 are quite varied, and no single one predominates. The most common events to trigger a decision to return to the church are serious illness or personal crisis, birth or baptism of a child, marital or family crisis, a move to a new parish or community, and having a religious experience. But all these are present in relatively low numbers.

We have noted that, sociologically, returnees are a lot like converts. This is especially true of those in their 20s or 30s who are concerned about their marriages or their children. The converts, for the most part, were not active in any church in the years prior to their conversion; most of them had dropped out during their teens or early 20s. These converts are little different from the Catholic returnees who also became active in the church at a similar age, for similar reasons. The returnees also had dropped out during their teens or early 20s, but they had dropped out of Catholic church life, not Protestant church life. We should not be surprised if the two groups are similar. And evangelistic efforts directed at them would be similar.

RELIGIOUS AND PERSONAL HISTORY

The returnees had much religious training; 98% said they had received religious training as children, and 66% said they had attended Catholic schools. Ninety-five percent were reared as Catholics. During their lifetimes 12% switched to religions that differed from the religion of their childhood; for 46% of these, the reason was marriage.

Marriage affected the returnees in other ways also. Currently, 77% are married (64% in their first marriages, 13% in second or third marriages), 9% are single, 11% are divorced or separated, and 3% are widowed. For those currently married, the median length of the marriage is nine years.

Surprisingly, of the currently married persons, only 74% are married to Catholics; 19% are married to Protestants or Jews, and 7%, to nonreligious spouses. We asked them what their religion was when they married, and 97% said Catholic. In short, about a fifth of these persons are now in a situation of religious intermarriage, and they recently returned to Catholic church life after a time away from it.

Most of the returnees have children. Forty-four percent have one or more children aged 0 to 6, 47% have children ranging from ages 6 to 18, and 18% have children 18 or older. This is comparable to the number of children the converts have.

Why had the returnees gone inactive some years earlier? This is a complex question, but we asked it straightforwardly. The reasons given may not be insightful or complete, but it is useful to know them. By far the most common reason the returnees gave was that the church was dull, and they were bored with it; 26% said this. Other responses were that they disagreed with some ideas and practices of the church (9%), that they were influenced by their spouses (7%), that they were divorced or had marital problems (7%), that they were married to non-Catholics (6%), that the church did not meet their needs (6%), that they had had unpleasant experiences with the church or with priests (5%), and that they had left the church out of general rebellion and wanted to enjoy freedom from family pressures (5%). Remarkably few said they left due to doubts about God or religion (1%).

These reasons are similar to those found in our sample of dropouts, in that in both groups the persons weary of church attendance or who were bored with it constituted the largest single category. For such persons, intrinsic motivation for church attendance was weak, and when some outside influence—such as family pressure; the wishes of a former spouse, fiancé, or fianceé; or the appeal of a particular church leader—ceased, they dropped out.

We asked all the returnees if, during the time they were inactive, they were active in other churches. Thirteen percent replied yes. Which denominations? They named the whole spectrum of Protestantism, with Baptist, Methodist, and Lutheran churches mentioned most frequently. Of the persons who were active in other churches, slightly less than half were members. We asked if they were active in the other churches until they became active Catholics, or if they became inactive in the other churches sometime earlier. About half said they were active in the other churches until recently. The other half had been inactive for one to five years. Why had they become inactive? The main reasons were that they had moved to different towns, or had had unpleasant experiences with the other churches or the ministers.

THE DECISION TO RETURN

Between two and ten years earlier these young adults—mostly in their 20s or 30s and mostly females—dropped out of church life. Now they returned. Why? We have already stated that the principal motivation was concern for family life and for children, but often alongside it was a personal spiritual need or a feeling of unease about being away from the church.

We asked a series of questions about factors that might have influenced the decision. (The responses given are shown in Table A.2, in Appendix A.) For 44%, the influence of other persons was very important; most influential were spouses, children, friends, relatives, and priests, approximately in this order. For 41%, feelings of need or of void in general were very important. For 37%, children were a very important factor—especially their education. For 27%, personal conversion experiences were central, and for 25%, personal or family problems (mainly family or marital crises, death of loved ones, personal illness, and divorce) had made a crucial difference. Other influences were only occasionally present, including participation in charismatic prayer groups, Marriage Encounter, cursillos, religious programs on radio or television, or religious reading.

The returnees had stronger inner spiritual motivation to return than did the new converts to become Catholics. More told of strong feelings of personal need, of conversion experiences, and of life-shattering crises. Apparently, a strong inner motivation was needed to overcome whatever barrier had kept the person away from the Catholic Church for a number of years.

Some individuals return to church life out of a desire for friends and personal contact. To assess the importance of this motivation, we asked, "Did you have a feeling of wanting more social involvement with other people when you were deciding whether to become an active Catholic?" Twenty-nine percent answered yes. This is apparently a secondary, not a foremost, motivation for returning.

How did the returnees choose the parishes to which they came back? We asked and found they had done little church-shopping. Seventy-six percent responded that they had chosen the closest parishes, their home parishes, or the only available parishes. In addition, 10% replied that friends or family members belonged to the

136

parishes chosen, and 10% said they liked the priests, the parishes, or the schools, or that they had participated in special groups or programs at these parishes.

THE RESULT OF RETURNING

The returnees are happy that they returned. We asked if, as a result of returning, there had been changes in their family life, and 54% responded yes. The main changes were that they had more family unity, better family life, and more contentment. We asked if there had been any changes in their personal outlook or attitude toward life, and 68% answered yes—mainly a more positive outlook, more satisfaction, more optimism, and more happiness. We asked if there had been any changes in their personal life practices or personal habits, and 40% answered yes—mainly that they spend more time going to church and in religious activity. Thirteen percent said they had stopped smoking, drinking, or using drugs, and 13% said they had better personal morality. We asked if they had changed their selection of friends or the groups with whom they socialize, and 24% replied yes.

In sum, the returnees are happier now that they have returned to church life. They affirm the spiritual benefits in their lives, and in many cases they have overcome earlier conflicts or burdens that had been troubling them. Their lives, for the most part, are more integrated and put together. Seventy-three percent attend Mass weekly or more often, and 70% say that religion is very important in their lives.

RELIGIOUS AND MORAL ATTITUDES

We have noted several times that returnees resemble new converts in terms of motivation. But in one respect they do not resemble them closely. Returnees, as a whole, are less committed to the Catholic Church and its teachings; religion is less important in their lives (70%, compared with 85% of the converts, said it is "very important"). They believe more than the converts do that to be a good Christian a person need not attend church. They report less belief than the converts in life after death. On these religious issues the returnees are similar to active Catholics, as found in nationwide polls.

On moral questions returnees are more liberal than new converts and active Catholics. More than the others, they favor remarriage of divorced Catholics in the church, liberalized standards regarding abortion, and liberalization of teachings about birth control (see Table A.3 in Appendix A).

Chapter
8

FOUR TYPES OF RETURNEES

RETURNEES FALL into more or less distinct types, much as the converts do. As our research got underway, we noted the similarities between the converts and returnees, and found the predispositions could be categorized in the same way—with the addition of one predisposition for the returnees, that of feelings of guilt for inactivity or for being away from the Sacraments. Thus the returnees break down into four types, three of which are equivalent to the three types of converts. These four are summarized in Table 8.1.

Marriage life returnees are equivalent to intermarriage converts. The dynamic of becoming active is closely related to marriage, comparable to the dynamic of conversion after intermarriage. About 8% of returnees are of this type.

Family life returnees, almost the same as family life converts, are clearly the largest type, making up about 55% of the total.

The third, *guilt-feeling returnees,* who feel guilty for inactivity or for being away from the church, constitute about 14% of the total.

Seeker returnees return to the church in search of an answer to spiritual need or from a sense of personal void. Eighteen percent of the sample are of this type.

For 5% of the sample we lacked sufficient information to categorize them. They probably resemble the seeker returnee category more than any other.

Some predispositions for returning tend to occur together. In our sample, two combinations represented almost all of them: the combination of family life concerns and feeling a spiritual need, and the combination of family life concerns and feeling guilt for being away

TABLE 8.1

FOUR TYPES OF RETURNEES

	Percent
1. **Marriage Life Returnees**. These persons feel concern for their marriages or are influenced by their spouses and relatives. About one fourth of these persons have spiritual motivations as well.	8
2. **Family Life Returnees**. These persons have children being reared as Catholics. They feel concern for the children's religious upbringing and desire family religious solidarity. About one third of these persons have spiritual motivations as well.	55
3. **Guilt-feeling Returnees**. These persons feel guilt for inactivity in the church or for being away from the Sacraments. Usually, they have had a strong Catholic upbringing. Life experiences created feelings inducing them to return to church life.	14
4. **Seeker Returnees**. These persons come back to the church in search of an answer to spiritual need or from a sense of void or meaninglessness.	18
Inadequate data	5
	100

from the church. These occurred in thirty-eight and twenty-seven cases respectively, and are classified with the family life returnees.

Our interviews included much information depicting the four types of returnees (see Table 8.2, page 140). The following sections review the distinctive characteristics of each type.

Marriage Life Returnees

The marriage life returnees have a median age of 30. Typically, they dropped out during the late teenage years or early 20s, and new influences connected with marriage brought them back. Of the fifteen persons of this type, eleven are currently married to Catholics, and four are engaged to marry Catholics. Three have gone through a divorce. Of the eleven Catholic spouses, three converted to the Catholic Church after marriage.

All the marriage life returnees have been influenced by their spouses, fiancés, or fiancées to return to Mass attendance. Of those married, the average time married before returning to the church was about three years.

139

TABLE 8.2

COMPARISON OF FOUR TYPES OF RETURNEES

	Marriage Life Return-ees	Family Life Return-ees	Guilt-feeling Return-ees	Seeker Return-ees
Age when dropped out (median)	19	21	26	19
Age when returned to Mass attendance (median)	30	30	37	29
Percent female	47	74	82	66
Percent with college degree or graduate degree	13	16	11	14
Percent single	13	0	14	20
Percent separated or divorced	13	9	11	20
If married, how long married before returning (median years)	3	7	14	4
Percent with children 0 to 6 years old	33	61	14	29
Percent with children 6 to 18 years old	13	66	43	20
Percent with children over 18 years old	27	6	50	20
If currently married, percent married to non-Catholic spouses	0	30	25	22
If currently married, percent who were influenced by spouses to return	100	40	20	22
Percent who took part in charismatic prayer groups	13	11	21	31
Percent who took part in Marriage Encounter	20	8	0	3
Percent who took part in cursillo or retreat	0	6	11	6
Percent influenced by radio or television	7	15	14	11
Percent influenced by religious books or periodicals	27	16	18	23
Percent for whom a feeling of void or spiritual need or emptiness was an important predisposition in their decision to return	27	35	14	100
Percent for whom a friend or neighbor was an important facilitator	13	8	21	17
Percent for whom a priest was an important facilitator	7	13	18	20

140

While inactive, six of the fifteen were active in non-Catholic churches, and four of these were active in these churches until they returned to the Catholic Church; they tended to be newly married or engaged to Catholics.

Of the four types of returnees, marriage life returnees seem to have the lowest percentage of inner converts. Their rate of Mass attendance is lowest, and their estimate of the importance of religion in their lives is lowest. Twenty percent had gone through Marriage Encounter recently, and for most, the experience was important. The influence of priests or of religious reading on the marriage life returnees is, by contrast, quite low.

The influence of spouses is not the sole motivation for returning to Mass attendance; 27% told of personal feelings of void or spiritual need that added to their motivation.

Ralph exemplifies the marriage life returnee. He returned to Mass attendance when he married a Catholic who felt strongly about it.

RALPH: WHAT HIS WIFE WANTS

Ralph, 32, is married and has two small children. He lives in an older neighborhood in a midwestern city. He was reared in a large family of loyal Catholic churchgoers and attended Catholic school for eight years. After high school he entered the military service and served in Vietnam.

As Ralph looks back on his upbringing, he thinks it was good. His family attitudes were rather strict but sound. "I can see now that it was just a good basic morality and code of ethics and belief in God." During his teenage years he did what his parents expected of him.

"I never rebelled against going to church, but I don't think my heart was in it. From junior high school until my second year in the army I went to church because everybody you knew was Catholic. You had to attend to fulfill your obligations to the public. But I didn't give any serious thought to what I was doing, probably. I didn't think of that. But I can see it now. That's one thing about religion—when you are young they make it a habit, and as long as you keep up the habit, I guess that's what everybody expects to see."

"Do you think it should be other than habit?"

"The way I look at it now anyhow, . . . I go to church on Sundays first because it's required. But I enjoy communicating with God in just my own way. Maybe I'm thinking what I should be doing during the coming week to help somebody. I

141

go because people expect it, and I also go because I enjoy that time when you can shut out the rest of the world for at least forty-five minutes to an hour and do some of your own thinking."

Soon after returning from Vietnam, Ralph married a Lutheran. "That is when I let the Catholic religion go by the wayside. I was active in the Lutheran Church, and that was because her family could accept this, and my family could accept my changing a lot easier than her family could accept her changing. I went to the Lutheran Church strictly for convenience on her family's part, and I still had the belief in God, but religion didn't mean that much to me."

"Some people with strict religious upbringing hesitate a lot before marrying outside their faith. Was this true for you? What were your feelings about this?"

"No, that wasn't true. The feelings were just that—it goes back to my basic belief, which is a belief in a creator or God. And it really didn't make much difference to me whether it was a Lutheran church or a Catholic church or whatever. You still have the *basic* belief. And it was easy for me to change and hard for her."

"What were your feelings about the Lutheran Church?"

"The Lutheran Church is so close to Catholic that it's hardly worth mentioning the differences. There was probably five years there when we were active as far as going to church, and the last year or so of that marriage maybe once a month we'd go to church. We just got lazy in it. In the back of my mind I always thought I was a Catholic. The thing about Lutheran was, you didn't go until ten-thirty on Sunday, and you didn't get out till twelve. And it was the same every Sunday. You didn't have a choice to go on Saturday night, or two or three times on Sunday. That was probably the biggest reason for becoming inactive."

"Were religious differences between you and your wife a problem in your first marriage? And were you happy being active in the Lutheran Church?"

"There were no problems, as far as religious differences. There's not that much difference, anyhow, between them, on basic things. And it wasn't a happy or unhappy thing. I think being 'passive' would be the correct description. I didn't think about that. I wasn't *un*happy—put it that way."

Ralph's first marriage had problems, and when the problems got bad, Ralph and his wife dropped out of the Lutheran Church completely. Soon they were divorced. After a time

142

Ralph began dating the woman who was to become his second wife. She was a Catholic.

"In between my first marriage and the second marriage I really put off doing something about a religious commitment of some sort. My present wife was good, I mean she had a real good effect on me. I started going to church with her when we were dating. We got married by a judge first."

"Did you have to think about it for a while before you decided you wanted to come back?"

"No, I really welcomed it and going with somebody. I don't know if I could have just walked into the Catholic Church all by myself and just started going again. It was strange to me after several years being away from it. You want somebody that you know to be there too."

"Here is a theoretical question. If you had married a Lutheran or other Protestant in your second marriage, do you think you would be in the Catholic Church now, or in any church?"

"I don't think I'd be in the Catholic Church. I would probably be—it's hard to say! I wasn't a very strong Lutheran when I was Lutheran. . . . I'd probably just go with whatever religion she's in."

Ralph's second wife is a strong Catholic, and she wanted to have the marriage blessed by the church. So they went to the pastor of her parish for aid. He was very helpful.

"Father Belini is the one who pushed through or did whatever he had to do to push through the archdiocese so we could get married in a Catholic church. We were married by a judge in September, and he pushed the paperwork and put a speedy thing on it, and we got married Christmas Eve in a Catholic church, three months later. He was a great help! He didn't give me a bad time at all about leaving the church. He's just a great guy. I think everybody down there would attest to that. He's probably been a terrific influence."

"Does your spouse have any effect on your religious and spiritual life?"

"If I feel really tired on a Sunday morning, she gets after me. To be honest with you, I might miss a Sunday if it wasn't for her, but only because of my belief that religion isn't as important as being in touch with God. I don't believe that you have to go to a fancy house or church to be in touch with God. In that respect she does have an effect on me."

"Do you and your wife agree on this kind of thing?"

"She could not justify missing. She's had some really strict

143

religious upbringing, and if she missed on Sunday she would probably think that she would go to hell, if she'd die during that week. We don't argue about that. That's the way she feels, and it won't break up our marriage."

Ralph is clearly a marriage life returnee, but he is unusual in his spineless approach to churchgoing. He goes along with what his spouse and "the public" expect of him, and if ever they do not appear to be urging him to go, he will taper off. He is personally uninterested in religious study or spiritual life, and therefore he sounds inarticulate about his own Christian commitment; in this respect he is atypical of returnees.

FAMILY LIFE RETURNEES

These persons returned to Mass attendance out of concern for their children's religious upbringing and family religious life. For the most part, they returned during their 20s or 30s (the median age is 30) after dropping out during their teens or early 20s (the median age is 21). Most are women, and all have children or expect children soon. At the time of the interview, 89% were married, and approximately the same percentage were married at the time of returning. The median length of these marriages is seven years. Of the marriages, 85% were first marriages and the rest were second or third marriages. Nine percent of the family life returnees were separated or divorced when interviewed.

Family life returnees are common in American Catholicism and indeed in all Christian churches. Every parish staff person knows many of this type of returnee. Of those in our sample, 99% had received religious training during childhood, and of these, 69% had attended Catholic schools. In the last few years 6% had been active in other churches before returning to the Catholic Church.

Of the spouses (mostly husbands), 70% are now Catholics; 64% were Catholics at the time of the marriage. The rest belong to various other churches or have no religion. Only 40% of the spouses had influenced their mates to return to Mass attendance, and of these, only 56% were considered very important influences in the decision. In short, the majority of spouses did not care. We asked the interviewees how important religion is in their spouses' lives, and 31% answered that it is very important. (This contrasts with 73% of marriage life returnees who replied that religion was very important to their spouses.) The persons interviewed usually stated that religion was more important in their lives than in their spouses' lives.

144

Sixty-four percent reported that other persons had influenced them to return to the church; the most frequently mentioned were children, spouses, priests, and friends. The influence of these persons was considered very important for 77%. Sixty percent said they had recently felt a sense of need or void in their feelings about life, and 40% of family life returnees thought these feelings were very important in the decision to return to church. Sixty-eight percent had thought about becoming active Catholics for some years before they actually did so.

Generally, the children of family life returnees are young; the majority are under age 10. Of the children of school age, 26% attend Catholic schools. We asked the parents of children younger than school age to which schools they would prefer to send their children—public, private, or Catholic—and 65% chose Catholic schools. Then we asked the interviewees if concern for their children's education influenced their decisions to become active Catholics, and 75% responded yes (for 54%, it was very important). Next we asked if their children were factors in other ways in their decisions to become active Catholics, and 73% answered yes—the main concerns were the children's religious training, family religious unity, and the desire to be examples for the children. For 61%, this was very important.

A small number of the family life returnees were influenced by charismatic prayer groups, Marriage Encounter, or cursillos. Likewise, radio, television, and books were secondary influences. In their theological and moral views they are similar to the total group of returnees (see Appendix A, Table A.3).

Sarah, a family life returnee, had a rather protected Catholic upbringing and later felt great confusion in harmonizing this upbringing with her experiences among non-Catholic friends. The adjustment was hard, and it caused her to drop out of the church. Later, after a difficult period in her marriage, she returned to the church to give her sons a sound religious upbringing and to make a new start in her own life.

Sarah: For Herself and Her Children

Sarah, 35, is married and has two children, aged 5 and 7. She lives in a large city in the Midwest, where she grew up. She is the oldest of seven children, and attended Catholic grade school and high school. The whole family attended Mass each Sunday. Her mother was "a really good Catholic" who did not believe in birth control but trusted God to lead her in life; she and Sarah prayed many times about her problems with miscarriages.

145

After high school Sarah started working and met new people. It was "a completely different influence, because you're not protected anymore." She had difficulties dealing with non-Catholics at work.

"That was an experience, because here I am from a big Catholic home, and a big Catholic school, and really no real experience with people that aren't Catholics. And now I got into people that went to the Lutheran Church, that went to this religion, that didn't go to church, that had all kinds of answers or questions for things, and I couldn't come up with all the answers. And it got worse and worse. The church didn't help at the time. Well, I shouldn't say that, because I didn't go to them for help."

"What years are you talking about now?"

"This was like in my early twenties. We're talking about in the sixties. And that was the time when they were studying birth control. Well, to me, birth control was a matter of faith and morals. There can be no birth control. Well, I knew the church was right on this, and I couldn't understand why if that's what we've been taught all along, that they should study something like that. You can't study God's law and change it. That's the way it is. It's like divorce. You can't study it and say, well, it's all right. You know—in this case it's not all right, and maybe if we study it we can find a loophole. To me, there wasn't any loopholes. Everything was black and white. That's the way we'd been taught, and that's what I believed. But it got more and more confusing, and it did because they were studying these things, and I couldn't understand why. My friends were saying, 'Oh, they're going to come around to it; the Catholic Church will come around to it.' And it wasn't any answer for it, because they had the fuel. They had the articles in the papers saying they're studying this. But what are they studying it for, if you can't change it? I said, 'Well, they can't change it.' But then there were priests that I thought were wrong, too. Now I'm not sure.

"When we go to a priest, we need more of an answer than 'Use your own conscience.' My girlfriend and I have discussed it, and she says, 'Well, if you use your conscience, you could come up with that birth control would be all right. I mean, not for any good reason, either, just selfishly.' And many people have told me that this is what a priest has told them. To me, that's wrong, not because I believe in no birth control, but because as far as the church has taught us and as far as what the pope says, the pope would never tell you this. Nothing I've

146

ever heard. Then why can this priest say something different than our pope is saying? And that's the part that I don't understand."

Another problem arose for Sarah when the priests in her home parish decided they would build a $400,000 rectory. Some people objected, saying the existing rectory was a nice house—better than many in the neighborhood—and that the money should be spent on Catholic schools in the city. This presented a conflict for Sarah and her family, since they did not want to refuse to pledge money. "None of the people seemed to want it, and they didn't do anything about it. They felt like, well, we can't say no to the priests. Well, they should have." Sarah finally decided to refuse to contribute, and now she wishes she had opposed the entire project, since it caused many people to fall away from the parish.

In time her non-Catholic friends influenced her attitudes. "It was easier just to join the crowd than it was to fight them. It was a time of confusion to me, too, because I wanted to get married and have seventeen babies. And it just didn't seem to go that way. And I think I kind of got mad at God, too, and disgusted with it. It seemed like the guys I met were all—even if they were Catholic, they believed in birth control, they believed in premarital sex—and it was just like, when we were kids we were taught that if we were good Catholics and did what was right, we got the things we wanted. And I wasn't getting the things I wanted (laugh). And it just like snowballed.

"At home we were very protected. My father was older, and he was—'Oh, you can't go here, you can't go there.' Once we got into our twenties where we were big enough to be out on our own and stuff, we were just kind of thrown out there, because we hadn't had any gradual entry into it."

"So there was a kind of taste of new freedom?"

"Yes, and putting aside what was old and restricting, religion included. And it just got so confusing to me that I just could not go anymore. And this broke my mother's heart at the time."

Sarah was too conflicted over sexual morals to continue taking the Sacraments, and when her mother reprimanded her for not doing so, she stopped going to church altogether. After once shouting it out with her mother, nothing more was said.

When she was 27, Sarah married a divorced man. He was nonreligious. They were married by a judge. In the first few years of marriage they began to have difficulties. Her husband was a bartender and a drinker. Sarah, too, had a drinking problem. She struggled to keep the marriage together. A year after they were married she had a son, which made her happy.

"It bothered me to a certain extent that I wasn't raising him Catholic. Not enough to go do it just for his sake. I knew it had to be for my sake. But I felt the twinges of guilt there, that I'm not doing anything for him. I didn't have him baptized, and my mother worried about that a little bit. She even talked to me about having him baptized, that I didn't have to go back to church, but I could have him baptized. But I just never got around to doing it."

Two years later she had another son. Because he was premature and in danger of dying, she had him baptized at the hospital. She was thankful when he survived.

Two years later the marital problems returned.

"My husband was drinking, he totaled a couple of cars, and I couldn't take it anymore. And I finally decided that I was a nervous wreck, and it wasn't good for the kids. It was a bad situation. I didn't believe in divorce, but I didn't know how to handle it anymore. And I'd tell myself that, well, you've just got to straighten up and accept it and do what's right for the kids, but somehow I couldn't do it. I just didn't have the strength to do it. So finally he totaled a car one night, and he called me up and was very obnoxious. He stayed over at his brother's that night. He wanted cabfare to come home. He said he didn't have any money and said, 'Will you pay the cab when I get there?' I said, 'I don't have any money,' and it was a lie—I had a hundred dollars in my purse, but I just didn't even want him home. I just had had it. I was through with it. And I felt bad about it, but I just couldn't stand the problems anymore. So the next day he didn't come home, and I knew he was right back out to drinking. The insurance man called me that night, and he wanted to know about the accident. And there was nothing I could tell him, since I hadn't been there. I said, 'He was drunk.' He said, 'Sarah, I know that, when accidents happen at one o'clock in the morning. You're not telling me anything.' I said, 'Well, I shouldn't be telling you this, though, you're our insurance man, but I'm just fed up. I don't know what to do. He needs something, and it isn't fair to you that he's totaling these cars all the time.' And he said, 'Well, Sarah, we've got to get that guy some help. He's just got to have some help.'

"Something clicked. I got off the phone and I thought, Here I am, I'm the one who's supposed to love him, I've got his kids, and I'm giving up on him. I don't care anymore. And here's an insurance man that he's ripping off. Here's this insurance man, practically a total stranger to us, and he's worried about him. I thought, Why am I not worried about him? What's wrong with me? And I started to think, and I think that's the first time I knew what 'meditate' meant. I thought about it, I thought about my part in it, I thought about my impatience—the part that I caused. There's never just one person that's to blame. It just went on and on to where it was one of the most amazing times of my life. I couldn't even get anything done. All I did was think. And well, instead of yelling at him, I got off his back. I decided you can't live other people's lives for them. They have to do their own thing. They have to have the right to be wrong. And it must have taken me a week that I went through this, and all of a sudden it was like the whole thing clicked into perspective, that it's the same with everything in life, that the marriage, you have to make it work. And the people—I make mistakes, he makes mistakes, we forgive each other, and we go on, and we build, and it's the same thing with the church. That's exactly the reason I threw the church out, is that they aren't perfect. But they can't be perfect because they're human beings. You've got something that's good to start with, and when you get off on the wrong track, you got to get back on. You don't throw the whole thing out and start with something entirely different.

"It was a neat feeling. And then I knew I had to go back to church. And then it was sort of like, oh, this is an awful big decision to make with all I've been through. It took me another whole week of thinking before I knew I was right.

"Then I talked to my husband about it. He's anti-Catholic, antireligion, anti—not even sure there's a God or a heaven. And so I just sat down and talked to him, and I told him that I would never try to influence him, because I knew what it was like having other people telling you what to do. I said I'd never try to force him into going, but that I wanted to go back, that I thought I was ready for it, and I really wanted to raise the kids that way. And he said, 'Well, it's up to the mother to raise the kids. You do what you want with them. I'll never complain about that. Just don't ever try to make me go to church.' And I said, 'Well, I never will. That's not my right. I'll pray for you, but I'll never harass you about it.' So then I went to my home parish first, and went down to confession and talked to a priest. He told me I'd have to have the marriage thing straightened out before he could ever hear my confession, and he told me I should go to my own parish. So I did. I told Monsignor the circumstances, because my husband was married before, but he was married to a divorced Catholic. The church would never recognize that."

The Monsignor helped Sarah's husband get an annulment; this took a long time, because they needed testimony from her husband's first wife. Finding this person was difficult, but finally the annulment came through.

"It was last year that I could go back to the Sacraments. It was a very happy day, because it was the day that my little boy made First Communion!"

"That's beautiful."

"Yes, it was."

The interviewer went on to ask her about her new parish. Sarah relates well to the priests, and she likes the parish life. The interviewer asked if she was involved in parish organizations.

"There's a lot of things I'd like to do, but it's hard for me with the kids. And I figure I have sort of my own cross with my family, my husband not being Catholic, that I don't want to push it to the point where that's all I'm doing, spending all my time at the church and ignoring my family. I think it would be a lot easier to be involved if your husband was Catholic and you did things together."

She is determined to give her boys a good Catholic upbringing.

Sarah had several motivations pushing her back to the church, mostly the need for religious training for the boys and for her own spiritual strength. She exemplifies the family life returnee who also has spiritual motivations. In Sarah's case no obvious facilitating person was present.

Guilt-feeling Returnees

These returnees, 80% of whom are females, dropped out and came back for distinctive reasons. They dropped out at all ages, including their teens, 20s, 30s, and 40s, and they came back a little later than other returnees. The median age for dropping out was 26; for returning, 37.

In their religious training and childhood they were no different from other returnees. Their Catholic training was no more intense than that of the others. We asked them why they had become inactive some years earlier; the most common responses were that they were dissatisfied with the teachings and practices of the church (19%), that

150

they were bored with the church (15%), that they had experienced marital problems or were divorced (15%), and that their life-styles conflicted with Catholic moral teachings—usually relating to sexuality. The guilt-feeling returnees, in short, left the church later than other dropouts, and they did so for reasons other than the typical youthful reasons. They seemed to find themselves in conflict with the church over questions of morality, and some were burdened with marital problems or divorces.

For the guilt-feeling returnees, the importance of religion in their lives five years ago was much greater than it was for the other returnees; 56% felt it was very important, compared with 25% for the other returnees. After leaving the Catholic Church, only 11% became active in other churches. Most did not turn to other religious groups.

At the time of returning, 71% were married, 14% were single, 11% were divorced or separated, and 4% were widowed. Of those married, 80% were in their first marriages. The median years married was fourteen (much longer than for other types of returnees). Few of the spouses were important influences in the interviewees' decisions to return—only 15%.

Sixty-one percent reported that other persons had influenced them to return to Mass attendance; most important were friends, priests, children, and relatives. We asked them if they had, in recent years, experienced a sense of need or void in their feelings about life, and all said they had. The feelings were mentioned at various points in the interviews. These feelings had apparently been present for some time. When we asked, "Had you thought about becoming an active Catholic for some years before you became active?" 78% replied yes. Apparently, specific events had triggered or strengthened the feelings, inducing the persons to return to the church. Indeed, guilt-feeling returnees had experienced more troubling events recently than the other returnees. More had recently experienced the death of a loved one (21%) or marital crisis (14%), than other returnees. Also, 29% had experienced personal illness or crisis (higher than all but the seeker returnees). These experiences were important in a restructuring of life that included reconciliation with the church and return to Mass attendance.

When we began the analysis we expected the guilt-feeling returnees to have had more intensive Catholic schooling than other returnees, hence greater guilt about being away from the church. But this was not so; the intensity of Catholic schooling was not greater. Possibly, their stronger feelings of guilt stemmed from the distinctive conflict situations in which these persons dropped out of church life, from the greater importance of religion in their lives, and from later, more troubling life experiences.

151

The guilt-feeling returnees include about the same number of inner converts as the average of all returnees. Their religious and moral attitudes are not distinctive.

Cathy is an example of a guilt-feeling returnee. Her life history contains additional elements, including a geographic move from an old-style ethnic parish near New York City to the more open-style middle-class Catholicism in the plains states. Her story also illustrates the ineffectiveness of parish religious education apart from the support and example of parents.

CATHY: GUILT WAS LIFTED

Cathy, 29, is married, has two children, and lives in a suburb in one of the plains states. She grew up in New Jersey, near New York City. Her parents were active in the church, and all the children in the family went to Catholic grade school. Cathy attended public high school but continued in Confraternity of Christian Doctrine (CCD). During high school she rebelled.

"In my early teens—ninth-, tenth-grade type—I just hit a stage that it seemed all boring. It wasn't something necessary to my way of life. It was an effort. I had to make an actual effort to go to church, and I think I played hookey more than I went.

"I was very resentful, but at that point it was because my father had stopped active church attendance. My mother went faithfully, but my father never went. He'd lay in bed on a Sunday morning and say, 'Get out of bed and get to church.' And I resented that. I resented that tremendously, because I felt, 'You have to set an example. You're telling me this is what has to be, and yet you don't do it yourself.' I said, 'Well, the heck with it, I'm not going to church.' And I'd spend many a Sunday in the diner, sipping a cup of coffee and eating an English muffin. And then I'd stop by the church just long enough to pick up a bulletin on the way home so I wouldn't get caught."

"As you look back on it, was there something about the way your parents handled your religious training that caused some of the rebellion?"

"Possibly. My parents didn't handle my religious training, with the exception of forcing us to go to church and to go to CCD. I don't remember my parents ever sitting down and explaining anything about my religion to me, why we went to church, you know, why I had to learn the catechism, why I had

152

to go to Catholic school. Nothing was ever said. It was just something that was expected of the nuns to teach us."

"Were you rebelling against the teaching at the time also?"

"I had questions. I was confused. But I don't think I ever really doubted God and Christ. I only doubted the church, some of the hypocrisy that I felt even then—money, mainly. You know, I could see my mother going back to work to put decent meals on our table, and then turn around and see the pastor of our church living what I felt was an extremely comfortable existence. And that bothered me.

"We got a money talk on an average of every other Sunday. And nothing was more frustrating than to be striving to put bread on the table and see a pastor with a beautiful new church and a gorgeous rectory driving around in a brand-new car every year crying out for more money. My mother was active in the Rosarians and everything, and I used to go with her to clean the rectory and to do the food shopping for the priests. And I'd see the food that they would eat and say, 'How come we never get steak? How come they get that and we don't?' And my mother would just kind of shrug her shoulders; she couldn't answer that. And I guess in my own way of thinking it wasn't fair that they should expect people, families, to support them where they could live so comfortably."

"So when did you actually make your break then?"

"I wasn't able to make a complete break until I was out of the house. There were times when I had no choice but to go to church, simply because it was a family time. Easters, Christmases, special holy days, certain Sundays my father would just up and decide he'd go to church, and when he went to church, everybody had to go with him. But I made the break when I got married, and that was when I was eighteen. We just stopped going to church altogether."

Cathy married Greg, a local boy, who, like Cathy, was from a strong Irish Catholic family. The interviewer asked if Greg had had an effect on her religious life.

"Only in the fact that we were inactive Catholics together. We never really discussed it. I think perhaps Greg felt as I did insofar as the guilt bit. We steered away from any conversation about becoming reactivated Catholics. Our friends ranged everywhere from atheistic to extremely pious. My husband's brother was in the seminary and had been since right out of grade school. We were fairly close to him. His influence about the church was informative and interesting, but he never crammed it—he never tried to force his views on us.

153

"I think the only thing that I can say we felt the same about was our feelings towards the financial hypocrisy in the church. That's the only thing that I think we really openly discussed. Beyond that, we really didn't discuss religion at all. It just became easier to not even talk about it. We avoided it."

"Was there anything that precipitated the stop?"

"No. Just convenience. At that point we had just gotten married, and we did not have the money, and I wasn't prepared to donate money to the church. And in not donating, I neither felt the need to go. To me, the church is your relationship with God. You don't need four walls and an altar to discuss your love directly to him, to communicate directly to God. And I don't believe in confession to the priest. If you're truly sorry for those sins which you've committed, God is the one who forgives you, not the priest."

Cathy told of the early years of the marriage, when she and Greg moved several times, in New Jersey. Except for the time Cathy attended a Brethren church for several months, they did not attend church.

"I guess I felt the need to be inside a building where I could be closer to God. I still did my own praying at home, but there was that void, that need to be closer to my upbringing, the idea that God is in the church. I started attending because the Reverend lived right behind our house, and he kind of connived me into coming (laugh). I did feel that I could reach out and talk to him. I discussed with him to some length my confusion over the Catholic Church. And he said, 'Well, we won't force you to any of our beliefs, nor will we expect your total participation until you are ready to give it.' That, I thought, was really neat."

"How long did you attend?"

"About four months."

"What caused you to stop?"

"I guess I got to a point where I just stopped. I never really felt comfortable with it. Well, it was just the idea that it wasn't a Catholic church. I felt guilty being inside it because of my earlier teaching that the only true church was the Catholic Church, and that you were not supposed to participate in any other ceremony or religious service at all. I was there, I was using their church as a way to get closer to my God, but I wasn't paying any attention at all to them and what they did.

"Also we had some marital problems about then, and I would say that that was the biggest reason why I stopped going. Soon afterward we moved out here. That was four years ago."

154

The interviewer then asked what happened when Cathy moved to the Midwest, especially what brought her back to the church.

"Marriage Encounter, I would have to say, is what did it."

"How did you get into Marriage Encounter?"

"We were forced to make a Marriage Encounter. I say 'forced' a little kiddingly, because Greg's brother out on the West Coast, in San Francisco, is very active in Marriage Encounter, and my husband goes on a lot of business trips for GM, and he'd go out there, and every time he went out there Ron would sit down and say, 'You've gotta make a weekend, you've gotta make a weekend.' And Greg would say, 'Yeah, one of these days, one of these days,' and put it off. And he was out there in January of last year, and his brother turned around and said, 'Look, have you guys decided on making a weekend yet?' and Greg of course said no, that we hadn't really talked about it seriously. And Ron turned around and said, 'Have you got ten bucks?'—they were in a restaurant at the time—and of course Greg said yeah, he had ten, and Ron said, 'You're now signed up for a Marriage Encounter weekend.' Fortunately, they're close enough that Ron could get away with that with Greg. I think the reason that Marriage Encounter was the deciding factor for us was that it was the first thing—or the first person or the first group—that's really made us believe in church—that's given us church in a way that we could handle it, understand it, and appreciate it.

"On the weekend three couples have several talks which they present on God and church and the apostolic community and your relationship with God. On the weekend you go through an 'I' phase, a 'we' phase, and 'we and God' phase, and a 'we, God, and the church' phase. And it was during that period of 'we and God' that religion came into the fore, and I started really, really thinking about active church life from the standpoint of my beliefs were worthy of church participation and worthy of community. I deserved that religious involvement as much as others did. It wasn't something that I owe God, but something that I wanted in my life. It lifted the guilt, I guess. And I felt so strongly about that—and Greg did, too—that we invited the team priest to talk. He was a fantastic priest, a Columban father. We invited him up to sit and talk to us, because we wanted to confess that guilt. We couldn't really accept the talks that the team couples were giving because there was still that guilt, you know—that we hadn't been church participants, and that we hadn't been active Catholics, and that

155

we had so many hang-ups about birth control and confession and things of that nature, and we sat and we talked to Father Wayne, and he was just so open and so honest and so down-to-earth. Gone was the idea of 'the man of the cloth.' He was a human being. I never ever once had thought of the pastor of our parish as being a human being. He was a priest, you know, you kissed his feet, and you walked a little to the side of him, you never kind of touched him or looked him in the eyes. He was something to fear and respect and be in awe of. And here was a priest sitting down next to us on the bed—which was about the only furniture in the room—and we were talking to him as if to another human being, as a friend, as a confidant, someone you could just pour your heart out to and not think twice about the fact that here was a man of the cloth. He didn't have a collar on; he was wearing a shirt and a tie and a pair of jeans or whatever. But it was the idea that we could relate to him as a human being, not a priest. And that was what finally broke us down. I went to confession that night and so did Greg. And the following morning, receiving Communion gave me such an uplift. It had been twelve years since the Host had passed my lips, and I felt all tingly! It was a real renewing experience. The idea that now I was back in it a hundred percent, that the guilt was gone, and I could participate and feel open and honest with God."

Cathy went on to tell of the spiritual joy she felt, and of how she and her husband went to Mass in their parish. The interviewer then asked if her feelings about the church changed in the following months.

"I would say yes. I can accept my religion on a much more human basis. I've lost that fear of God from the standpoint of the Baltimore Catechism. I've been able to take my religion out of the grade school level and bring it up to date, put it on a par with an adult standing. After having been an inactive Catholic for twelve years, I missed the greater part of the changes that happened. The last time I had been to church actively, the Mass was still in Latin, and none of the changes that are in effect now had even begun then. Father Wayne told me one thing I think that was foremost in my ability to start reacclimating my thinking. He said, 'You are the church, and a particular building does not make the church.' I had kept my religious views, my religious thinking, on a grade school level. Now I can accept the church. Maybe I don't agree with everything they do, maybe I don't agree with some of the changes. But I can accept it."

Cathy did not agree with everything she found, but the sources of greatest alienation when she lived in New Jersey—the money problem, the rote catechetical training, the elevated status of the priests—were not present in her suburban parish. She was amazed that some priests accepted the concept of church-shopping.

"The idea that you could shop around for a church, my God, this was heresy! That's impossible. And I guess I finally realized that you can. You know, one priest does not the Catholic Church make, and if you disagree with the attitudes or the personality of one priest, then fine. Go someplace where you feel comfortable with the church and the priest."

The oldest of Cathy's two children is aged 10. The interviewer asked if the children had been influencing factors.

"I guess it bothered me when the first child was old enough that things started coming back at us. Once we had a funeral to go to. I think it was my husband's uncle that died. And when we came back from the funeral we brought home one of those little funeral cards—the Mass cards. And on it was a picture of the Crucifixion. And our son Mike was at that time about six. And he asked me why the man was hanging on the cross. And I explained the Crucifixion to him and the fact that people didn't believe in Jesus and they were afraid of him, and they felt the only way to eliminate him was to kill him. And Mike couldn't understand why they would do that. Why would they hang him if he didn't do anything wrong? And his infantile honesty, that total naiveté—and he went to bed that night and several nights afterward with that little Mass card underneath his pillow. It affected him that much. And I sat back and thought, 'What am I doing to him by not bringing him up in the Catholic religion? He has no idea, he at six years old is an infant in his religious understanding.' I was worried about it.

"He started CCD just this past September. We've tried since then to talk to him, and we went out and got a children's Bible, and we read the stories to him. . . . I was looking through the CCD books, and I was so pleased to see the way they're teaching them now. Back in my time, everything was based around the Baltimore Catechism. It was a question-and-answer memorization process. And fear, too. Fear was a large part of it."

Cathy talked at length about her ideas of how religious education should be handled. Her family has times set aside for Bible story reading. She discusses Catholicism whenever the

157

children bring up something relating to it. And she and Greg belong to a Marriage Encounter sharing group that meets for dialogue and Bible study.

Some changes in the church have surprised her.

"My first experience with a nun out of habit, at close range, was such a shock to me. I think poor Sister Doris must think I'm some sort of a raving lunatic. I had to sign up Mike for CCD after Mass one of the first Sundays when we had come back to church, and I had spoken to her over the phone, but I had no idea what she looked like. And she said, 'Well, after church on Sunday, there will be somebody with registration forms.' Well, I came out of church and walked up to this lady who was sitting in a chair behind a card table. She was really cute. She had on a nice flowered peasant dress, her hair was all curled up, and she had earrings in her ears. I filled out my form, handed it to her, and said, 'Sister Doris told me to bring this to your attention.' She said, 'Are you Cathy N_____?' And I said, 'Yes.' She said, 'I'm Sister Doris.' My mouth must have gaped right down to my belly button. I didn't say anything for a solid five minutes, I'm sure. And she just kept looking at me, like, what's the matter? And I couldn't tell her. And afterwards I came home, and I shared this with Greg, and I said, 'Greg, I've never been so shocked in my life.' The idea that they've finally come out of the habits. And I felt so good about it after I thought about it. I thought, thank God, we need this."

Cathy's experience demonstrates clearly the importance of facilitating persons and relationships. The brother-in-law and the priest at Marriage Encounter broke through a set of defenses that were destructive to Cathy and Greg. And the Vatican II changes were in the right direction for them, helping them to affirm the church as they found it after ten years. Now Cathy and Greg are committed members of their parish and of the Marriage Encounter movement.

Seeker Returnees

Seeker returnees have several characteristics in common with seeker converts: Both types include relatively high numbers of single, divorced, and separated persons; both include persons influenced more than the average by charismatic prayer groups and by individuals who have had conversion experiences; both include many persons telling of the importance of priests in their decisions to change.

The seeker returnees dropped out mostly during their late teens and 20s (median age is 19) and returned in their 20s and early 30s (median age is 29). Their childhood religious training was similar to that of other returnees, as were the reasons they went inactive. Twenty percent were active in other churches during the time they were inactive Catholics.

At the time of interviewing, 54% were married, 20% were single, 20% were separated or divorced, and 6% were widowed. Those who were divorced had been so only one, two, or three years, so the return to Mass attendance was probably part of the readjustments of divorce. Similarly, those widowed had been so only one or two years, suggesting that the return to Mass attendance came at about the same time.

Of those married, 78% are married to Catholics, but the spouses were not very important in their decision to return to Mass attendance; only 5% reported that their spouses' influence was very important. Twenty-nine percent said that the influence of other persons was very important, foremost of which were friends, relatives, and priests.

Most important to the seeker returnees were the impact of personal problems and the impact of feelings of personal need. Sixty-nine percent said they had experienced personal or family problems recently that had influenced their religious viewpoints; most prominent were death of loved ones, personal illness, and divorce. Forty percent of the seeker returnees said that this influence was very important in their decisions to return to the church. Also, 80% said they had recently felt a sense of need or void about life; 43% felt that this played a very important part in their decisions to return. We asked, "Did you have a feeling of wanting more social involvement with other people when you were deciding to become an active Catholic?" and 43% answered yes; this percentage is higher than for the other types of returnees. To sum up, these persons had been hit by life-shattering events and by strong feelings of meaninglessness. They came back to the Catholic Church out of spiritual need.

Thirty-one percent had taken part in charismatic prayer groups, and 11% thought this was very important in their decisions to return to the church. Also, 14% believed that religious reading was very important in their decisions.

The seeker returnees are the type with the most inner converts. Their lives have changed the most as a consequence of their decisions to return to the church. At present they attend Mass more frequently than the other types (89% attend weekly or more often), and they are more active in parish groups and committees. They report a remarkably great increase in the importance of religion in their lives—much greater than the other three types (see Appendix A, Table A.6).

159

The theological and moral attitudes of the seeker returnees are not distinctive. What is distinctive about them is their strong spiritual need, their life-changing conversions, and their strong commitment to the church now. They came to the church quite apart from any marriage- or family-related motivations.

Richard is a clear case of a seeker returnee. He dropped out of churchgoing at age 20 or 21, after an early marriage to a non-Catholic, while he was going through a stressful time. Only after much personal turmoil and growth did he gravitate back to the church.

RICHARD: A NEW LIFE

Richard, 34, is divorced and lives in an industrial town in New England. He is one of fourteen children in a French Catholic family. During his childhood the whole family attended church weekly, and all the children went to Catholic schools. Richard looks back at his Catholic schooling with a good feeling. He has maintained good ties with his brothers and sisters.

As a teenager, Richard rebelled against parental discipline in that he hung out with the boys, boozed it up, and stayed out much later than his parents allowed. But as wild as he and his brothers were, they were still involved in parish life. They would do jobs around the church, and they spent time with some of the teachers in the schools. They felt at home at the church, since it was right there in the neighborhood. But the Mass bored him.

"I always felt like the church wasn't really doing anything for us. You'd go Sunday after Sunday, and you'd hear the same things, but they wouldn't really relate to your everyday life. I felt like the church wasn't doing enough in that area."

After high school Richard began working.

"Then I went into the reserves. After I came out of there, my girl told me that she was expecting, so (laugh) . . ."

"So you got married."

"Yeah. I was twenty."

"How did that relate to your spiritual life, that you were married and working and a father?"

"I think that's probably the decline (laugh). For a while I'd get up for Mass on Sunday and stuff, and it got to be hard after a while. You see, Pam was not Catholic, and she never went. So she's still in bed, and you're going, and you don't know why after a while. Of course, I was going through a lot

160

of inner things then. Like, you're married, and a year later you have a child, and I really don't think I was ready for it. I don't think either one of us was ready for it."

"How old was Pam when you got married?"

"Eighteen. She was about a year and a half younger than I. There's still so many periods of growth that you have to go through that you're not aware of then. You're wondering if you really love her, and you're wondering if you really care. You don't like yourself very much because you're stuck in a job you didn't really much care for but felt you had to do it because you've got a family now to take care of. So you would rebel and take a lot of time out from work, and I almost got canned a few times, but I just wanted to get out! I felt like I was trapped, you know? And I'd take it out on her. You know, I was trying to explain to her—Pam was the kind of person I really couldn't express my feelings to because she's very insecure. So I couldn't really express myself fully with her. It would just get bottled up. And when I would tell her things, they would come out wrong, or she would take them the wrong way, and it was crazy. Crazy! I would end up telling her things like I'm not sure if I love her anymore, simply because of the things I was going through inside. I didn't love myself very much. So I felt like I wasn't really capable of giving any love. That's something you look back on later and say, 'Oh yes, that's why I felt that way,' but when you're going through it, you don't understand it at all. Somehow we got through it.

"I started playing in a band when I was about twenty-five. A rock group. I guess I had to have an outlet, an emotional outlet or a creative outlet, which I didn't have at home. And I guess I kind of went off the deep end. I started seeing a girl that I had met at the club. Just a crazy time. For a few weeks I was seeing her and just ended up telling my wife about it, and the whole thing. And she took me back, and that had a real profound effect on me. I guess from then on my love for her really began growing. A year later we had another child. And then we bought a home. I guess about then her feelings began going. Or maybe it was when I had the affair. Mine were coming up the other way and hers were going down. And then she started seeing another guy. She was working by that time. I guess for a year this thing was going on, and I didn't know anything about it. You knew something was wrong, but I guess I didn't want to. But that's what it was. Finally I found out. It just tore me apart. So there were like five separations that year. I went to live with a guy who was playing in the band, I went out and got a place of my own, I lived upstairs in my parents' home for a while, just to let her get her head straightened out. As it turned out she was still seeing the guy even while I wasn't gone, so she wasn't really trying. I guess she felt this was what she wanted, that we had nothing left. So we went ahead with a divorce. She married the other guy, and then their marriage broke up simply because she was so screwed up. She was in counseling for a while. She went through some heavy emotional stuff."

"What was your wife's attitude about the church and religious matters?"

"I don't think she ever really felt that it was anything. She was an Episcopalian, but like I said, she never really practiced her faith. I guess she felt like she could take it or leave it, like she didn't really think about it one way or the other."

"Your own spiritual life, meanwhile, was all tied up with this terrific turmoil. Did the church help?"

"I guess I didn't really seek that help. I never really did. And I guess the only thing that was going through my mind was that as far as the church was concerned, if you're divorced or separated, well, they kind of look down on it, and supposedly you're not able to receive the Sacraments. I guess that's changed. But I felt like I still could, and I always did receive the Sacraments. If I felt I wanted to go to church and Communion, I did. I guess I felt it was between myself and God, and I was trying to make my peace with him. I was alone in the house I guess a year after she moved out, and then my brother came in. He was being divorced, too, and he moved in with me. It was just good having someone else in the house. It was tough coming home to an empty house. I was really having a tough time coping. I would scream at God, and I would swear at him, What the hell are you doing? My work was going bad, and the harder I tried at work, the more I would screw up, and it just seemed like every part of my life was just totally going down the tubes. I even contemplated suicide. I was going to pull my car into the garage one night and sit in it and just let it run. I was pulling up in the driveway, ready to pull my car in, and I looked in the garage. A couple of weeks earlier my sister had asked me if she could bring a bunch of her furniture in and store it in the garage. And I pulled up to the garage, and all this furniture was there, and I couldn't even bring the car in. At the time I was even mad at God for that! And it was just a whole turnaround from that point on in my life."

162

"What brought it?"

"I don't know! I didn't see it that particular night, but as the days went on I began feeling—and I'm sure God had a lot to do with it—I began feeling there is a purpose. I've never known why I'm here, and I'm the kind of a guy who has always, well, I'll go along and see what happens, and I began feeling that way more and more. It's bad now, but it's got to be better. And I'm sure it's a feeling that he was putting into me. I went to LaSalette shrine a few times and prayed in the chapel. It's in Attleboro. So I began going there once and a while. It was kind of my little getaway, I guess. I was away. And I would always come out of there feeling very peaceful, even with all this turmoil going on. I would just feel peaceful. And I know he was helping; I know he was doing something for me. I don't know why. I didn't know why then. But I think since then it's been kind of an upward . . . up-seeking. I guess back then he was reaching out to me, and I guess right now I'm reaching back."

Richard told how he began to spend more time with his children and got to know the person Pam had married. Richard felt better and found he did not have to hate Pam for leaving him—he could still love her. In fact he was able to open up to her more at that time than earlier. It was a relief.

"Some people find the Lord on their own, and others through groups. Which was it for you?"

"Well . . . I've had helpers. People who have been there along the way when I really needed them, and that's been beautiful for me, looking back on it. One of them is my brother. Another is this guy, Allen, who was in the band that I was in, and he's a guy that I lived with for a while. My brother went through a lot too. He had an accident a few years ago, and he couldn't walk for a while. And he's got three kids, and he wasn't working, and his wife wasn't working. They had no way of collecting, because it was all tied up in insurance. I don't know how he made it, how he got through those days. Just recently he's opened up to me about it. I guess he got involved with a prayer group at church. They prayed over him and laid on hands, and he feels that he was really helped by it. The doctors told him he wouldn't even be able to walk without a limp, and now he's walking real fine. He's got a new job. His family is back together."

Next, the interviewer asked about Richard's return to the church.

"I guess alongside these things you came back to Mass

attendance, right?"

"Yes."

"Was that important or was it like a side thing?"

"For a while there, I didn't think it was important. I felt like, I believe in God, and he knows I do. I talk to him, and I felt like I didn't have to go to Mass just to show that. I guess more and more I began feeling . . . Well, I had been part of a folk group at church, and we sang for some of the Masses."

"How'd you get involved in that?"

"Through my brother. He was the director. I was in it, I guess, when he first started it. And I guess I began feeling—I do sing, I've sung professionally—that this is something I can bring to the Lord. This is something I can bring to the church. I feel more involved if I'm up there singing. I feel like I'm giving something back rather than just sitting there and going through the rituals. I need it. I really feel like I need it right now. It's no longer a thing that I can or cannot do."

"So the folk group brought you back to the church?"

"Pretty much, yes. I guess I never really realized how much I enjoyed singing with them and just how much it meant to me to be there."

Richard also got involved in the community theater group. They were performing *Jesus Christ Superstar* in Richard's parish, and he was asked to play the part of Jesus. "I was just overwhelmed. What a way to start! Everything's downhill from there (laugh)! So we did it! People loved it! We ended up doing it again about a month later."

Slowly, Richard began reaching out to other people. He felt the urge to talk with his pastor, which he hadn't done for years. He attended the charismatic prayer group in the parish for a while. And he went with his folk group friends to a charismatic healing meeting in a nearby city. Soon he had a strong feeling that he was being called to greater ministry. He felt he should go to seminary and become a priest.

"I just felt like this is what the Lord has called me for. I talked with my sister (a nun) about it, I talked to my mom about it, I talked to my girlfriend about it, and she said, 'I'm not surprised.' I guess even during my times when I wasn't really involved in the church, I've always on the inside been a religious person. I think since then what's coming into me is that there are other ways I can minister other than being a priest. I feel that's the way I'm being called right now. I feel like maybe that was a test, you know—am I willing to do this? And I *was* willing to do it. So I don't know. I think God has his answer, and he's moving in my mind."

"What does your girlfriend think about this?"

"Well, we're discussing marriage. It's a matter of when the annulment takes place. She is aware of how I felt back then and what was going on inside of me and what I thought the Lord was calling me for, and she respects that. And it's kind of a let's-wait-and-see type of thing."

Richard has now begun participating in prayer meetings at church on a regular basis. He asked the pastor if he could teach CCD. He feels the urge to spread the good news of God's love, possibly through his gift of music—maybe as a singer or songwriter. Above all, he is open to the movement of the Spirit.

Richard's life exemplifies the joy and expansiveness that we found in many returnees. He is a clear case of a seeker returnee whose route back to the church was one element in a manifold life transformation. Interestingly, questions of moral teachings of the church did not affect him much. He took Communion when he felt he wanted to, and at the end of the interview he mentioned that he is now living with his girlfriend.

Richard was never seriously alienated from the church as Cathy was (earlier in this chapter), so he felt freer to return to the church in several tentative ways. His associations with the folk group, his brother, his sister, and the charismatic prayer group have clearly facilitated his return. Now he is a committed Catholic with a magnetic personality and contagious joy.

Chapter

9

CONCLUDING THOUGHTS ON RELIGIOUS CHANGE

OUR EXPERIENCES in carrying out this research have been absorbing, and have clarified some fuzziness in past theorizing about religious change and evangelization. A topic as complex as religious behavior can be approached from various angles, and we have looked at it from social science theory. Hence the foregoing chapters are filled with talk of predispositions, facilitating persons, roles, and the like. They are devoid of theological analyses and of discussions of prevenient grace, revelation, or the movement of the Holy Spirit. The genuine movements of the Holy Spirit are not labeled as such in this account. In this chapter we state a few conclusions we have reached as a result of our experiences.

FOCUS ON MASS ATTENDANCE

At the outset we decided this study would be of church involvement as measured by Mass attendance, not of inner spiritual life or piety. This decision had numerous consequences for our work that must be kept clearly in mind. People who attend Mass even occasionally are considered active Catholics in this study. We know relatively little about their inner motivations for doing so. Some attend out of intrinsic religious motivations, and others do so for external or nonreligious motivations, such as family pressure or the desire to enhance their reputations. Conversely, a portion of those who do not attend may be

166

just as inwardly religious as those who do, and in certain cases they may have stopped for what they view as highly religious reasons. So our study of Mass dropouts was not of people who left Christianity; on the contrary, almost all still considered themselves Christian, and the majority still considered themselves Catholic. The religious change we studied had more to do with the church than with their inward lives. Forty-seven percent of the dropouts told us that religion is now very important in their lives. The dropouts, for the most part, are still believing Christians, but they are individualistic Christians who argue that Mass attendance is not obligatory for a Christian life.[1]

Religious individualism is high in American society. A 1978 Gallup poll found that 80% of Americans agreed with the statement, "An individual should arrive at his or her own religious beliefs independent of any churches or synagogues." In such a social setting we should not be surprised that many people see church life as a resource, not a requirement, for Christian or upright living.[2] We should not be surprised that theological arguments are less effective in reinvolving inactive Catholics than are real human experiences demonstrating the value of involvement in a Christian faith-community for their lives. The strongest case for the church is made by life experiences.

THE ROLE OF HUMAN RELATIONSHIPS

The present study stresses the importance of human relationships more than most writings on religious change. This is done deliberately. We hope to accord human relationships the place they should rightly have in discussions of evangelization. We do not diminish the impact of the preached gospel or the movement of the Spirit. But human beings are usually their mediators. Christians bear in their persons as well as in their words both the gospel and God's grace.

In stressing human relationships we are not talking about mechanical personal skills such as might be used in salesmanship, but about authentic relationships of one Christian to others. We are talking about an ongoing reaching-out of one person to another in a way that says, "I affirm you, brother, or sister, and let us praise God and seek God's will together." Evangelization is always to a particular group, and usually to a particular group with a particular leader. It is not to religion in general, to the Catholic Church in general, or to a purely personal faith. Church leaders should be constantly aware that they are instruments of grace not only in their offices, but especially in their human personhood.

Several implications of this conclusion may be mentioned. We stated in chapter 1 that evangelization should be visualized as matchmaking—individuals are matched with particular groups. Our research has looked mostly at the individuals, much less at the religious groups. But we can make a few statements about religious groups (usually, parishes) that help them with matchmaking. Personal relationships within the parish are crucial, so that staff and laypeople feel free to be open with one another, and the laity have a sense of ownership of the parish. Then person-to-person relationships with outsiders will more easily be transformed into person-to-parish relationships, and outsiders will desire to join the parish community. Laypersons who feel little personal identity with their parish will not reach out as effectively to friends.

Clergy and especially pastors should take seriously their inevitable role as symbols of the parish. The more they can forge authentic personal relationships with people in the community, through various activities and leadership roles, the more approachable the parish will appear to outsiders. Priests should mix with the people as much as they can, so that they come to know as many as possible personally. Rapid changes in parish staffing hinder this relationship-building process and should be avoided; generally, the most successful parishes in evangelization have had stability in pastors and staff.

It helps in forging bonds between parishioners and parishes if the parishes take on individual identity and distinctive coloration, as an outgrowth of the styles and experiences of the people. Then the people acquire pride in their parish as "the most _____ in this area" or "the parish which does _____." If various parishes in a city or suburban area take on distinctive identities, it would help in the matchmaking process, since some parishes would be able to appeal to certain types of persons—perhaps young families, or those in a college community, or those from a certain type of background. Also a diocesan attitude of toleration toward parish shopping by parishioners new in the area would help the matchmaking process, since the chances of successful matchmaking would be higher if the people visited several distinctive parishes.

ASSIMILATION AND CULTURAL CHANGE

In chapter 1 we argued that assimilation of Catholics into American culture accounts for many of the changes visible in American Catholicism since the 1960s. In addition we should note that American culture is undergoing change in its own right, so that mainstream culture to which immigrants are assimilating is itself moving away from the Old World ways. One might expect that cultural creativity in

America would be found more in the Midwest and the Far West than in the East, since the eastern cities maintain the European culture relatively intact, but only in the pluralistic, individualistic West and Midwest do new forms germinate. Our experiences indicate that this is so.

Some observers of American Catholicism have stated that the Midwest is the most creative region, since it is some distance from the Old World culture and the immigrant experience, yet enough Catholics are found there to provide a critical mass for new cultural forms. This sounds plausible. In American society generally, the movement of cultural innovation seems to be more west-to-east than vice versa, a reversal from what it was a century ago. As someone has said, "The great teeter-totter has tipped." [3]

Analysts of social change have found that in America, youth and young adults have changed more than older people and that youth today give great importance to personal freedoms in behavior. In fact, youth have gained quite a few new freedoms in most of American society in the past two decades. Anyone who is familiar with the history of higher education in America will see quickly how restriction after restriction was removed from the student body. First, it was obligatory chapel attendance, then dormitory hours, then the requirement that parties be chaperoned, then geographic segregation of sexes on campus. Today youth enjoy more personal autonomy than in the 1940s and 1950s, and they feel it is their right.

This has had an effect on religious behavior too, and it is seen in attitudes toward Mass attendance. We heard many older persons talk about Mass attendance as an obligation to God. A study done in the 1950s described this viewpoint well: "The people come to Mass to offer an objective debt of worship to God. They are not interested primarily in fulfilling any of their own individual needs through the service. Often, from the viewpoint of the individual, there is little about the service itself that is attractive." [4] The argument that Mass attendance is an obligation of the Catholic has small impact on freedom-oriented youth today. We found little sentiment among young people that they should come to Mass to fulfill an obligation to God or to make a sacrifice of their time and money to God. For this they were criticized by a portion of the adults, who saw them as irresponsible or excessively self-centered. Adults would shake their heads and say, in effect, "I don't know what to make of those youngsters today."

The religion of obligation strongly felt and practiced by some of the older Catholic community is indeed weak—almost absent—among the young Catholics we talked with. Attempts by their elders to sustain traditional church attendance by arguments about obligation are unlikely to succeed, given the social changes of the past several decades.

In chapter 1 we argued that an individual's religious change must often be understood not in itself but within a larger package of life changes. We introduced Daniel Levinson's concept "life structure," denoting the total structure of involvements and areas of participation in any period of life. When some important elements in this structure are altered by events such as marriage, change of career, birth of children, or divorce, other elements soon modify in a kind of chain reaction. This pattern applies to many cases of converting, dropping out, and returning that we studied. In short, predispositions for a religious change may be absent one year but present the next year, because of intervening life experiences changing the total life structure. Thus the mission field is ever being renewed.

Church involvement or noninvolvement, that is, depends partly on adult life experiences. Many of these are covered explicitly by Catholic moral teachings, making the moral teachings a key factor in church involvement or noninvolvement. Our interviewees discussed Catholic moral teachings much more often than doctrinal teachings. The most salient moral teachings are in the areas of marriage and sexuality, and they are important to the individual's overall life-style. An individual's choice of life-style is thus often related to his or her church involvement or noninvolvement.

To oversimplify a bit, we found that churchgoing is integral to one kind of life-style but foreign to another kind. We heard over and over the assumption made by interviewees that the church is a natural ally of family life, good child-rearing, respectability, and responsible citizenship, and that persons who hold these ideals feel affirmed by the church. Such people feel almost obliged to be active in the church, since the church is a supporting pillar of this life-style. By contrast, persons who deviate from "straight" traditional living—who engage in some sort of free-wheeling or deviant life-style—feel strong tension between themselves and the church, and they pull away from it. In their attitudes, although not always consciously, the church is the domain of the traditional and the straight and not of others.

One could almost say that the church is a civilizing agent in a culture filled with roughshod elements, and when a person opts for a straight or free-swinging life-style, his or her decision concerning church involvement is already halfway made. Case after case of young people sowing their wild oats showed how they dropped away from the church, and case after case of former prodigals "finding themselves" and becoming respectable adults showed how they returned to the church.

In this perspective we can understand why so much religious

change is concentrated in the teenage and young adult years. The reason is largely that life structures change most in these years. The typical American life cycle involves participation in two families—first the family into which the person is born, and later a new family that he or she forms and in which the next generation is reared. But there is typically a period after the person leaves the first family, and before he or she forms the second, and this period is one of freedom, experimentation, and movement. The young person often moves from setting to setting and from friendship group to friendship group. Many decisions need to be made during this time regarding career, marriage, and even sex role. The life structure during this time has a temporary, changeable character, and of course, much dropping out and returning to the church takes place. As an adult grows older, changes decelerate. Sociological studies have amply demonstrated how attitudes become more stable, geographic moves more infrequent, and life-styles more constant. Religious changes also become more infrequent.

VIEWS ABOUT THE FUTURE OF THE CHURCH

In all the interviews we asked what the direction of the Catholic church should be in the years ahead. (For a summary of responses, see Table A.3 in Appendix A.) In the personal interviews this topic was discussed at length. The viewpoints varied widely, but despite the diversity four general themes can be discerned.

First, people want personal and accessible priests. Many asked that the priests get out more with their parishioners, try to understand the problems in people's lives, and avoid aloofness. Persons in parishes with such priests praised them, and other persons whose parishes did not seem to have such priests complained. Everyone appreciated priests who are open and human, and most hoped for reduced clergy-lay distances in future parish life.

Second, many hoped for warmer, more personal parishes. We heard a number of complaints, especially from people in large and impersonal parishes, that it was hard to relate to the parish. People often asked for more fellowship and more diverse opportunities to become involved. The size of the parish was not mentioned as much as its climate, but generally, smaller-than-average parishes were preferred.

Third, the problem of birth control was discussed many times. Most persons hope for more flexibility and more personal decision-making on this question.

171

Fourth, we heard people call for more support for family living. This included religious education, adult education, and family-oriented programs.

In addition to these four themes we got strong feelings from some people on the question of divorce. Not a large number mentioned the issue, but those who did had intense feelings. This was especially true among recently divorced people who complained of little help from the church and who desired to return to full sacramental church participation after remarriage.

In short, we received both positive and negative comments. Many people were happy with the church and expressed their support and joy in what it is doing. Others were negative. But virtually all thought seriously about what it is and what it might be, then suggested areas on which the church could work. They shared the hope that the church can carry out its God-given work.

Chapter

10

EVANGELIZATION IN THE 1980S
The Rev. Alvin A. Illig, C.S.P.
Executive Director, National Conference
of Catholic Bishops' Committee on Evangelization

THE STUDY on which this book is based has provided new information on people being evangelized to the Catholic Church, both formerly inactive Catholics who have been invited to return and new converts. The research has shown how important the human factors are and how closely religious life is related to the rest of life. This chapter examines evangelization in the 1980s—our hopes, our theological grounding, and some lessons we have learned from research and experience.

What might we hope for and pray for, as American Catholic evangelizers in the 1980s? I hope and pray that by 1990, Catholic evangelization will have achieved these goals:

- 85% of the archdioceses and dioceses in the United States (150 of the present 173) will have full-time offices for evangelization, with a special focus on inactive Catholics and the unchurched.
- 65% of the parishes in the United States (12,500 of the present 19,000) will have a Committee on Evangelization and Growth as part of the normal life of the Catholic community.
- 20% of American Catholics (10 million of the present 50 million active Catholics) will have an evangelizing mentality, regularly reaching out in friendship to their inactive Catholic friends, relatives, and neighbors to invite them to come back, and reaching out in friendship to the unchurched to invite them to sample the Catholic way of life to see if it can enrich their lives.

Concrete suggestions by Alvin A. Illig, C.S.P., to stimulate creative thinking on evangelization are given in Appendix B.

173

· 10 converts per 1,000 active Catholics will come into the Catholic Church each year. In 1950 the number of converts per 1,000 active Catholics was 4.3, and in 1980, this figure dropped to 1.6 converts per 1,000 active Catholics. Based on the present census of 50 million active Catholics, 10 converts per 1,000 active Catholics would translate to 500,000 converts per year.

The national office of the Bishops' Committee on Evangelization is striving to attain these goals by:

· stimulating within the Catholic community a ministry to those who are not active in any church or synagogue, and to those who have become estranged from the Catholic faith.
· gathering and sharing information on the work being done by dioceses, parishes, religious communities, and individuals in this area of ministry, and encouraging those at work.
· inviting dioceses and Catholic organizations to join with American bishops to help raise public awareness to the reality of inactive Catholics and the unchurched by focusing some programs on this area of ministry.
· distributing model programs of what is being done within parishes and dioceses to minister to the inactive and the unchurched; preparing and distributing models of evangelization efforts in the U.S. Hispanic community and in other groups with special needs.
· conducting conferences and workshops for clergy, religious communities, dioceses, and national organizations on the evangelization of the unchurched and the inactive in the various cultures.

Whenever we begin to move toward realizing these objectives and to plan for Catholic evangelization in the 1980s, three areas of immediate concern emerge: (1) theological grounding for contemporary evangelization, (2) the basic guiding principles to be applied in evangelization efforts, and (3) the concrete steps that can make our work more effective. On the following pages I offer a starting point for your reflection in each of these areas.

THEOLOGICAL GROUNDING FOR CONTEMPORARY CATHOLIC EVANGELIZATION

On December 8, 1975 Pope Paul VI published a magnificent document titled *Evangelii Nuntiandi* (The Gospels Must Be Proclaimed), more popularly known as *Evangelization in the Modern World*. In this apostolic exhortation he gives Catholics a twenty-five-year charter for evangelization, "for these years which mark the eve of a new century, the eve also of the third millennium of Christianity" (EN #81).

Evangelii Nuntiandi is a 23,000-word reaffirmation of a 2,000-year-old Catholic missionary heritage, and a call to find more effective contemporary methods of evangelization. It is my hope the following brief summary of this classic work will encourage people to become familiar with the full document.[1] The numbers refer to paragraphs of the text.

A *Summary of* Evangelization in the Modern World

Introduction

Proclaiming the gospel is a service rendered to the Christian community and to all humanity (#1). It is only in the Christian message that people can find the answers to their deepest questions and the energy for their commitment to human solidarity (#3).

The presentation of the gospel message is not an optional contribution of the church. It is the duty on the church by the command of the Lord Jesus, so that people can believe and be saved (#5).

From Christ the Evangelizer to the Evangelizing Church

"I must proclaim the good news of the kingdom of God" without doubt has enormous consequences, for it sums up the whole mission of Jesus: "The Spirit of the Lord has been given to me, for he has anointed me. He has sent me to bring the good news to the poor [Luke 4:18]" (#6).

Jesus was the first and greatest evangelizer (#7). As an evangelizer, Christ first of all proclaims a kingdom, the kingdom of God. The kernel and center of Christ's good news is salvation, this great gift of God which is liberation from everything that oppresses men and women, which is, above all, liberation from sin and the devil. Each person can gain this kingdom and salvation through a radical conversion, a profound change of heart and mind, a total interior renewal (#10).

Through his untiring preaching of the Word which has no equal, Christ proclaims the kingdom of God. Christ manifests the divine content of this proclamation by innumerable signs and miracles, but more especially by his death and resurrection, and by sending of the Holy Spirit (#12).

Those who sincerely accept the good news can and must communicate and share it with others (#13). The church clearly exists in order to evangelize, i.e., in order to preach and teach, to be the channel of the gift of grace, to reconcile sinners with God, and to

175

perpetuate Christ's sacrifice in the Mass (#14). Anyone who reads the gospel sees that the church is linked to evangelization in its most intimate being (#15).

What Is Evangelization?

Evangelizing, an action whose complexity, dynamism, and richness defies partial definition, means bringing the good news into all strata of humanity in order to transform it and make it new: "I make all things new [Apoc. 21:5]." In proclaiming the gospel the church seeks to upset and replace the prevailing values of society with those of Christ (#17-19). The starting point for this work must be the individual as he or she is found, within a culture. The life of each person and of each culture can then be regenerated by the gospel (#20).

All Christians are called first to the "silent proclamation of the good news," a witness expressed in action that sets an example and a foretaste of the kingdom for all to see. At some point, however, Christian witness must become explicit, through the spoken and written word. To be true evangelization, the Christian message must proclaim the teaching, the life, the promises, the kingdom, and the mystery of Jesus of Nazareth, Son of God, crucified and risen (#21-22).

A twofold response can be expected of a community that has been evangelized: adherence to the kingdom expressed in the beginning of a "new world"—a new state of things, a new manner of living that the gospel inaugurates; and a new zeal to bring others to the kingdom, to evangelize, by those who have been evangelized (#23-24).

The Content of Evangelization

To evangelize is to bear witness, in a simple and direct way, to God revealed by Jesus Christ, in the Holy Spirit. The center of the message is this: salvation in Jesus Christ in a manner that exceeds all temporal limits, and reaches fulfillment in communion with the one and only divine Absolute. The transcendent and eschatological aspects of the message are the culmination of the kingdom inaugurated with the preaching of the gospel on earth: thus, in proclamation the church begins by emphasizing the immediate rights and duties of every human being in the family and in society. The church has the duty to proclaim the message of liberation from famine, chronic disease, illiteracy, poverty, and cultural and economic neo-colonialism; the people of God are responsible for assisting in the birth of this liberation. This essential message cannot be changed, although the presentation of secondary elements, of accidentals, depends greatly on changing circumstances (#25-30).

The authentic advancement of humankind through development and liberation is an integral part of the message of the gospel. In our time the church has become increasingly aware of the need for liberation and of its place in evangelization. When preaching liberation, however, the church recognizes that to turn its mission into a solely temporal project would render the uniqueness of the gospel meaningless. The spiritual and transcendent fundamentals of the church have primacy in its task, making liberation a step toward total fulfillment in God (#31-38).

The Methods of Evangelization

The question of how to evangelize is permanently relevant because the methods vary according to time, place, and culture. Still, the first and foremost means of evangelization is the example of a Christian life. St. Peter expressed this well when he held up the example of a reverent and chaste life that wins unbelievers by example (1 Peter 3:1). Second, preaching, the verbal proclamation of the message, is always indispensable (#40-42). Preaching to evangelize takes many forms. One of them is the homily, which is to be used in all Sacraments, paraliturgies, and assemblies of the faithful. Neither must catechetics be neglected, whether in the training of children or in the catechumenate and neo-catechumenate for adults and young people who are touched by grace and feel the need to give themselves to Christ (#43-44).

Several other methods assist evangelization. Mass media enable the good news to reach millions of people. Side by side with the collective means of transmission the person-to-person approach is valid and important. The Lord often used it (for example, with Nicodemus, Zacchaeus, the Samaritan woman, Simon the Pharisee), and so did the apostles. Yet evangelization is more than simply teaching and preaching a doctrine; it exercises its full capacity when it touches life, establishing a permanent bond between Word and sacrament. Popular piety can be a true encounter with God in Jesus Christ for multitudes of our people, if it is well oriented (#45-48).

The Beneficiaries of Evangelization

Jesus' last words in St. Mark's Gospel entrust to his apostles a limitless universality: "Go out to the whole world; proclaim the good news to all creation [Mark 16:15]." In the course of twenty centuries this commission has met with resistance from people being addressed by evangelizers, tempting the church to narrow the field of mission. Yet the church has survived such adversities and has renewed its inspiration to follow through: To the whole world! To all creation! Right to the ends of the earth! (#49-50).

To reveal Jesus Christ and his gospel to those who do not know them has been the fundamental program the church received from its founder.

In addition to reaching those who have never heard the gospel, it is also necessary to address this first proclamation to people who have been baptized but who accept the values of a dechristianized world.

The church esteems and respects non-Christian religions, because they carry within them the echo of thousands of years of searching for God; they are all impregnated with innumerable "seeds of the Word" and can constitute a true "preparation for the Gospel." Yet, even in the face of worthy natural religious expressions, the church finds support in the fact that the religion of Jesus, which it proclaims through evangelization, objectively places humankind in relation with the plan of God (#53).

Unflagging attention is also to be paid to those who have received the faith and who have been in contact with the gospel for generations, that they may further advance in the Christian life (#54-57).

Ecclesial basic communities, which flourish throughout the church, will be a hope for the universal church as they grow in missionary zeal, love of the Word of God, and the desire to share their gifts (#58).

Workers for Evangelization

The duty of going out into the whole world and preaching the gospel to every creature rests on the whole church. The church has the task of transmitting the gospel in the language each individual people can best understand yet maintaining utter fidelity to the content of evangelization (#59-66).

Each member of the church can serve this goal in many ways. In union with the successor of Peter, the Bishops receive authority to teach the revealed truth in the church. Associated with their ministry is that of priests and religious, whose consecrated lives are a privileged means of evangelization (#67-69). Lay people, whose particular vocation places them in the midst of the world and in charge of the most varied temporal tasks, exercise a special form of evangelization. Their own field of evangelizing activity is the vast and complicated world of politics, society, and economics, and also the world of culture, the sciences, the arts, international life, and the mass media. Within the variety of ministries for the laity, the role of the family—"the domestic Church"—and that of youth are especially necessary. In some instances, the laity may feel called to work with pastors in service of the ecclesial community. We owe special esteem to them, and must seek to offer serious preparation for all workers for evangelization (#70-73).

The Spirit of Evangelization

Evangelizers, be worthy of your vocation. The Holy Spirit inspires you, but only you can live what you proclaim and offer this age the authenticity for which it thirsts. Divisions among Christians, lack of reverence for truth, lack of love and fervor are some of the great obstacles to evangelization today. Yet, as we enter the third millennium of Christianity the light of Christ shines on those setting out to evangelize in these times that are both difficult and full of hope (#74-82).

This summary conveys some of the key elements of evangelization spelled out in *Evangelization in the Modern World*. Evangelization is to both individuals and to cultures. It conveys the message of salvation, the culmination of the kingdom, liberation, and human fulfillment. It is performed in many ways and involves all Catholics.

The next section outlines some practical implications of this book for evangelization today.

FOURTEEN BASIC PRINCIPLES FOR DESIGNING PROGRAMS OF EVANGELIZATION

1. "Go, therefore, make disciples of all nations; baptize them in the name of the Father, and of the Son and of the Holy Spirit, and teach them to observe all the commands I gave you [Matt. 28:18-20]." Most Christians accept this text as Christ's last will and final testament, often called the Great Commission. However, the unique contemporary challenge to today's Catholic is to find the best way to evangelize effectively—to develop ways by which today's committed Christians can share the good news and mediate, especially to the unchurched, Christ's call to faith and ecclesial community in today's context. While Christ clearly tells Christians they must evangelize, the method is left up to each evangelizer. The evangelizer is encouraged in this search by the knowledge that God who wills the end, wills the means.

The particular form evangelization will take will be determined (1) by the personal charisma, the unique talents, the special gifts that each evangelizer brings to this joyful task, and (2) by the audience being served, e.g., active Catholics; inactive Catholics; the unchurched; urban, suburban, and rural communities; blacks; Hispanics; Native Americans; the handicapped, etc.

2. Those attracted to this aspect of the mission of Christ must approach the task with the firm conviction that they most certainly have something of value to share with others, that they come to enrich the lives of others, that they are indeed God's messengers, that they are truly resurrection people. Evangelization programs must be positive, filled with hope, oriented toward the future, and rooted in the example of Jesus Christ, who said, "I must proclaim the good news of the kingdom of God. That is what I was sent to do [Luke 4:43]."

3. The basic attitude of the evangelizer must be one of friendship. As the words of Pope John XXIII gave witness—chiseled on the entrance wall of the Vatican Pavilion at the 1965 World's Fair in New York, "We come not to conquer, we come to serve." Our commission as Christians is to invite those in search of a religious family to investigate the Catholic family, and to create the opportunities and the atmosphere for the inquirers to sample our way of life to see if it can enrich their lives.

4. Because the challenge of evangelizing all peoples is so great, it must be approached simultaneously at all levels of action: interpersonal dialogue, parish programs, diocesan offices of evangelization, and national—as well as international—efforts at evangelization. Without question, however, the most effective programs of evangelization are interpersonal. As this research study documents, four out of five individuals who investigate the Catholic community do so because friends, relatives, or neighbors extended personal invitations.

5. Ecumenism and evangelization are not incompatible, but can and must work together if both challenges are to be met. Poor principles of evangelization result in bad ecumenism and vice versa. Ecumenism is the effort to undo the scandal of disunity among the 50 million active Catholics and the 75 million other Christians in America. Primary evangelization, however, is the effort to share the gospel of Christ with 80 million unchurched Americans. Ecumenism and primary evangelization serve different and distinct communities; both are vitally important to the life of the church and both must work together.

6. When designing programs to serve the needs of the unchurched, the evangelizer must have an appreciation of the human and psychological needs of the inquirer, since the inquirer usually does not accept scripture or authority. At times everyone needs hope, in the face of a world threatened by atomic holocaust. At times everyone yearns for stability, rootedness, and authority. At times everyone needs challenge and individual help to be the person each of us wants to be: a man or woman of goodness, justice, understanding, strength, purity, peace, sacrifice, and love—a person who loves even his or her enemies. The evangelizer might begin the dialogue with the four great fears of humankind: fear of failure, fear of rejection, fear of physical and psychological pain, and fear of death and annihilation. The evangelizer can raise the questions of life and death, pain and sorrow, what awaits each of us after death: Why do you exist? Where are you going? It is the evangelizer's task to show how Christ, being fully human and fully divine, confronted these human conditions, and to suggest that by coming to know Christ, the lonely, the frightened, the searching, the spiritually impoverished will be able to see God's loving

plan in their lives, as Christ saw it in his life. Then they will be better prepared to cope with their human problems, achieving a fuller sense of well-being and a clearer direction for their lives. The final step is to show that in Word, Sacraments, and Christian community, Christ lives in his people, the church. Even though we Christians often blemish him by our personal sins, he has promised that he will stay with us, even to the end of the world.

7. Social and spiritual ministry are but two sides of the same coin that says we are to love God with our whole heart and our neighbor as ourselves (Matthew 22:37-40). Evangelizing is neither social ministry nor spiritual ministry; it is both. The more the Catholic community shows genuine concern and effective action in alleviating social ills and liberating the poor, the more believable will its gospel be. Conversely, social ministry will transcend itself only if the gospel is explicitly proclaimed side by side with action and concern.

8. Because we find ourselves living in an existential age, a visual age, a here-and-now age, the evangelizer must develop an increasing sympathy for the emotional and the experiential, for flowers, music, color, beauty, design. "Taste and see the goodness of the Lord," the psalmist writes. But note that first we are to taste and then we shall see. This is especially true of the less educated and the less sophisticated. In evangelization, people frequently act their way into thinking, rather than think their way into acting. Experiential evangelization, through renewal endeavors such as Marriage Encounter, the charismatic movement, and the Cursillo, is one of the features which distinguishes current evangelization from that practiced before Vatican Council II. This understanding of the human condition is clearly reflected in the 1972 Rite of the Christian Initiation of Adults.

9. Evangelizers have to be open to a multiplicity of approaches, using an array of tools, because each one is trying to reach all manner of people. No one method, no one style, no one program can possibly reach everyone. The evangelizer will continually want to develop new models for different situations and different peoples. There will be long-range programs as well as short-range programs, indirect approaches as well as direct approaches, the use of print media as well as nonprint, formal liturgical services as well as bumper stickers.

10. One of the greatest strengths for Catholic evangelization is the nationwide network of 19,000 parish families. More than 95% of Americans live within a thirty-minute drive of a Catholic parish. For stability and follow-through, therefore, evangelization programs should be parish-based. The task of the Catholic evangelizer is to invite the inactive Catholic to come back, and to invite the unchurched to become part of a community of believing people on a pilgrimage to an eternal destiny, a pilgrim people who gather regularly to give honor

and glory to God and to support one another on this life journey.

11. Another strength for the evangelizer, one more important than the network of 19,000 parishes, is the 50 million active Catholics (in addition to an estimated 15 million inactive Catholics) who make up these parishes. This is the greatest single hope that Catholic evangelization will realize success during the 1980s. Today's laity are a fire-tried people who have been forced to make a reaffirmation and a recommitment to Christ in the past fifteen years. They remain Catholics because they want to, not because they have to. The laity are in daily contact with the very people the church is trying to evangelize. Even if 190,000 priests, sisters, brothers, and deacons could do the job alone—and they certainly cannot—it is neither theologically desirable nor pedagogically sound that they do. Evangelization programs are most effective when constructed on a peer-to-peer basis. Like Andrew who found Christ and then introduced his brother Peter to the Lord, so evangelization will flourish when the laity introduce their brothers and sisters to Christ.

12. Evangelization does not need more structures, more buildings, more things, or even large amounts of money. The American Catholic community, for the most part, has passed through the brick-and-mortar stage of its development. Now it has ample structures waiting to be used. What Catholic evangelization does need is people, ideas, dedication, and a modest amount of financing to help communicate the message. A blend of time, talent, and treasure is required.

13. Part of the mystery and the beauty of evangelization is what it does to the evangelizer. As you become more involved in sharing Christ with others, you become painfully alert to the fact that you cannot share someone you yourself do not first know. Through prayer, reflection, and study you come to realize that you will be effective to the extent that you are a branch grafted to the vine that is Christ. The first one to be evangelized is the evangelizer. The first group to be enriched is the active Catholic parish that makes up the evangelizing community.

14. If the evangelizer insists on waiting until the total Catholic community is in exemplary spiritual condition, with all questions and doubts resolved and with all Christians living in harmony, he or she will never do anything. Remember, Christ did not found his church for saints and angels, but for sinners—sinners who strive for goodness yet know that the spirit is willing, but the flesh is weak. For two thousand years Christ's people have not been in perfect order, and they never will be. Even while telling us to preach the good news of hope, liberation, and salvation, Christ warned us that scandals would always plague our footsteps (Luke 17:1-2). Read the epistles of Paul, remembering that the sins and the excesses of which he is writing were

being committed not only by the pagans, but also by the early Christians. We are a sinful people in need of daily conversion. So the evangelizer accepts this humbling reality, works with whatever there is to work with, does his or her best, and leaves the outcome in God's hands. Writing to the Corinthians, St. Paul says, "I did the planting, Apollos did the watering, but God made things grow. Neither the planter nor the waterer matters: only God who makes things grow. . . . We are fellow workers with God [1 Cor. 3:6]."

Appendix

A

RESEARCH PROCEDURE

PRETESTS

IN JANUARY 1979 we asked a group of priests in the Archdiocese of Washingon to give us names of recent converts, dropouts, or returnees in their parishes whom we could interview in a pretest. We asked them to notify the persons if they preferred. They gave us forty-five names, and I interviewed thirty-five in person. This was an introduction to the kinds of persons and problems we would be working with in the final study. I gained experience in how to conduct the interviews. For example, I learned that a third person cannot be in the room, and if a spouse seems curious about the study, that it is best to interview the spouse as well. The interviews were somewhat unstructured so that I could follow the lead of the interviewee and pursue topics that seemed important. One principal finding of this first pretest was the need for clear definitions in selecting interviewees.

The second pretest was done to see if telephone canvassing from parish census lists would work. It was done in two suburban Maryland parishes that were known to have good census lists. Bernard Stratman and I called households on the lists from about 6 to 9 P.M. on two evenings, and we discovered that we could find one interviewee fitting the dropout or the returnee definition and agreeing to be interviewed per eleven or twelve calls. In this pretest we asked for persons who had dropped out or returned within the past *two* years, not three. Since the canvassing was somewhat laborious and discouraging, we worried about the morale of persons helping us in the final study, and we asked Father Illig if we could do the final study on persons who dropped out or returned within the past *three* years, to increase the yield from the canvassing. He agreed. But as it turned out, the yield in the final study was still about one in twelve, since we had unknowingly picked two pretest parishes with relatively high yield rates.

The second pretest included twenty-three personal interviews with persons found by telephone canvassing. The interview form was semistructured. We hired additional interviewers and pretested our method of training and paying them. The most troubling aspect of the second pretest was the high rate of refusals. Many individuals did not want to take the time to be interviewed in person. We discussed the problem with the advisory committee, who suggested we try doing all the interviewing, as well as the canvassing, by telephone. This would entail tightening up our interview structure and shortening it, but it promised fewer refusals and lower interview cost.

The third pretest tried out a structured telephone interview rather than a personal interview. Again we canvassed in the parishes to generate interviewees, but this time we asked when we could call back with a telephone interview. We completed fifteen interviews, which lasted twenty to thirty-five minutes each. The results were favorable, so we decided to do all the structured interviews by telephone. We revised the interview form a final time, then had separate versions printed for converts, dropouts, and returnees.

The interview schedule included seventeen questions borrowed verbatim from recent nationwide surveys so that we could use the churchgoing Catholics from the nationwide surveys as a control group. The surveys were the 1977 survey done by Gallup for the Catholic Press Association (Gallup, 1978b), the 1978 Gallup survey on unchurched Americans (Gallup, 1978a), and the NORC General Social Surveys of 1977 and 1978. From these nationwide surveys we took the data from Catholics who attend church weekly, thus allowing us to compare the attitudes of new converts, dropouts, and returnees with active Catholics. These comparisons are shown in Table A.3 below.

TELEPHONE CANVASSING

We asked the thirty-two pastors for their census lists and for the names of converts within the past three years. Also, we asked them to notify the converts about the study—if they thought it best—and to announce the study to all the parish.

It turned out that about half the parishes had recent house-to-house censuses, either totally or partially complete. The other half of the parishes had only a registry list, and we used this. From the lists, our volunteer helpers called names randomly, phoning between 6 and 9

P.M. on weekdays and all day on Saturdays. The telephone interviews were scheduled when the people preferred. In each diocese the canvassing took six to ten days to complete.

The yield from the canvassing—that is, the number of interviews achieved per 100 or 500 canvassing calls to households—varied greatly from parish to parish. This was an unexpected occurrence and represented a research finding in its own right. In the most favorable parishes, from a canvassing point of view, the yield was about one interviewee who agreed to an interview per six calls. In the most unfavorable the yield was less than one per fifty calls. The average was about one per twelve calls.

Yield rates were mostly a function of the demographic characteristics of the parishes; they were only slightly a function of high or low willingness of the persons to be interviewed. And we doubt if they are much related to institutional factors in the parish churches. Yield rates were highest where the neighborhoods were filled with young adults. A second factor influencing yield rates was the amount of movement in and out of the community; suburbs with people constantly moving in and out had more dropouts and returnees than old urban neighborhoods or small towns. A third factor was educational level, in that persons who had more education were a bit more receptive to being interviewed.

In short, the lowest yield rates were in old ethnic neighborhoods now inhabited mostly by old people, in ghetto-like blighted urban neighborhoods, and in stable small towns. The highest rates were in growing suburbs having fast influx of young educated adults rearing families.

BIASES

Several biases in the telephone canvassing and interviewing can be identified. First, we had no way of reaching someone whose family had no telephone. This is a small bias. Second, often we could not reach a family whose number was unlisted. Sometimes the parish had the number, or we were referred to the person by another family member who had the number. But some bias resulted.

The main bias came from refusals. Among the new converts this was only a small problem, since the refusals were only 5% or 10%. Among the returnees the refusal rate was about 10% to 20% in every location except Providence, where it was higher—about 25% to 35%. The reasons for the refusals, when we could obtain them, usually had little to do with the content of our survey. Rather, the people refused to

187

give interviews to anyone for any survey, or they were too busy, or they had visitors, or the like. We offered to call some back in a week, and when we did, they often were willing to be interviewed.

The problem of refusals was worst in the dropout group. This was partly because many inactive people feel unpleasant when the church is discussed, therefore they do not want to talk about it. Sometimes they feel guilty for being inactive. Among young people there is often family tension over their inactivity, and they do not want to talk to a researcher who may increase their feelings of guilt. Especially among young men aged 18 to 22, many refused to talk with us, and by talking with other family members we found that these persons were in the wild oats syndrome, leading a freedom-loving, hot-rodding style of life. Many young men with this life-style drop out of church life and also keep arm's length from social researchers. The same phenomenon occurred among young women but to a lesser extent.

We estimate that among dropouts aged 18 to 22 the refusal rate was 40% to 50% everywhere except in Providence, where it was 60% to 70%. Among the other dropouts the refusal rate was 20% to 30%, except in Providence, where it was 35% to 45%.

Refusal rates in Providence were the highest we experienced, and the reason for this was a topic of much discussion. We found that persons living in old ethnic neighborhoods were unwilling to talk with us. Also, our friends speculated that New England reticence was a factor. We do not know.

Spanish-speaking Catholics in San Antonio

Data gathering in the Archdiocese of San Antonio, where the Catholic population is largely Hispanic, presented special problems. The interview forms were translated into Spanish, and Cecilio Morales Jr., a Spanish-speaking journalist at the National Conference of Catholic Bishops, went along to help. Most of the interviewers were bilingual, so interviews were done in both languages.

Two characteristics of Hispanic Catholicism in Texas posed problems. First, cultural norms about church attendance are different, so that some Hispanic persons who should be considered active might be inactive by our definition. Hispanic religiosity stresses home religious rituals and special fiestas as much as regular Mass attendance. We decided to keep the definitions in our study intact for sake of continuity but to consider a Hispanic person as active if he or she attended at least twice in the past year, including the fiestas.

Second, Hispanic Catholics do not hesitate to attend different churches of different denominations for different purposes. A person may go to Bible study and prayer groups in Baptist or Lutheran churches while attending Mass occasionally at the Catholic parish. This posed no problem for our study, but it introduced a fluidity in the dropout category in that some Hispanics shift denominations easily—and temporarily.

GLOBAL CODING

A principal goal of our study is a descriptive typology of converts, dropouts, and returnees. For maximal usefulness, a typology must be tied to theoretical and practical needs. In this study we deemed it best to construct each typology on the basis of predispositions for the change. Put simply, *what motivated* the person to make the change? Predispositions must be inferred from interview data, and we considered doing this either by computer or by human judgment. We chose the latter as being more reliable. Therefore, Kenneth McGuire and I jointly made a global code for each telephone interview. Each of us did the task separately, then we met and hammered out differences to arrive at a code.

In this way we coded predispositions, facilitating persons or relationships, and facilitating events. The events had to have been within two years of the person's religious decision. The coding scheme allowed coding up to three predispositions, two facilitating persons or relationships, and two facilitating events in any single case, since in reality more than one was often present. The categories were arrived at inductively, after we reviewed a large number of interview forms. It turned out that global coding categories were the same for converts and returnees, but different categories were required for the dropouts.

This coding scheme is the most accurate method of typologizing the cases, but it proved too complex to use in communicating our findings to other persons. Hence we simplified it by combining some categories. In the case of the converts, the four predispositions we identified for the global code were easily reduced to three, since one of the four (dissatisfaction with another church) rarely occurred alone. Likewise, in the case of returnees, the five predispositions in the global code were easily reduced to four, because one usually occurred in combination with others. When two or more predispositions were coded for any case, we assigned the case to one or the other type after reviewing all the interviews similarly affected and making the most realistic decision.

In the case of dropouts, the problem was more complex. The

189

predispositions were divided into eight categories not obviously combinable. After reviewing the cases with multiple predispositions and trying various ways of combining the categories, we used a method of identifying five basic types of dropouts. Problems of where to assign those with multiple predispositions were again decided after reviewing all the interviews involved.

TABLE A.1

DESCRIPTION OF ACTIVE CATHOLICS, CONVERTS, DROPOUTS, AND RETURNEES

	Active Catholics[a]	Con- verts	Dropouts[b]		Return- ees
			Young	Older	
1. Sex: percent female	59	62	c	c	71
2. Age at time of religious change: median		31	18	35	30
3. Education: percent with some college or higher	28	57	56	50	50
4. Marital status: percent married at time of religious change (approximately)		81	20	86	82
5. Did you receive any religious training as a child? (percent yes)	92	85	100	98	98
6. Percent who attended religious or parochial school as a child	58	8	75	62	68
7. When you were in elementary or grade school, how often did you attend Sunday school or church? (percent "every week")	91	68	91	86	86
8. Think back about five years. How important was religion in your life at that time? (percent "very important")		39	28	32	29
9. How important would you say religion is in your life? (percent "very important")	74	85	38	52	70

[a]"Active Catholic" data are for Catholics who attend church weekly, from nationwide polls in 1977 or 1978.

[b]Young = dropout at age 22 or younger; older = dropout at age 23 or older.

[c]Due to known bias resulting from refusals, our data are inaccurate.

SELF-REPORTED "VERY IMPORTANT" INFLUENCES ON DECISIONS TO BECOME A
CONVERT, TO STOP MASS ATTENDANCE, OR TO BECOME AN ACTIVE CATHOLIC

	Percent for whom this was a "very important" influence			
	Decision to become a convert	Decision to stop Mass attendance		Decision to become active
		Young	Older[a]	
1. Someone influenced me to _____.	40	13	8	44
2. Had a personal problem or a problem in the family in recent years that had an influence on my religious viewpoint.	10	3	19	25
3. In recent years experienced a sense of need or void in my feelings about life.	23	14	15	41
4. Felt a dissatisfaction with the other church or religious group in which I was active in the past.	14	*	*	*
5. Had a personal conversion experience in the past 3 or 4 years.	18	16	13	27
6. (if "no" on #5) There was a definite time in the past 3 or 4 years when I had an important religious experience and made a new personal religious commitment.	10	0	0	11
7. Have children, and feel a concern for their education.	12 }	2[b]	8[b]	31
8. Have children, and they were a factor in some other way.	18 }			37
9. Took part in a charismatic prayer group in recent years.	5	0	3	6
10. Took part in a Marriage Encounter weekend in recent years.	6	0	0	4
11. Took part in a cursillo or retreat in recent years.	0	0	0	3
12. Listened to or watched radio or television programs sponsored by religious organizations.	2	0	1	4
13. Read religious books or periodicals in recent years (not including those in the inquiry class).	10	3	4	9
14. Felt a dissatisfaction with the Catholic Church or its teachings.	*	42	47	*

(continued)

191

	Decision to become a convert	Decision to stop Mass attendance		Decision to become active
		Young	Older	
15. The views of the Catholic Church about sexuality are well known. My own views about sexual values and practices influenced me to become an inactive Catholic.	*	9	14	*
16. In recent years felt conflict or tension between myself and the priests or nuns.	*	13	17	*
17. In recent years felt conflict or tension between myself and other members of the parish.	*	6	2	*
18. Found spiritual help or religious truth in another religious group.	*	17	18	*

[a]Young = dropout at age 22 or younger; older = dropout at age 23 or older.

[b]A single question asked whether children were a factor in any way. No question asked how important a factor, but based on other similar items, about half would have said "very important." These figures are approximations.

*Not asked.

ATTITUDES OF FOUR GROUPS: PERCENTAGES

	Actives	Con-verts	Drop-outs	Return-ees

Religion and the Church

1. How important would you say religion is
   in your life--would you say it is very
   important, fairly important, or not
   very important?

	Actives	Con-verts	Drop-outs	Return-ees
Very important	74	85	47	70
Fairly important	22	15	35	27
Not very important	2	0	16	2
Don't know	2	1	3	1

2. Most churches and synagogues today have
   lost the real spiritual part of
   religion.

Strongly agree	16	14	37	15
Moderately agree	32	18	29	27
Uncertain	10	8	9	6
Moderately disagree	28	31	17	24
Strongly disagree	16	29	9	29

3. An individual should arrive at his or
   her own religious beliefs independent
   of any church or synagogue.

Strongly agree	46	29	37	34
Moderately agree	27	19	23	21
Uncertain	9	7	8	7
Moderately disagree	12	23	18	17
Strongly disagree	6	22	14	21

4. Do you think a person can be a good
   Christian or Jew if he or she doesn't
   attend church or synagogue?

Yes	78	52	82	77
No	18	45	15	22
Don't know	4	3	3	1

5. Do you believe there is life after death?

Yes	84	90	75	77
No	11	4	7	9
Don't know	5	6	19	15

Moral Issues

6. Please tell me whether or not you think
   it should be possible for a pregnant
   woman to obtain a legal abortion if she
   is married and does not want any more
   children?

Yes	30	14	28	23
No	63	80	64	66
Don't know	7	6	8	11

(continued)

	Actives	Con-verts	Drop-outs	Return-ees
7. There's been a lot of discussion about the way morals and attitudes about sex are changing in this country. If a man and a woman have sex relations before marriage, do you think it is always wrong, almost always wrong, wrong only sometimes, or not wrong at all?				
Always wrong	41	36	32	24
Almost always wrong	15	20	8	15
Wrong only sometimes	22	30	33	36
Not wrong at all	21	8	25	17
Don't know	1	8	3	7

Issues Facing the Catholic Church

	Actives	Con-verts	Drop-outs	Return-ees
8. A. Divorced Catholics should be permitted to remarry in the Catholic Church. B. Divorced Catholics should not be permitted to remarry in the Catholic Church.				
A.	67	71	79	81
B.	28	23	12	11
Don't know	5	5	9	8
9. A. Catholics should be allowed to practice artificial means of birth control. B. Catholics should not be allowed to practice artificial means of birth control.				
A.	70	77	89	83
B.	25	18	8	10
Don't know	5	5	3	8
10. A. The Catholic Church should relax its standards forbidding all abortions under any circumstances. B. The Catholic Church should not relax its standards forbidding all abortions under any circumstances.				
A.	36	37	54	51
B.	58	59	42	43
Don't know	6	5	5	6
11. A. In general, I approve of the changes in the Catholic Church since Vatican II. B. In general, I disapprove of the changes in the Catholic Church since Vatican II.				
A.	73	84	54	79
B.	21	4	30	17
Don't know	6	12	16	5

(continued)

194

	Actives	Con-verts	Drop-outs	Return-ees

Direction for the Catholic Church

12. In your opinion, what should be the direction of the Catholic Church in the years ahead? What should the church stress, or how should it move? What would you recommend? (open-ended answers categorized by coders)

	Actives	Con-verts	Drop-outs	Return-ees
General: stricter, more formal; church is too modern		4	19	10
General: remain firm on moral issues; remain stable and firm		9	5	6
General: more lenient, more liberal		4	8	3
General: update the church, move forward		8	7	5
General: more voice of the people, listen to the people		2	7	9
General: church is too bureaucratic, should be more people-oriented; awareness of people instead of rules		2	9	9
General: return to Bible or basics; personal relationship to Jesus Christ; more spiritual		7	21	11
More stress on community; more parish activities		3	3	7
More outreach; evangelization		9	6	4
More help to families; stress family		11	5	7
Abortion: liberalize		4	6	8
Abortion: don't liberalize		8	2	1
Birth control: liberalize		11	13	17
Birth control: don't liberalize		2	0	1
Divorce: liberalize		6	9	13
Divorce: don't liberalize		1	0	5
Women: open up, more participation		4	4	6
Women: don't open up		2	2	3
Nuns should return to formal habits		3	2	2
Celibacy: liberalize		3	4	6
Celibacy: remain firm		2	1	1
More ministry to youth		11	6	4
More ministry to elderly		1	1	0
More emphasis on children's religious education		3	5	4
Provide more courses; more adult education; forums for people to meet and discuss		6	3	3
More Bible study		3	7	5
Better Mass or liturgy; less boring; more lay participation		8	9	11
Need interpretation of recent changes, guidelines, and Vatican II		1	0	3

TABLE A.4

RESULTS OF CONVERSION: PERCENTAGES

	Inter-marriage Converts	Family-life Converts	Seeker Converts
1. As a result of your becoming a baptized Catholic, has there been any change in your family life? Yes.	50	64	60
2. As a result of your becoming a baptized Catholic, has there been any change in your personal outlook or attitude toward life? Yes.	73	79	81
3. Has there been any change in your personal life practices or your personal habits? Yes.	34	51	54
4. Has there been any change in your selection of friends or the group of people you socialize with? Yes.	29	32	23
5. In recent months, how often have you attended Mass? Weekly or oftener.	85	79	85
6. Are you active in any group or committee in the parish, such as the ushers, the school committee, the altar guild, or any other? Yes.	28	36	31
7. Are you active in any Catholic organizations, action groups, or movements other than those in the parish? Yes.	6	10	15
8. How important would you say religion is in your life? (Same question was asked about five years ago.) Change in percent saying "very important" from five years ago till now.	+43	+46	+50

RESULTS OF DROPPING OUT OF CHURCH LIFE: PERCENTAGES

	Family-tension Dropouts	Weary Dropouts	Life-style Dropouts	Spiritual-need Dropouts	Anti-change Dropouts
1. As a result of becoming an inactive Catholic, has there been any change in your family life? Yes.	27	22	20	54[a]	14[a]
2. As a result of becoming an inactive Catholic, has there been any change in your personal outlook or attitude toward life? Yes.	44	33	38	58	0
3. Has there been any change in your personal life practices or your personal habits? Yes.	35	24	25	31	0
4. Has there been any change in your selection of friends or the group of people you socialize with? Yes.	27	19	10	29	0
5. How important would you say religion is in your life? (Same question was asked about five years ago.) Change in percent saying "very important" from five years ago till now.	+14	+20	+2	+7	+21

[a]Because of a low number of cases, percentages in the last two columns are rough approximations.

197

TABLE A.6

RESULTS OF RETURNING TO ACTIVE CHURCH LIFE: PERCENTAGES

	Marriage-life Returnees	Family-life Returnees	Guilt-feeling Returnees	Seeker Returnees
1. As a result of becoming an active Catholic, has there been any change in your family life? Yes.	60	58	36	51
2. As a result of becoming an active Catholic, has there been any change in your personal outlook or attitude toward life? Yes.	33	66	82	83
3. Has there been any change in your personal life practices or your personal habits? Yes.	33	38	43	43
4. Has there been any change in your selection of friends or the group of people you socialize with? Yes.	29	19	25	37
5. In recent months, how often have you attended Mass? Weekly or oftener.	60	67	71	89
6. Are you active in any group or committee in the parish, such as the ushers, the school committee, the altar guild, or any other? Yes.	20	26	29	29
7. Are you active in any Catholic organizations, action groups, or movements other than those in the parish? Yes.	20	6	4	23
8. How important would you say religion is in your life? (Same question was asked about five years ago.) Change in percent saying "very important" from five years ago till now.	+20	+39	+19	+63

198

Appendix

B

CONCRETE SUGGESTIONS TO STIMULATE CREATIVE THINKING
THE REV. ALVIN A. ILLIG, C.S.P.

1. The parish council should establish a Committee on Evangelization and Growth as part of the regular parish structure. This committee would address itself solely to ministering to inactive Catholics and the unchurched, as well as to ecumenical and interreligious matters. The focus of this committee would be on those not active in the parish.

2. Mention the evangelization of the inactive and the unchurched frequently in the prayers of the faithful. Pray that the spirit of inviting everyone to share in the good news of Christ will come alive in the parish and will be reflected in the hearts and in the activities of Catholics. Hold a monthly prayer vigil, or Holy Hour, for inactive Catholics in the parish. Invite parishioners to come and pray for particular persons.

3. For a broad understanding of evangelization, purchase for use in study groups and in adult education programs Pope Paul VI's magnificent statement of evangelization titled *Evangelii Nuntiandi*—"The Gospels Must Be Proclaimed."* $2 per copy.

4. Purchase quantities of the popular summary of *Evangelii Nuntiandi* titled *Evangelization in the Modern World,* for mass distribution and discussion among parishioners. 20 cents per copy plus postage; minimum order 50 copies. For a free sample copy, send a stamped, self-addressed #10 envelope.

5. Consider employing a permanent deacon, a sister, a brother, or a layperson to work full time (much like a director of religious

*All materials mentioned in this appendix are available from the Paulist Catholic Evangelization Center, 3031 Fourth Street, NE, Washington, DC 20017.

education) in evangelizing inactive Catholics and the unchurched. Basically, the task of this person is to (1) compile and maintain a list of all residences in the parish, (2) recruit and train lay volunteers to be part of a team for evangelization and growth, (3) design and send five saturation mailings per year to every residence in the parish, (4) design and conduct special social, educational, and religious programs so guests can sample Catholic life in action, (5) visit personally each home in the parish once a year, (6) help initiate into the Catholic community those inquiring into the Catholic way of life, (7) help new Catholics integrate more smoothly into the parish family. A tested and documented model of a year-long, parish-based, clergy/laity evangelization program is available. Write for the St. Bernadette Year-Long Evangelization Model. $4 per copy plus postage.

6. To help compile a list of every residence in your parish, investigate AMERICALIST, Haines & Company, 8050 Freedom, N.W., North Canton, OH 44720. This company makes available on computer tape a listing of most residences in the United States, according to zip code. Write them for an estimate on the cost of supplying you with a list of all the residences—but not the personal names—for your parish community. Consult your local library for the Haines Criss-Cross Street Directory. The best way to compile your listing of every residence is to ask your parish societies to canvass every street in the parish and to mark down every house and apartment number, street by street.

7. Conduct an annual Visitor's Sunday and regular Open House. Mail invitations to all residences in the parish. Encourage the parishioners to bring their friends to Mass on Visitor's Sunday and then to tour the parish facilities. Conduct an Open House, and invite the community to tour the parish facilities, i.e., the church, the school, the rectory, the convent. Serve light refreshments. The Evangelization Center has prepared a 24-page booklet titled Welcome to Our Open House, to help you conduct an Open House. 20 cents per copy; minimum order 50 copies. For a free sample copy, send a stamped, self-addressed #10 envelope.

8. Ask one of your major parish societies to sponsor an annual Banquet of Friendship for the unchurched and the inactive Catholics. The purpose of this free banquet of friendship is to say, "We are here. We would like to introduce our parish family to you. We hope you will investigate our parish family if you ever feel that a religious family can enrich your life." Send a stamped, self-addressed envelope for a free sample of the letter used to conduct such a program.

9. Prepare a booklet about the parish, the parish staff, the services

200

and societies in the parish, and the people who lead the societies, along with a warm welcome to strangers and newcomers. Instruct the ushers to give these booklets to visitors and also to leave them in the pews. Invite visitors to fill out the cards attached to the booklets and place the cards in the collection basket, or to give the cards to an usher or a staff member. Follow up with a letter of welcome from the pastor and a personal visit from members of the Committee on Evangelization and Growth.

10. Each fall mail the booklet about the parish to every residence in the parish, inviting everyone to participate in services and societies that appeal to them. The covering letter will focus this invitation on the unchurched and on the inactive Catholic.

11. About every three months conduct a social evening in the rectory for newcomers to the parish, so they can meet the leadership of the parish family and be invited to participate in one or more parish activities.

12. Occasionally, distribute forms to those attending Mass, requesting that active Catholics list the names and addresses of inactive Catholics living in the parish. Assign about ten names to each member of the Committee on Evangelization and Growth to visit personally just before Christmas and just before Easter. The purpose of these visits is to invite brother and sister Catholics to "come home for the holidays because we miss you, and we are sorry for what we may have done to alienate you."

13. Each fall send a third-class, nonprofit mailing to all residences in the parish announcing the beginning of a program on the teachings and life of Christ, as proclaimed by the Catholic community. The weekly series is for those interested in investigating the Catholic way of life, for Catholics desiring better knowledge of their faith, and for those curious about the Catholic church.

14. Members of the Committee on Evangelization and Growth can function as coinstructors and helpers for those seeking entrance into the Catholic community of believers. Committee members can accompany inquirers to Mass and to parish functions, follow up when someone has missed an instruction, prepare the meeting room, keep records, help with major presentations and with audiovisual presentations, serve light refreshments.

15. About ten days before Christmas, and about ten days before Easter, send out a mailing to all residences in the parish inviting those with no church family—especially inactive Catholics—to worship with the Catholic family on these holidays.

16. Design posters and signs reading, "Welcome, Neighbor," and display them in the church vestibule, the parish hall, and the

rectory foyer. When newcomers move into the parish let them know they are welcome. Some will come for weddings, funerals, or sometimes just to sit and meditate in our churches. Others come for social and recreational events. Signs tell all who read them—active Catholic and visitor—how happy we are these persons are with us.

17. The admissions department of the local hospital can supply you with a listing of new patients who have indicated they are Catholics or who have no religious preference. Send everyone listed as being Catholic or without religious preference a small bouquet of flowers. Attach a card that indicates the local Catholic parish family is praying for the recovery of the patient, noting, "If I can be of any help to you spiritually, please phone me." Give the rectory phone number, and sign the card with the pastor's name. If you wish not to use flowers, send a get-well card with the same message.

18. Working with the churches and synagogues that encompass your parish, prepare a small booklet, using one page per church in the area to list the name of the church and its address, professional staff, phone, religious services, social services, and lay leadership people. Consider this project an ecumenical welcome wagon program. When newcomers move into the area, two people representing the church community should visit them, welcoming them on behalf of the churches in the area and asking them what their religious heritage is. The visitors present a copy of the booklet to each newcomer, open to the page featuring the church that best corresponds to this person's spiritual heritage. The visitors should offer to contact local priests, ministers, or rabbis so that the appropriate clergy can call on the newcomers personally. If the newcomers have no church community, their names are given to all participating churches.

19. Here is an idea that works well in an inner-city setting or on a college campus, wherever people mill about freely in the streets. Each Saturday afternoon, weather permitting, station your musical group on a different street corner someplace in the parish, and have them practice the music for the Mass which will be celebrated that afternoon or evening. About fifteen minutes before the Mass, invite those who have gathered to come with the musical group as it marches off to church to give honor and glory to God. Done week after week, this effort will draw positive attention to the Catholic community and will give you high visibility among inactive Catholics and the unchurched.

20. Introduce your parishioners to *Share the Word,* a magazine of regular home Bible study and small-group sharing that is based on

the scripture readings of each Sunday. This magazine is designed to help the Catholic laity reach out in friendship to inactive Catholics and the unchurched in their neighborhoods. Individual subscriptions are free. Write for a sample copy of this program. Up to 100 sample bulk copies will be sent free to pastors to help them introduce this program to parish leaders.

21. Write for information on the Film Training Program for Lay Evangelizers. Four thirty-minute sound color films are available to pastors to assist in training parishioners to be evangelizers. These films can be rented in either 16mm film or ¾″ videocassettes. Special materials designed to stimulate discussion accompany the films. This is an excellent way to help pastoral teams introduce parishioners to Catholic evangelization and to show how the laity can effectively evangelize.

22. In an effort to create a friendlier atmosphere, consider husband-and-wife usher teams, stressing that a major function of the usher is to be an official greeter for the pastor and the parish community, especially greeting and welcoming strangers and visitors.

23. Urge your diocese to have an annual Catholic Lay Celebration of Evangelization, modeled on the National Catholic Lay Celebration of Evangelization, featuring local examples of the projects underway to build up the Catholic community. Write for a free brochure on the National Lay Celebration so you can see how you might design your own evangelization celebration.

24. Write for a free copy of the *Goodnewsletter,* published ten times per year for Catholic evangelizers. It will help keep you up to date on Catholic evangelization.

25. A comprehensive Introductory Kit on Evangelization for parish communities, containing many of the materials mentioned above, plus background materials, minority evangelization materials, sample posters, diocesan models, and so on, is available for $15 plus postage.

NOTES

1. For overviews of denominational research on evangelization and church growth, see David O. Moberg, *The Church as a Social Institution* (Englewood Cliffs, NJ: Prentice-Hall, 1962); Donald McGavran, *Understanding Church Growth* (Grand Rapids, MI: Eerdmans, 1970); Ezra Earl Jones, *Strategies for New Churches* (New York: Harper & Row, 1976); and James E. Anderson and Ezra Earl Jones, *The Management of Ministry* (New York: Harper & Row, 1978).

2. *The Unchurched American* (Princeton, NJ: Gallup, 1978).

3. We would like to thank the Rev. David Bava, the Rev. Frank Benham, the Rev. Andrew Cassin, Msgr. David Foley, the Rev. Ron Jameson, the Rev. Patrick McCaffrey, the Rev. John Scanlon, and the Rev. George Stallings for their help.

4. Two other definitional points must be noted. First, the word convert is used here in the institutional sense, as in "How many converts did the parish have?" It carries no meaning about inner change in the person. To denote a person experiencing inner changes, we use the term inner convert. Of course, not all converts are inner converts and vice versa. Converts who show no evidence of inner change or of spiritual effect of becoming Catholics we call switchers, since in effect they "switched brands."

   Second, adult converts who have been baptized in a Christian denomination recognized by the Catholic Church are not rebaptized when entering the Catholic Church, but are merely confirmed. It is cumbersome to say "baptized or confirmed" each time, so we simply use the word baptized.

The minimum age for inclusion in the study was 18 at the time of interviewing.

5. See *The Unchurched American,* op. cit., which describes churched and unchurched Americans using the same definitions employed in the present study. The Gallup survey looked at both active and inactive persons, while the present study looks at individuals who *moved* from one category to another within the past three years. Our definition of active is similar to Fichter's definition of distinguishing "nuclear" and "modal" from "marginal" and "dormant" Catholics (1954). In Fichter's study of parishes in Louisiana, marginal and dormant Catholics were those persons who had not attended Mass or made their Easter duties (Eucharist and confession) in the past year. By this measure 51% of Catholics living in the parish territories were marginal or dormant. By our definition of inactive (not persons who changed, but all inactive people) the percentage inactive would be about the same.

6. We would like to thank the Rev. Desmond Murphy, of Holy Family parish, and the Rev. Noel O'Callaghan, of Mount Calvary parish, for their help.

7. We would like to thank the Rev. Frank Ponce, of the United States Catholic Conference, and Bishop Raymond Peña, then of the Archdiocese of San Antonio, for their help. Cecilio Morales reflected on some characteristics of Hispanic religion in Texas in an article in *America* ("Hispanic Home Religion," April 19, 1980, pp. 344-45).

8. More detailed life stories of some of these persons have been published separately by the Committee on Evangelization. For more information write to the National Conference of Catholic Bishops, Committee on Evangelization, 3031 Fourth Street, NE, Washington, DC 20017.

9. See Joseph H. Fichter, *Social Relations in the Urban Parish* (Chicago: University of Chicago Press, 1954), for a summary of his classic southern parish studies.

10. Ibid., pp. 76ff.

11. Ruth A. Wallace, "A Model of Change of Religion Affiliation," *Journal for the Scientific Study of Religion,* 14:345-55 (1975).

12. Reginald W. Bibby and Merlin B. Brinkerhoff, "The Circulation of the Saints: A Study of People Who Join Conservative Churches," *Journal for the Scientific Study of Religion,* 12:273-83 (1973); also see Reginald W. Bibby and Merlin B. Brinkerhoff, "Sources of Religious Involvement: Issues for Future Empirical Investigation," *Review of Religious Research,* 15:71-79 (1974).

13. Edward A. Rauff, *Why People Join the Church* (Washington, DC: Glenmary; New York: The Pilgrim Press, 1979). Many Protestant studies of new members in churches have been done, typically by interviewing people who joined certain churches or types of churches. They are only partly relevant to Catholics, since Protestant churches in any community are in competition with one another, and most Protestants readily switch denominations if they like a local church of a different denomination. For summaries of this research, see Lyle E. Schaller, *Assimilating New Members* (Nashville: Abingdon Press, 1978), and "Evaluating the Potential for Growth," *Christian Ministry*, 10:55-58 (1979); and C. Peter Wagner, *Your Church Can Grow* (Glendale, CA: G/L Regal, 1976). Personal relationships have been found to be foremost in these studies, as stated by Schaller in the following table (from "Evaluating the Potential for Growth," op. cit.; used by permission):

Where Do New Members Come From?

Walk in on own initiative	3% to 8%
Come because of program	4% to 10%
Pastor	10% to 20%
Response to visitation-evangelism	10% to 25%
Sunday church school	3% to 6%
Brought by friend or relative	60% to 90%

14. John N. Kotre, *The View from the Border* (Chicago: Aldine Atherton, 1971).

15. Many other studies of college students have been done, but none so directly relevant as the Kotre study. See Robert Wuthnow and Charles Y. Glock, "Religious Loyalty, Defection, and Experimentation Among College Youth," *Journal for the Scientific Study of Religion*, 12:157-80 (1973); Robert Wuthnow, *Experimentation in American Religion* (Berkeley, CA: University of California Press, 1978); David Caplovitz and Fred Sherrow, *The Religious Drop-outs: Apostasy Among College Graduates* (Beverly Hills, CA: Sage Publications, 1977); and Philip K. Hastings and Dean R. Hoge, "Changes in Religion Among College Students, 1948 to 1974," *Journal for the Scientific Study of Religion*, 15:237-49 (1976), for examples and reviews of research. On church dropouts during the high-school years, see Robert J. Havighurst and Barry Keating, "The Religion of Youth," in M.P. Strommen, ed., *Research in Religious Development* (New York: Hawthorn, 1971), pp. 686-723; and Dean R. Hoge and Gregory H. Petrillo, "Determinants of Church Participation and Attitudes Among High School Youth," *Journal for the Scientific Study of Religion*, 17:359-79 (1978).

16. David A. Roozen, "Church Dropouts: Changing Patterns of Disengagement and Re-entry," *Review of Religious Research,* 21:427-50 (1980).

17. J. Russell Hale, *Who Are the Unchurched? An Exploratory Study* (Washington, DC: Glenmary, 1977), p. 89.

18. John S. Savage, *The Apathetic and Bored Church Member* (Pittsford, NY: LEAD Consultants, 1976), p. 58.

19. Warren J. Hartman, *Membership Trends* (Nashville: Discipleship Resources, United Methodist Church, 1976), p. 42.

20. John Lofland and Rodney Stark, "Becoming a World-saver: A Theory of Conversion to a Deviant Perspective," *American Sociological Review,* 30:862-75 (1965).

21. John Lofland, "Becoming a World-saver Revisited," *American Behavioral Scientist,* 20:805-18 (1977), p. 815. For a critique of parts of the model, see James T. Richardson, Mary W. Stewart, and Robert B. Simmonds, *Organized Miracles* (New Brunswick, NJ: Transaction Books, 1979), chap. 9.

22. Luther P. Gerlach and Virginia H. Hine, *People, Power, Change: Movements of Social Transformation* (Indianapolis: Bobbs-Merrill, 1970). For extensions of the model, see Bibby and Brinkerhoff, "Sources of Religious Involvement," op. cit., and Max Heirich, "Change of Heart: A Test of Some Widely Held Theories About Religious Conversion," *American Journal of Sociology,* 83:653-80 (1977). James A. Beckford, "Organization, Ideology and Recruitment: The Structure of the Watch Tower Movement," *Sociological Review,* 23:893-909 (1975), found it to fit the Jehovah's Witnesses despite their practice of laborious house-to-house calling.

23. This conclusion conflicts with some current ideas about mass evangelism. Researchers have not found evidence that mass evangelism crusades, such as those conducted by Billy Graham, in themselves contribute much to church growth. Most persons attending Billy Graham rallies are already church members, and an estimated 75% attend church regularly. About 55% of the persons going forward to make a decision for Christ in a Graham crusade are doing it for the second or third time in their lives; for them, it represents a rededication of their lives to Christ. Only a few percent of the persons making decisions at a rally represent previously unchurched people who subsequently become active in church life for any length of time (see Kurt Lang and Gladys Engel Lang, "Decisions for Christ: Billy Graham in New York City," in Maurice R. Stein, ed., *Identity and Anxiety* [Glencoe, IL: Free Press, 1960], pp. 415-27; Frederick L. Whitam, "Adolescence and Mass Persuasion: A Study of Teen-Age Decision-making at a Billy Graham Crusade," unpublished Ph.D. dissertation, Indiana

University, pp. 36ff; and Weldon T. Johnson, "The Religious Crusade: Revival or Ritual?" *American Journal of Sociology*, 76:873-90 [1971]). The weakness of mass evangelism in aiding church growth is increasingly recognized by revivalists, so that, for example, Leighton Ford now insists on coordinating any crusade with a simultaneous calling or canvassing program by church members in the city.

24. Rodney Stark and William Sims Bainbridge, "Networks of Faith: Interpersonal Bonds and Recruitment to Cults and Sects," *American Journal of Sociology*, 85:1376-95 (1980). See also Michael I. Harrison, "Sources of Recruitment to Catholic Pentecostalism," *Journal for the Scientific Study of Religion*, 13:49-64 (1974), and Heirich, "Change of Heart," op. cit.

25. David A. Snow, Louis A. Zurcher, Jr., and Sheldon Ekland-Olson, "Social Networks and Social Movements: A Microstructural Approach to Differential Recruitment," *American Sociological Review*, 45:787-801 (1980).

26. The Mormon manual is cited in Stark and Bainbridge, "Networks of Faith," op. cit., pp. 1386-89.

27. For examples of this type of theory see Neil J. Smelser, *Theory of Collective Behavior* (Glencoe, IL: Free Press, 1963), and Hans Toch, *The Social Psychology of Social Movements* (Indianapolis: Bobbs-Merrill, 1965).

28. Snow, et al., "Social Networks and Social Movements," op. cit.

29. Daniel J. Levinson, *The Seasons of a Man's Life* (New York: Ballantine Books, 1978). Two other important works in this tradition are George E. Vaillant, *Adaptation to Life* (Boston: Little, Brown, 1977), and Roger L. Gould, *Transformations: Growth and Change in Adult Life* (New York: Simon & Schuster, 1978).

30. Levinson, *The Seasons of a Man's Life*, op. cit., p. 44.

31. The telephone interviews included an open-ended question asking what should be the direction of the Catholic Church in the years ahead and what the church should stress, and the taped interviews included a series of questions about what makes a good parish and what the person would do if he or she were a bishop today. These questions elicited some views about parishes. Also, in a separate research effort, liaison persons from twenty dioceses to the Office of Evangelization wrote up case studies of successfully evangelizing parishes, which we were able to review. The case studies were done partly for the United States Catholic Conference, Office of Parish Renewal, directed by the Rev. Philip Murnion. We would like to thank the twenty persons who did the case studies and Father Murnion for their cooperation and help.

32. The Committee on Evangelization in 1980 began publishing two

series of booklets describing parishes that are exemplary in evangelization. One contains portraits of Hispanic parishes and the other has portraits of other Catholic parishes. For more information write to the National Conference of Catholic Bishops, Committee on Evangelization, 3031 Fourth Street, NE, Washington, DC 20017.

33. John Cogley, *Catholic America* (Garden City, NY: Doubleday, 1974), p. 95.
34. Andrew M. Greeley, William C. McCready, and Kathleen McCourt, *Catholic Schools in a Declining Church* (Kansas City: Sheed & Ward, 1976), p. 10.
35. James Hennesey, S.J., "American Catholicism," unpublished manuscript, p. 397.
36. Ibid., p. 485.
37. See David J. O'Brien, *The Renewal of American Catholicism* (New York: Oxford University Press, 1972), and David Bohr, *Evangelization in America* (New York: Paulist Press, 1977), p. 234.
38. Thomas F. O'Dea, *American Catholic Dilemma* (New York: Mentor Omega, 1962).
39. Avery Dulles, *The Resilient Church* (Garden City, NY: Doubleday, 1977), pp. 109ff.
40. Greeley, McCready, and McCourt, *Catholic Schools in a Declining Church*, op. cit., p. 152. Greeley's argument has been widely discussed. In our view it is overstated, since even without *Humanae Vitae*, church authority was destined to weaken gradually as a result of assimilation to prevailing American values, which for two centuries have included rather weak church authority.
41. Ibid., p. 56.
42. Recent sociological studies have documented the convergence between American Catholic and Protestant life-styles. On convergence of views on church authority, see Douglas B. Koller, "Belief in the Right to Question Church Teachings, 1958-71," *Social Forces*, 58:290-304 (1979). On convergence on birth control, fertility, and attitudes toward abortion, see Charles F. Westoff, "The blending of Catholic reproductive behavior," in Robert Wuthnow, ed., *The Religious Dimension: New Directions in Quantitative Research* (New York: Academic Press, 1979), pp. 231-40.
43. Harold J. Abramson, *Ethnic Diversity in Catholic America* (New York: John Wiley & Sons, 1973); Greeley, McCready, and McCourt, *Catholic Schools in a Declining Church*, op. cit., chap. 3; Mario Vizcaino, "The Hispanic Americans: A Prophetic Church," *New Catholic World*, July/August 1980, pp. 175-76; U.S. Census Bureau, "Persons of Spanish Origin in the United States: March, 1977," *Current Population Reports*, Series P-20, No. 329, September 1978.

44. See Andrew M. Greeley, "Ethnic Variations in Religious Commitment," in Robert Wuthnow, ed., *The Religious Dimension: New Directions in Quantitative Research* (New York: Academic Press, 1979) for an analysis of ethnic differences in Catholic religiosity, based on nationwide surveys. Briefly, he found that both German and French Catholics have the highest levels of church attendance, and Italian and Hispanic Catholics the lowest. Slavic and Irish Catholics have the firmest religious convictions, and Italian and Hispanic Catholics the weakest.

45. Andrew M. Greeley, et al., "A Profile of the American Catholic Family," *America*, September 27, 1980, pp. 155-60.

46. Andrew M. Greeley, "Church Authority: Beyond the Problem," *National Catholic Reporter*, September 26, 1980, pp. 7-9.

47. *U.S. Catholics and the Catholic Press* (Princeton, NJ: Gallup, 1978).

48. Thomas P. Sweetser, *The Catholic Parish: Shifting Membership in a Changing Church* (Chicago: Center for the Scientific Study of Religion, 1974), p. 80; Greeley, McCready, and McCourt, *Catholic Schools in a Declining Church*, op. cit., p. 32; George Gallup, Jr. and David Poling, *The Search for America's Faith* (Nashville: Abingdon Press, 1980), p. 62.

49. See Joseph H. Fichter, *The Catholic Cult of the Paraclete* (New York: Sheed & Ward, 1975); Kilian McDonnell, *Charismatic Renewal and the Churches* (New York: Seabury Press, 1976); Kenneth H. McGuire, "People, Prayer, and Promise: An Anthropological Analysis of a Catholic Charismatic Covenant Community," Ph.D. dissertation, Department of Anthropology, Ohio State University.

50. See Virginia H. McDowell, *Re-Creating: The Experiences of Life-Change and Religion* (Boston: Beacon Press, 1978).

Chapter 2. Who Are the Converts?

1. On sex ratios in church attendance, see Michael Argyle and Benjamin Beit-Hallahmi, *The Social Psychology of Religion* (London: Routledge & Kegan Paul, 1975). In a 1978 Gallup survey, the ratio of females to males who attended church at least twice monthly, in all denominations, was 1.56 to 1.

2. W. Charles Arn, in an article "Receptivity-Rating Scale," *Church Growth: America*, Summer 1978, p. 3, states: "Unchurched people are most responsive to a change in life-style (i.e., becoming Christians and responsible church members) during *periods of transition*. A period of transition is a span of time in which an individual's or family's normal everyday behavior patterns are disrupted by some irregular event that requires an unfamiliar response." Arn proposed use of the Holmes-Rahe Social

Readjustment Rating Scale, an interesting list of forty-one events rated as to their typical stressfulness for Americans. (See Thomas H. Holmes and R.H. Rahe, "The Social Readjustment Rating Scale," *Journal of Psychosomatric Research*, 11:213-8 [1967]). The most stressful experiences and their ratings are (1) death of spouse, 100; (2) divorce, 73; (3) marital separation, 65; (4) jail term, 63: (5) death of close family member, 63; (6) personal injury or illness, 53; (7) marriage, 50; (8) fired at work, 47; (9) marital reconciliation, 45; (10) retirement, 45. We had hoped to include a shortened Holmes-Rahe scale in our interview, but time limitations prevented it.

A study by Michael J. Coyner, "Why People Join: Research into the Events and Motivations Which Lead Persons to Join Local Churches in the North Indiana Conference of the United Methodist Church," unpublished D.Min. dissertation, Drew Theological School, included interviews with twenty new members of United Methodist churches in Indiana. Coyner looked at facilitating events (he calls them "precipitant events") in some detail and scored them on the Holmes-Rahe scale. All twenty new members had discernible precipitant events, and the mean Holmes-Rahe scores were 88.6 for males and 72.3 for females. These persons waited an average of 6.7 weeks between the main precipitant events and first attending church, and they waited another 24.7 weeks before joining the churches formally. All twenty had attended other churches earlier in life, and none mentioned television programs, radio evangelism, crusades, or other highly publicized events as important in their decision to become active United Methodists.

3. Murray H. Leiffer, *The Effective City Church* (Nashville: Abingdon Press, 1961), and Ezra Earl Jones, *Strategies for New Churches* (New York: Harper & Row, 1976).

Chapter 3. Three Types of Converts

1. The two main combinations of predispositions were (1) feeling concern for marriage to a Catholic plus feeling a spiritual need, and (2) feeling concern for children plus feeling a spiritual need. The sample has eighteen cases of the first and thirty-two cases of the second. The other combinations are much smaller in number. See the technical supplement for details and for the method of making the typology. In cases of multiple predispositions we assigned the case to the intermarriage convert or family life convert type if the first or second predisposition in Table 2.1 was present.

2. To clarify, we may note that more than 11% actually expressed dissatisfaction with their former church during the interviews, but in our global coding we included it only if the dissatisfaction was clearly present in the few years preceding the conversion. Some interviewees answered yes to the question about dissatisfaction with their former churches and said that it was important, even if they also told us that they had dropped out many years before converting to the Catholic Church. In such cases we did not include this predisposition in our global code.

Chapter 4. Interfaith Marriage in America

1. Andrew M. Greeley, *Crisis in the Church* (Chicago: Thomas More Press, 1979), p. 150. Disidentification with Catholicism—that is, saying that one's religious preference is no longer Catholicism—is different from stopping Mass attendance and is done less frequently. Our own research was on persons stopping Mass attendance.

2. Larry Bumpass, "The Trend of Interfaith Marriage in the United States," *Social Biology*, 17:253-59 (1970); Samuel A. Mueller, "The New Triple Melting Pot: Herberg Revisited," *Review of Religious Research*, 13:18-33 (1971); and Greeley, *Crisis in the Church*, op. cit.

3. Bumpass, "The Trend of Interfaith Marriage," op. cit., p. 255.

4. The data on various dioceses in 1950 are from John L. Thomas, "The Factor of Religion in the Selection of Marriage Mates," *American Sociological Review*, 16:487-91 (1951).

5. Bumpass, "The Trend of Interfaith Marriage," op. cit., and Andrew M. Greeley, William C. McCready, and Kathleen McCourt, *Catholic Schools in a Declining Church* (Kansas City: Sheed & Ward, 1976) depict the change.

6. Albert Gordon, *Intermarriage: Interfaith, Interracial, Interethnic* (Boston: Beacon Press, 1964), p. 52.

7. Leo Rosten, "Intermarriage—Statistics, Opinions, and Conversion Data: Catholics, Protestants and Jews," in *Religions of America: Ferment and Faith in an Age of Crisis* (New York: Simon & Schuster, 1975), pp. 549-62; "The 70's: Decade of Second Thoughts, *Public Opinion Magazine*, December/January 1980, pp. 19-42.

8. John E. Lynch, "Mixed Marriages in the Aftermath of *Matrimonia mixta*," *Journal of Ecumenical Studies*, 11:637-58 (1974), p. 640.

9. John Alston, William McIntosh, and Louise Wright, "Extent of Interfaith Marriages Among ·White Americans," *Sociological Analysis*, 37:261-64 (1976), and Thomas Monahan, "The Extent of Interdenominational Marriage in the United States," *Journal for the Scientific Study of Religion*, 10:85-92, (1971) p. 89.

10. R.C. Bealer, K.F. Willits, and G.W. Benger, "Religious Exogamy: A Study of Social Distance," *Sociology and Social Research,* 48:69-79 (1963).

11. Jerald Heiss, "Premarital Characteristics of the Religiously Intermarried in an Urban Area," *American Sociological Review,* 25:47-55 (1960); William F. Kenkel, Joyce Hemler, and Leonard Cole, "Religious Socialization, Present Devoutness and Willingness to Enter a Mixed Religion Marriage," *Sociological Analysis,* 26:30-37 (1965).

12. Thomas, "The Factor of Religion," op. cit.; Paul H. Besanceney, "Unbroken Protestant-Catholic Marriages in the Detroit Area," *American Catholic Sociological Review,* 23:3-20 (1962); Alfred J. Prince, "A Study of 194 Cross-religion Marriages," *Family Life Coordinator,* 11:3-7 (1962).

13. Heiss, "Premarital Characteristics," op. cit.; Eric Rosenthal, "Divorce and Religious Intermarriage: The Effect of Previous Marital Status upon Subsequent Marital Behavior," *Journal of Marriage and the Family,* 32:435-40 (1970); Thomas Monahan, "Some Dimensions of Interreligious Marriages in Indiana, 1962-1967," *Social Forces,* 52:195-203 (1973); Greeley, *Crisis in the Church,* op. cit.

14. Lee Burchinal and Loren E. Chancellor, "Ages at Marriage, Occupation of Grooms and Interreligious Marriage Rates," *Social Forces,* 40:348-54 (1962), p. 349.

15. Ibid.; Kenkel, Hemler, and Cole, "Religious Socialization," op. cit.

16. Paul H. Besanceney, "Interfaith Marriages of Catholics in the Detroit Area," *Sociological Analysis,* 26:38-44 (1965); Kenkel, Hemler, and Cole, "Religious Socialization," op. cit., p. 37.

17. LaVell E. Saunders, "The Gradient of Ecumenism and Opposition to Religious Intermarriage, *Review of Religious Research,* 17:107-19 (1976).

18. Heiss, "Premarital Characteristics," op. cit., p. 53; Greeley, *Crisis in the Church,* op. cit., p. 132; see also John Wilson, *Religion in American Society* (Englewood Cliffs, NJ: Prentice-Hall, 1978), p. 249.

19. J. Milton Yinger, "A Research Note on Interfaith Marriage," *Journal for the Scientific Study of Religion,* 7:97-103 (1968), p. 100.

20. Greeley, *Crisis in the Church,* op. cit., p. 127.

21. W. Seward Salisbury, "Religious Identification, Mixed Marriage and Conversion," *Journal for the Scientific Study of Religion,* 8:125-29 (1969); see also Harry Crockett, "Change in Religious Affiliation and Family Stability: A Second Study," *Journal of Marriage and the Family,* 31:464-68 (1969).

22. Alston, McIntosh, and Wright, "Extent of Interfaith Marriages Among White Americans," op. cit., p. 263.
23. Ibid., p. 264.
24. Jerald Heiss, "Interfaith Marriage and Social Participation," *Journal of Religion and Health,* 5:324-33 (1961).
25. Judson T. Landis, "Marriages of Mixed and Non-mixed Religious Faith," *American Sociological Review,* 14:401-6 (1949); Alfred J. Prince, A Study of 194 Cross-religion Marriages," *Family Life Coordinator,* 11:3-7 (1962); Robert L. Blood, Jr. and Donald M. Wolfe, *Husbands and Wives: The Dynamics of Married Living* (New York: The Free Press, 1960); and Rosten, "Intermarriage," op. cit., p. 561.
26. Larry Bumpass and James Sweet, "Differentials in Marital Instability: 1970," *American Sociological Review,* 37:754-66 (1972), p. 764.
27. Lee Burchinal and Loren E. Chancellor, "Survival Rates Among Religiously Homogamous and Interreligious Marriages," *Social Forces,* 41:353-62 (1963); see also Wilson, *Religion in American Society,* op. cit., p. 261.

Chapter 5. Who Are the Dropouts?

1. Another issue arose during the research, regarding older disabled persons. Some elderly persons stop Mass attendance when they find it too hard to get out or are obligated to stay at home to care for disabled spouses or relatives. These persons technically fit the dropout category, since they have stopped Mass attendance in the past three years. When we began the study we decided to include these persons if we found them during the random canvassing, partly because the 1978 Gallup survey had done so. But we encountered two difficulties. First, many did not see themselves as dropouts merely because they could not get to the church, and in some cases they told us they received Communion from the priests or deacons in their homes, or they watched Mass on television. It is indeed a question whether they should be seen as dropouts like others. The second difficulty was that most refused to be interviewed. Usually they saw no point to it, since the reason for their nonattendance was obvious. We succeeded in interviewing only three such dropouts until we changed our minds and stopped trying. As a result we have only three disabled older persons in our dropout sample, and before we divided the dropouts into types we deleted these three from the data. Hence our analysis provides no information on such persons.

2. David A. Roozen, "Church Dropouts: Changing Patterns of Disengagement and Re-entry," *Review of Religious Research,* 21:427-50 (1980).

3. See Dean R. Hoge and Gregory H. Petrillo, "Determinants of Church Participation and Attitudes Among High School Youth," *Journal for the Scientific Study of Religion,* 17:359-79 (1978).

4. John H. Westerhoff III, *Will Our Children Have Faith?* (New York: Seabury Press, 1976), chap. 4; see also Jim Fowler and Sam Keen, *Life Maps: Conversations on the Journey of Faith* (Waco, TX: Word Books, 1978).

5. See Appendix A, Table A.3, for the attitudes of all three groups in our study.

Chapter 7. Who Are the Returnees?

1. David A. Roozen, "Church Dropouts: Changing Patterns of Disengagement and Re-entry," *Review of Religious Research,* 21:427-50 (1980).

Chapter 9. Concluding Thoughts on Religious Change

1. Related to this point is a criticism made of our study by some persons, most often those in the charismatic movement or in a similar religious group. They said we were missing the boat by researching church involvement, since true religious life has to do with a personal relationship with Jesus Christ; church involvement is at best optional and at worst a serious obstacle. Ron, whom we described in chapter 6, made this argument forcefully. We can understand the argument, but it is sociologically wrong. The argument is aimed at established churches but not at the charismatic meetings, and nobody argued that the charismatic meetings were optional for the Christian life. That is, *some* churchlike involvement is intrinsic to Christian living, in our view, whether it be in established parishes or in prayer groups. This is a sociological truth: Apart from supportive groups no religious commitment persists long. To study group behavior, in the church or in informal groups, is not at all to miss the boat in analyzing religiousness.

2. For an analysis of life-style as a factor in church attendance, see Wade Clark Roof and Dean R. Hoge, "Church Involvement in America: Social Factors Affecting Membership and Participation," *Review of Religious Research,* 21:405-26 (1980).

3. An intriguing sidelight in our interviews with youth was a recurring image of California as a land of religious hope for the

alienated or constrained. Several persons in the 18-to-24 age range disaffected with the institutional church had toured California on a spiritual quest or had fervently wanted to get there to experience the new religious scene.

4. William Ashdown, *Motivation and Response in Religion: A Report on Religious Motivation, Attitudes, and Response* (Glendale, OH: Glenmary Home Missioners, 1962), p. 55.

Chapter 10. Evangelization in the 1980s

1. For a copy of the full document, send $2 to the Paulist Catholic Evangelization Center, 3031 Fourth Street, N.E., Washington, DC 20017. A popular summary, 14 pages in length, may be useful for mass distribution or for discussion groups. Free sample copy sent on request. Price per copy is 20 cents plus postage with minimum orders of fifty copies.

BIBLIOGRAPHY

ABRAMSON, HAROLD J.
  1973 *Ethnic Diversity in Catholic America.* New York: John Wiley & Sons.
ALSTON, JOHN, WILLIAM MCINTOSH, and LOUISE WRIGHT
  1976 "Extent of interfaith marriages among white Americans." *Sociological Analysis* 37:261-64.
ANDERSON, JAMES D., and EZRA EARL JONES
  1978 *The Management of Ministry.* New York: Harper & Row.
ARGYLE, MICHAEL and BENJAMIN BEIT-HALLAHMI
  1975 *The Social Psychology of Religion.* London: Routledge & Kegan Paul.
ASHDOWN, WILLIAM
  1962 *Motivation and Response in Religion: A Report on Religious Motivation, Attitudes, and Response.* Glendale, OH: Glenmary Home Missioners.
BEALER, R.C., K.F. WILLITS, and G.W. BENGER
  1963 "Religious exogamy: a study of social distance." *Sociology and Social Research* 48:69-79.
BECKFORD, JAMES A.
  1975 "Organization, ideology and recruitment: the structure of the Watch Tower Movement." *Sociological Review* 23:893-909.
BESANCENEY, PAUL H.
  1962 "Unbroken Protestant-Catholic marriages in the Detroit area." *American Catholic Sociological Review* 23:3-20.
  1965 "Interfaith marriages of Catholics in the Detroit area." *Sociological Analysis* 26:38-44.

BIBBY, REGINALD W. and MERLIN B. BRINKERHOFF
  1973   "The circulation of the saints: a study of people who join conservative churches." *Journal for the Scientific Study of Religion* 12:273-83.
  1974   "Sources of religious involvement: issues for future empirical investigation." *Review of Religious Research* 15:71-79.
BLANSHARD, PAUL
  1949   *American Freedom and Catholic Power.* Boston: Beacon Press.
BLOOD, ROBERT O., JR. and DONALD M. WOLFE
  1960   *Husbands and Wives: The Dynamics of Married Living.* New York: The Free Press.
BOHR, DAVID
  1977   *Evangelization in America.* New York: Paulist Press.
BUMPASS, LARRY
  1970   "The trend of interfaith marriage in the United States." *Social Biology* 17:253-59.
BUMPASS, LARRY and JAMES SWEET
  1972   "Differentials in marital instability: 1970." *American Sociological Review* 37:754-66.
BURCHINAL, LEE and LOREN E. CHANCELLOR
  1962   "Ages at marriage, occupation of grooms and interreligious marriage rates." *Social Forces* 40:348-54.
  1963   "Survival rates among religiously homogamous and interreligious marriages." *Social Forces* 41:353-62.
CAPLOVITZ, DAVID and FRED SHERROW
  1977   *The Religious Drop-Outs: Apostasy Among College Graduates.* Beverly Hills: Sage Publications.
COGLEY, JOHN
  1974   *Catholic America.* Garden City, NY: Doubleday.
COYNER, MICHAEL J.
  1980   "Why people join: research into the events and motivations which lead persons to join local churches in the North Indiana Conference of the United Methodist Church." Unpublished D.Min. dissertation, Drew Theological School.
CROCKETT, HARRY
  1969   "Change in religious affiliation and family stability: a second study." *Journal of Marriage and the Family* 31:464-68.
DULLES, AVERY
  1977   *The Resilient Church.* Garden City, NY: Doubleday.
ELLIS, JOHN TRACY
  1969   *American Catholicism.* Chicago: University of Chicago Press.
FICHTER, JOSEPH H.
  1954   *Social Relations in the Urban Parish.* Chicago: University of Chicago Press.

1975 *The Catholic Cult of the Paraclete.* New York: Sheed & Ward.

FOWLER, JIM, and SAM KEEN
1978 *Life Maps: Conversations on the Journey of Faith.* Waco. TX: Word Books.

GALLUP, GEORGE, JR. and DAVID POLING
1980 *The Search for America's Faith.* Nashville: Abingdon Press.

GALLUP ORGANIZATION
1978a *The Unchurched American.* Princeton, NJ: Gallup.

1978b *U.S. Catholics and the Catholic Press.* Princeton, NJ: Gallup.

GERLACH, LUTHER P. and VIRGINIA H. HINE
1970 *People, Power, Change: Movements of Social Transformation.* Indianapolis: Bobbs-Merrill.

GORDON, ALBERT
1964 *Intermarriage: Interfaith, Interracial, Interethnic.* Boston: Beacon Press.

GOULD, ROGER L.
1978 *Transformations: Growth and Change in Adult Life.* New York: Simon & Schuster.

GREELEY, ANDREW M.
1977 *The American Catholic: A Social Portrait.* New York: Basic Books.

1979a *Crisis in the Church.* Chicago: Thomas More Press.

1979b "Ethnic variations in religious commitment," in R. Wuthnow, ed., *The Religious Dimension: New Directions in Quantitative Research.* New York: Academic Press, pp. 113-34.

1980 "Church authority: beyond the problem." *National Catholic Reporter* 16:42 (September 26):7-9.

GREELEY, ANDREW M., WILLIAM C. MCCREADY, and KATHLEEN MCCOURT
1976 *Catholic Schools in a Declining Church.* Kansas City: Sheed & Ward.

GREELEY, ANDREW M., WILLIAM MCCREADY, TERESA SULLIVAN, and JOAN FEE
1980 "A profile of the American Catholic family." *America* 43:8 (September 27):155-60.

HALE, J. RUSSELL
1977 *Who Are the Unchurched? An Exploratory Study.* Washington, DC: Glenmary.

HARRISON, MICHAEL I.
1974 "Sources of recruitment to Catholic Pentecostalism." *Journal for the Scientific Study of Religion* 13:49-64.

HARTMAN, WARREN J.
1976 *Membership Trends.* Nashville: Discipleship Resources, United Methodist Church.

HASTINGS, PHILIP K. and DEAN R. HOGE
1976 "Changes in religion among college students, 1948 to 1974."

Journal for the Scientific Study of Religion 15:237-49.

HAVIGHURST, ROBERT J. and BARRY KEATING
1971 "The religion of youth," in M.P. Strommen, ed., *Research in Religious Development*. New York: Hawthorn, pp. 686-723.

HEIRICH, MAX
1977 "Change of heart: a test of some widely held theories about religious conversion." *American Journal of Sociology* 83:653-80.

HEISS, JERALD
1960 "Premarital characteristics of the religiously intermarried in an urban area." *American Sociological Review* 25:47-55.
1961 "Interfaith marriage and social participation." *Journal of Religion and Health* 5:324-33.

HENNESEY, JAMES, S.J.
1980 "American Catholicism." Unpublished manuscript.

HOGE, DEAN R. and GREGORY H. PETRILLO
1978 "Determinants of church participation and attitudes among high school youth." *Journal for the Scientific Study of Religion* 17:359-79.

HOLMES, THOMAS H. and R.H. RAHE
1967 "The social readjustment rating scale." *Journal of Psychosomatric Research* 11:213-18.

JOHNSON, WELDON T.
1971 "The religious crusade: revival or ritual?" *American Journal of Sociology* 76:873-90.

JONES, EZRA EARL
1976 *Strategies for New Churches*. New York: Harper & Row.

KENKEL, WILLIAM F., JOYCE HEMLER, and LEONARD COLE
1965 "Religious socialization, present devoutness and willingness to enter a mixed religion marriage." *Sociological Analysis* 26:30-37.

KOLLER, DOUGLAS B.
1979 "Belief in the right to question church teachings, 1958-71." *Social Forces* 58:290-304.

KOTRE, JOHN N.
1971 *The View from the Border*. Chicago: Aldine Atherton.

LANDIS, JUDSON T.
1949 "Marriages of mixed and non mixed religious faith." *American Sociological Review* 14:401-6.

LANG, KURT and GLADYS ENGEL LANG
1960 "Decisions for Christ: Billy Graham in New York City," in Maurice R. Stein, ed., *Identity and Anxiety*. Glencoe, IL: Free Press, pp. 415-27.

LEIFFER, MURRAY H.
1961 *The Effective City Church*. Nashville: Abingdon Press.

LEVINSON, DANIEL J.
   1978   *The Seasons of a Man's Life.* New York: Ballantine Books.
LOFLAND, JOHN
   1977   "Becoming a world-saver revisited." *American Behavioral Scientist* 20:805-18.
LOFLAND, JOHN and RODNEY STARK
   1965   "Becoming a world-saver: a theory of conversion to a deviant perspective." *American Sociological Review* 30:862-75.
LYNCH, JOHN E.
   1974   "Mixed marriages in the aftermath of *Matrimonia mixta.*" *Journal of Ecumenical Studies* 11:637-58.
MCDONNELL, KILIAN
   1976   *Charismatic Renewal and the Churches.* New York: Seabury Press.
MCDOWELL, VIRGINIA H.
   1978   *Re–Creating: The Experience of Life-Change and Religion.* Boston: Beacon Press.
MCGAVRAN, DONALD
   1970   *Understanding Church Growth.* Grand Rapids: Eerdmans.
MCGUIRE, KENNETH H.
   1976   "People, prayer and promise: an anthropological analysis of a Catholic charismatic covenant community." Ph.D. dissertation, Department of Anthropology, Ohio State University.
MOBERG, DAVID O.
   1962   *The Church as a Social Institution.* Englewood Cliffs, NJ: Prentice-Hall.
MONAHAN, THOMAS
   1971   "The extent of interdenominational marriage in the United States." *Journal for the Scientific Study of Religion* 10:85-92.
   1973   "Some dimensions of interreligious marriages in Indiana, 1962-1967." *Social Forces* 52:195-203.
MORALES, CECILIO, JR.
   1980   "Hispanic home religion." *America,* April 19, 344-45.
MUELLER, SAMUEL A.
   1971   "The new triple melting pot: Herberg revisited." *Review of Religious Research* 13:18-33.
O'BRIEN, DAVID J.
   1972   *The Renewal of American Catholicism.* New York: Oxford University Press.
O'DEA, THOMAS F.
   1962   *American Catholic Dilemma.* New York: Mentor Omega.
PRINCE, ALFRED J.
   1962   "A study of 194 cross-religion marriages." *Family Life Coordinator* 11:3-7.

PUBLIC OPINION MAGAZINE
1980 "The 70's: decade of second thoughts." December-January, 19-42.

RAUFF, EDWARD A.
1979 *Why People Join the Church*. Washington, DC: Glenmary; New York: The Pilgrim Press.

RICHARDSON, JAMES T., MARY W. STEWART, and ROBERT B. SIMMONDS
1979 *Organized Miracles*. New Brunswick, NJ: Transaction Books.

ROOF, WADE CLARK, and DEAN R. HOGE
1980 "Church involvement in America: social factors affecting membership and participation." *Review of Religious Research* 21:405-26.

ROOZEN, DAVID A.
1980 "Church dropouts: changing patterns of disengagement and re-entry." *Review of Religious Research* 21:427-50.

ROSENTHAL, ERIC
1970 "Divorce and religious intermarriage: the effect of previous marital status upon subsequent marital behavior." *Journal of Marriage and the Family* 32:435-40.

ROSTEN, LEO
1975 "Intermarriage—statistics, opinions, and conversion data: Catholics, Protestants and Jews," *Religions of America: Ferment and Faith in an Age of Crisis*. New York: Simon & Schuster, pp. 549-62.

SALISBURY, W. SEWARD
1969 "Religious identification, mixed marriage and conversion." *Journal for the Scientific Study of Religion* 8:125-29.

SAUNDERS, LAVELL E.
1976 "The gradient of ecumenism and opposition to religious intermarriage." *Review of Religious Research* 17:107-19.

SAVAGE, JOHN S.
1976 *The Apathetic and Bored Church Member*. Pittsford, NY.: LEAD Consultants.

SCHALLER, LYLE E.
1978 *Assimilating New Members*. Nashville: Abingdon Press.
1979 "Evaluating the potential for growth." *Christian Ministry* 10:55-58.

SMELSER, NEIL J.
1963 *Theory of Collective Behavior*. Glencoe, IL: Free Press.

SNOW, DAVID A., LOUIS A. ZURCHER, JR., and SHELDON EKLAND-OLSON
1980 "Social networks and social movements: a microstructural approach to differential recruitment." *American Sociological Review* 45:787-801.

224

STARK, RODNEY and WILLIAM SIMS BAINBRIDGE
1980 "Networks of faith: interpersonal bonds and recruitment to cults and sects." *American Journal of Sociology* 85:1376-95.

SWEETSER, THOMAS P.
1974 *The Catholic Parish: Shifting Membership in a Changing Church.* Chicago: Center for the Scientific Study of Religion.

THOMAS, JOHN L.
1951 "The factor of religion in the selection of marriage mates." *American Sociological Review* 16:487-91.

TOCH, HANS
1965 *The Social Psychology of Social Movements.* Indianapolis: Bobbs-Merrill.

U.S. CENSUS BUREAU
1978 "Persons of Spanish origin in the United States: March, 1977." *Current Population Reports.* Series P-20, No. 329 (September).

VAILLANT, GEORGE E.
1977 *Adaptation to Life.* Boston: Little, Brown.

VIZCAINO, MARIO
1980 "The Hispanic Americans: a prophetic church." *New Catholic World* July/August:175-76.

WAGNER, C. PETER
1976 *Your Church Can Grow.* Glendale, CA: G/L Regal.

WALLACE, RUTH A.
1975 "A model of change of religious affiliation." *Journal for the Scientific Study of Religion* 14:345-55.

WESTERHOFF, JOHN H. III
1976 *Will Our Children Have Faith?* New York: Seabury Press.

WESTOFF, CHARLES F.
1979 "The blending of Catholic reproductive behavior," in Robert Wuthnow, ed., *The Religious Dimension: New Directions in Quantitative Research.* New York: Academic Press, pp. 231-40.

WHITAM, FREDERICK L.
1965 "Adolescence and mass persuasion: a study of teen-age decision-making at a Billy Graham crusade." Unpublished Ph.D. dissertation, Indiana University.

WILSON, JOHN
1978 *Religion in American Society.* Englewood Cliffs, NJ: Prentice-Hall.

WUTHNOW, ROBERT
1978 *Experimentation in American Religion.* Berkeley, CA: University of California Press.

WUTHNOW, ROBERT and CHARLES Y. GLOCK
1973 "Religious loyalty, defection, and experimentation among college youth." *Journal for the Scientific Study of Religion* 12:157-80.
YINGER, J. MILTON
1968 "A research note on interfaith marriage." *Journal for the Scientific Study of Religion* 7:97-103.